SO-BDM-802

PRAISE FOR
A LIVING SPIRIT OF REVOLT

"The great contribution of Žiga Vodovnik is that his writing rescues anarchism from its dogma, its rigidity, its isolation from the majority of the human race. He reveals the natural anarchism of our everyday lives, and in doing so, enlarges the possibilities for a truly human society, in which our imaginations, our compassion, can have full play."

> —Howard Zinn, author of *A People's History of the United States*, from the Introduction

"Like Marx's old mole, the instinct for freedom keeps burrowing, and periodically breaks through to the light of day in novel and exciting forms. That is happening again right now in many parts of the world, often inspired by, and revitalizing, the anarchist tradition that is examined in Vodovnik's book. *A Living Spirit of Revolt* is a deeply informed and thoughtful work, which offers us very timely and instructive lessons."

> —Noam Chomsky, MIT

"Žiga Vodovnik's *A Living Sprit of Revolt* is an original and brilliant exploration of the great tapestry of theory and praxis that belongs in the anarchist tradition and its contemporary forms. For the first time he makes a striking case that the Transcendentalists and their intellectual cousins belong firmly in this tradition. No library of contemporary or historical radicalism can be without it."

> —James C. Scott, professor of political science and anthropology, Yale University

"Žiga Vodovnik has made a fresh and original contribution to our understanding of anarchism, by unearthing its importance for the New England Transcendentalists and their impact on radical politics in America. *A Living Spirit of Revolt* is interesting, relevant, and is sure to be widely read and enjoyed."

—Uri Gordon, author of *Anarchy Alive: Anti-authoritarian Politics from Practice to Theory*

"This book with its felicitous title is an important and essential work, honest, painstaking, and intelligent. Unlike so many political scientists, Žiga Vodovnik understands anarchism. It is unlikely that anyone can read *A Living Spirit of Revolt* without gaining a wholly new perspective on the history and future of the anarchist movement. In a period that promises to spawn exciting transformations and occupations of politics, this brilliant work offers a degree of real understanding, and therefore cannot be too much commended."

—Andrej Grubačić, author of *Don't Mourn Balkanize! Essays After Yugoslavia* and coauthor of *Wobblies and Zapatistas: Conversations on Anarchism, Marxism, and Radical History*

A LIVING SPIRIT OF REVOLT
OF REVOLT
The Infrapolitics of Anarchism

Žiga Vodovnik

A Living Sprit of Revolt: The Infrapolitics of Anarchism
Žiga Vodovnik

© PM Press 2013
All rights reserved. No part of this book may be transmitted by any
means without permission in writing from the publisher.

PO Box 23912
Oakland, CA 94623
www.pmpress.org

Cover design by John Yates
Layout by Jonathan Rowland

ISBN: 978-1-60486-523-3
LCCN: 2012913632

10 9 8 7 6 5 4 3 2 1

Printed in the USA by the Employee Owners of
Thomson-Shore in Dexter, Michigan.
www.thomsonshore.com

This book was financially supported by the Slovenian Book Agency.

Dedicated to the memory of my mother, Ana Vodovnik (1944–2010), and my friend Howard Zinn (1922–2010). In a way, they are both responsible for this book.

Contents

A FRESH LOOK AT ANARCHISM

IT IS TIME TO BREATHE SOME CLEAN, REFRESHING AIR INTO THE stale, nonsense-filled discussions of anarchism which have occupied the attention of people on all sides of the political spectrum—right, left, center. This is what Žiga Vodovnik sets out to do in his original and imaginative analysis of anarchism.

Anarchism deserves to be liberated from all the ideological debris it has accumulated for over a hundred years. Anarchism, properly cleansed of myth and pretense, has never been more needed than in our time, when every system, every culture, has been corrupted by the profit motive or the hubris of leaders, and has led the people of the earth into a morass of injustice and violence.

The word *anarchy* still unsettles most people in the Western world; it suggests disorder, violence, uncertainty. We have good reasons for fearing those conditions, because we have been living with them for a long time, not in anarchist societies but in exactly those societies most fearful of anarchy—the powerful nation-states of modern times. At no time in human history has there been such social chaos. Millions starving, or in prisons, or in mental institutions. Inner turmoil to the point of large-scale alienation, confusion, unhappiness. Outer turmoil symbolized by huge armies, stores of nerve gas, and stockpiles of hydrogen bombs. Wherever men, women, and children are even a bit conscious of the world outside their local borders, they have been living with the ultimate uncertainty: whether or not the human race itself will survive into the next generation. It is these conditions that the anarchists have wanted to end: to bring a kind of order to the world for the first time. We have never listened to them carefully, except through the hearing aids supplied by the guardians of disorder.

The institution of capitalism, anarchists believe, is destructive, irrational, inhumane. It feeds ravenously on the immense resources of the earth, and then churns out (this is its achievement—it is an immense stupid churn) huge quantities of products. Those products have only an accidental relationship to what is most needed by people, because the organizers and distributors of goods care not about human need; they are great business enterprises motivated only by profit. Therefore, bombs, guns, office buildings, and deodorants take priority over food, homes, and recreation areas. Is there anything closer to "anarchy" (in the common use of the word, meaning confusion) than the incredibly wild and wasteful economic system in America?

It was both ironic and appropriate that anarchism should arise as a philosophy and guide to action exactly in that period—the late nineteenth and early twentieth century—when capitalism, professing to enrich the world, kept so many in poverty, when nationalism, professing to unify people around a common identity, instead unified them in violence and war against other nations, when imperialism, professing to bring freedom and civilization to "backward" societies, brought them exploitation, repression, death.

What has modern civilization, with its "rule of law," its giant industrial enterprises, its "representative democracy," brought? Nuclear missiles already aimed and ready for the destruction of the world, and populations of a mind to accept this madness. Civilization has failed on two counts: it has perverted the natural resources of the earth, which have capacity to make our lives joyful, and also the natural resources of people, which have potential for genius and love.

It seems that revolutionary changes are needed—in the sense of profound transformations of our work processes, or decision-making arrangements, our sex and family relations, our thought and culture—toward a humane society. But this kind of revolution—changing our minds as well as institutions—cannot be accomplished by customary methods: neither by military action to overthrow governments, as some tradition-bound radicals suggest, nor by that slow process of electoral reform, which traditional liberals urge on us.

As I have already written elsewhere, the state of the world today reflects the limitations of both those methods. The anarchist rather sees revolutionary change as something immediate, something we must do now, where we are, where we live, where we work. It means starting this moment to do away with authoritarian, cruel relationships—between men and women, between parents and children, between one kind of worker and another kind. Such revolutionary action cannot be crushed like an armed uprising. It takes place in everyday life, in the tiny crannies where the powerful but clumsy hands of state power cannot easily reach. It is not centralized and isolated, so that it cannot be wiped out by the rich, the police, the military. It takes place in a hundred thousand places at once, in families, on streets, in neighborhoods, in places of work. It is a revolution of the whole culture. Squelched in one place, it springs up in another, until it is everywhere. Such a revolution is an art. That is, it requires the courage not only of resistance, but of imagination.

However, the anarchist movements that flourished in Europe, Latin America, and the United States barely survived the First World War, and with the Bolshevik Revolution, the radical spirit was taken over by the world Communist movement, which then smothered it in state capitalism, bureaucracy, and dictatorship, exactly those concentrations of power which anarchists had always opposed. Today, there are small anarchist groups here and there, in the United States, in Europe, in Latin America, which put out publications with tiny circulations, which hold meetings with a handful of people, and these tiny groups sometimes split into tinier factions, arguing over obscure theoretical or tactical issues.

Nevertheless, the need for a true radical spirit has never been greater. Capitalism is clearly incompetent in meeting the needs of people all over the world. The existence of poverty and violence in the most capitalist of countries—the United States—is clear proof of its failure. With the collapse of the Soviet Union, the radical movement has rid itself of an enormous burden, and now can reemerge with clean hands to face a world desperate for change. The ideas of anarchism—a global community free of national antagonism, an economy based on cooperation free of the profit motive, a culture of equality and imagination—have never been so relevant as they are today.

Those ideas need to be freed from the small circles that call themselves anarchist. They need to be connected with the far larger world, embracing a majority of the human race, whose instincts are anarchist without using the name. Most people do not want war, most people want to live in a neighborly way with others. There is a natural urge to be free of domination, whether in the family, the workplace, or the community.

Indeed, whenever historical circumstances allowed, whenever human beings could break away from domination, could find spaces in which their natural instincts could have free play, they have acted in accord with anarchist principles without using the language or identifying the theory. History is full of such examples: early Christian communities, the egalitarian culture of Indian tribes in north America, the utopian communities of New England, the Communards of Paris who in 1871 sent balloons over the countryside declaring to all that "our interests are the same."

Occasionally, an oasis of freedom would declare itself "anarchist," as in Barcelona in the early months of the Spanish Civil War, described by George Orwell in *Homage to Catalonia*. But for the most part, people acted out their desires for freedom without identifying themselves as anarchists. For instance, the young black people who formed the Student Nonviolent Coordinating Committee in the South in the early 1960s rejected centralized leadership or monetary gain. They worked with local people in the black communities of the Deep South, sharing their living quarters, their food, while sharing also the dangers of challenging racism. In Mexico, the Zapatistas of Chiapas and the striking teachers of Oaxaca showed the flaming spirit of grassroots anarchism without calling it by name.

The great contribution of Žiga Vodovnik is that his writing rescues anarchism from its dogma, its rigidity, its isolation from the majority of the human race. He reveals the natural anarchism of our everyday lives and, in doing so, enlarges the possibilities for a truly human society, in which our imaginations, our compassion, can have full play.

Howard Zinn

PREFACE

IN HIS BOOK *UNDER THREE FLAGS: ANARCHISM AND THE ANTI-colonial Imagination*, Benedict Anderson assessed that at the end of the nineteenth century, the anarchist movement was the first global anti-system movement at a center of revolutionary tumult. At the start of the new millennium, then, we can legitimately put forward an even bolder thesis: anarchism is not only the most revolutionary political current today but, for the first time in history, the only one left. This is an even more provocative thesis given the historical development of anarchist thought and practice in the "short twentieth century."

At the end of the nineteenth century, it seemed that humankind was set to witness a "century of anarchism." Yet, political developments, as Robert Graham remarked, again showed that the "contest of ideas" throughout history has never been a fair one.[1] At the Hague Congress of the First International in 1872, Mikhail Bakunin and many other anarchists and anarchist organizations were expelled or forced to resign on the grounds of their disapproval of Marx's view of the objectives and means of political struggle. In the beginning, the struggle against the anarchist "heresy" merely

---

1   Robert Graham, ed., *Anarchism: A Documentary History of Libertarian Ideas, Vol. 2: The Emergence of the New Anarchism, 1939–1977* (Montreal: Black Rose Books, 2009).

resulted in the marginalization of anarchism, but in 1921 this process culminated in a bloody crushing of an independent Soviet and the revolt of the libertarian-minded (anarchist!) sailors in Kronstadt. Let us not forget the Spanish Civil War and various efforts by communists, liberals, and Francoists against the anarchists. Thanks to this collective sabotage, the "dangerous" (in that it promoted the idea of people's actual freedom) anarchist experiment was crushed.

In the United States, the physical destruction of anarchism started when eight prominent members of the anarchist movement were arrested after the 1886 Haymarket tragedy in Chicago.[2] Seven of them were given the death penalty. This response by the authorities and the political motive of the trial were unsurprising considering the explanation the chief judge gave the accused: "Not because you caused the Haymarket bomb, but because you are Anarchists, you are on trial."

In the same year that the Kronstadt commune was suppressed in blood, the new U.S. president, Theodore Roosevelt, labeled anarchism in his address to Congress as "a crime against the whole human race" and called on humankind to "band together against the anarchist." In 1894, a law had been adopted by Congress prohibiting anarchists and "all those who do not believe in or oppose to organized authority" from entering the United States. The 1917 and 1918 Espionage Act and Sedition Act led to the deportation of 247 anarchists (including Emma Goldman and Alexander Berkman) on the S.S. *Buford* (the so-called Soviet Ark) for agitation against the draft and U.S. war efforts.

In the period of "reaction," many protagonists of the anarchist movement were murdered for their ideas and

---

2   On May 4, 1886, a rally in support of an eight-hour workday was held at Haymarket Square in Chicago. A fight broke out, and an unknown person threw a dynamite bomb at the police. The blast and ensuing gunfire resulted in the deaths of at least four civilians and seven police officers.

ideals (e.g., Gustav Landauer, Francisco Ferrer, August Spies, Albert Parsons, and Erich Mühsam), others died in prisons or met a premature death after having been imprisoned for many years (e.g., Mikhail Bakunin, Johann Most, and Nestor Makhno), and some committed suicide (e.g., Louis Lingg and Alexander Berkman). These events are only a few examples of a systematic process of trivialization and suppression of global anarchism that helped bring an end to the period when the global anarchist movement was fueled by just enough action potential to mobilize the broad public and ensure the necessary support and legitimacy for its activities.

It is not surprising that in 1960 George Woodcock reckoned that anarchism as a movement was dead. He was compelled to revise his conclusions just a few years later when the black and red flags of anarchy—in all their complexity (i.e., feminist, ecological, cultural, and pacifist dimensions)—again fluttered in London, Paris, Amsterdam, Berlin, Chicago, Mexico City, Buenos Aires, and Tokyo during the 1968 student protests. According to Woodcock, the anarchist imagination returned as an "important and central element in the pluralistic spectrum of new radicalism and its thought," whereby "anarchism has come down to the New Radicals not through direct reading but through remnants and ideas which still pervade the air of certain settings in New York, Los Angeles, Vancouver, and Montreal."[3]

In its struggle against capitalism, state socialism, and the pyramidal structure of power within the university, factory, state and family, the new radicalism reflected and reactualized traditional anarchist principles such as mutual aid, self-management, participatory democracy, and decentralization. Like Bakunin, the participants in this new radicalism found revolutionary potential in the "left-outs," the "have-nots," the lumpenproletariat, the marginalized and *declassé* elements

---

3   George Woodcock, *Anarchism: A History of Libertarian Ideas and Movements* (Peterborough: Broadview Press, 2003), 403.

of modern society. By building alternative institutions, they faithfully followed Bakunin's idea that the seeds of future society should be sown in the existing social system. But the new radicalism was largely unaware of its own anarchist aspirations. Since it lacked explicit historical inclinations, it drew anarchist conclusions from simply the analysis of the current state of affairs and a pragmatic acceptance of practical ideas.

A similar waning and waxing cycle of anarchist imagination has been witnessed over the past three decades. With the abatement of the "eros effect" in the early 1970s, theses announcing the end of anarchism were again advanced.[4] Following the fall of the Berlin Wall and breakup of the Soviet bloc, these considerations were further supported by conclusions about the end of history.

There is no need to stress that, within the "post-Seattle" alterglobalization movement, anarchism offers space to the most creative and most lucid radical turmoil. Yet, the return of anarchism offers both a relief and a new problem. Anarchism has always ideationally fluid and flexible, accommodating a host of occasionally contradictory ideas. A bifurcation of anarchist thought and practice has been noticed in past years, leading to the point where diffusion and heterogeneity make it practically impossible to demarcate the boundaries of anarchism. The anarchist principles of non-authoritarian organization have spread to such an extent that many social movements can be classified as anarchist even without assuming this identity. By contrast, many anarchists intentionally refuse to declare themselves anarchists, often due to extreme adherence to the anarchist ideas of an anti-cult attitude, openness, and flexibility, whereby complete emancipation also encompasses emancipation from the rigidity of identity.

---

4   The "eros effect" is a concept forwarded by professor, sociologist, and author George Katsiaficas to explain the transcendental, transformative qualities of social movements that seem to occur during historical moments of popular upheaval.

Despite all these limitations, my reading has attempted to avoid the pitfall of equating anarchism with a single dimension by leaving the task of identifying the relevant and the anachronistic within the new anarchism to the reader. The book currently in your hands does not aim to justify true anarchism (is that even possible?) and is also not an uncritical and naïve list of cases proving that anarchism is possible and needed. As Uri Gordon suggests, such a book—considering the plethora of works over the past two centuries that have done this job excellently—would really be an unnecessary and inexcusable waste of trees.[5]

My purpose is therefore more challenging: to enrich social scientific and humanistic thought with the contributions of modern anarchism. Even more, I hope that these lines will contribute not only to what Bakunin referred to as the "creation of ideas but also the facts of the future itself," although I am aware that the book itself is a negligible contribution to the process of changing the existing social relations. Nevertheless, there is a hope that it could offer a stepping-stone to critically considering and inventing completely new political practices or recuperating the forgotten ones.

Then again, allow me to point to another, more political danger or dilemma. If this text brings to the forefront heterogeneity rather than providing clarity and unique answers, and if it raises questions about anarchism's inner contradictoriness, then the goal has been achieved. Noam Chomsky states that, due to the fossilization of anarchism, the anarchist tradition too often assumes the purist positions that "legislate what the doctrine *is*, and with various degrees of fury (often great) denounce those who depart from what they have declared to be the True Principles." With its theoretical purity, anarchism has preserved its radicalness but often shattered its actuality: by being "torn between a

---

5   Uri Gordon, *Anarchy Alive! Anti-authoritarian Politics from Practice to Theory* (London: Pluto Press, 2008), 6.

tragic past and impossible future, it has lost the present."[6]
Featherstone, Henwood, and Parenti have further established that theoretical purism within individual segments of
the alterglobalization movement can be carried to such an
extreme that it is now possible to speak of a new (post)ideol-
ogy of *activistism* or *actionism*.[7]

According to Adorno (and I am well aware he is not a
proper reference for a discussion on anarchism), the problem
of this new nonideology is that it means an inconsiderate collective compulsion to positivism that requires its immediate transformation into practice. Although it is applied by
people who consider themselves radical agitators, actionism
(with its thoughtless compulsion for mere action) is only a
reflection of pragmatic empiricism of the dominant culture
(also by separating physical and mental work). Actionism is
inevitably regressive, as it allows no reflection on its own
impotence.[8] These assessments are greatly exaggerated and,
fortunately, are not considered anarchist currents within the
"movement of movements," although they are still a welcome warning against the problem or crisis which can manifest itself in the future when the anarchist movement will
require self-reflection as a necessary party of transformation.
That we should take these warnings and instructions with
a grain of salt was a word of advice from Emma Goldman,
who established a hundred years ago that anarchism is not a
theory about a future system but a "living force in the affairs
of our life, constantly creating new conditions; the spirit of

6   Hakim Bey, *T.A.Z.: The Temporary Autonomous Zone, Ontological
Anarchy, Poetic Terrorism* (Brooklyn: Autonomedia, 2003), 60.

7   Liza Featherstone, Doug Henwood, and Christian Parenti,
"Activistism: Left Anti-Intellectualism and Its Discontents" in
Confronting Capitalism: Dispatches from a Global Movement, eds. Eddie
Yuen, Daniel Burton-Rose, and George Katsiaficas (New York: Soft
Skull Press).

8   Nigel Gibson and Andrew Rubin, eds., *Adorno: A Critical Reader*
(Malden, MA: Blackwell Publishers, 2002), 182.

revolt, in whatever form, against everything that hinders human growth."[9]

Because of my teaching work, it has taken me much longer to write this book than I dare admit. But my students inspire me time and again to broaden my perspective and look at the complexity of certain phenomena under a magnifying glass; this book is also partly theirs.

This work would not have been possible, at least not in its present shape, without the help and advice of many "co-conspirators" who have left their indelible (ideational) mark: A-Infoshop, AK Press, Zach Blue, Lawrence Buell, Noam Chomsky, Uri Gordon, Andrej Grubačić, Craig O'Hara, the Institute for Anarchist Studies, Ramsey Kanaan, Andrej Kurnik, Cindy Milstein, Gregory Nipper, John Petrovato, PM Press, Raven Used Books, Rudi Rizman, Jonathan Rowland, James C. Scott, Chris Spannos, Matjaž Šprajc, Tamara Vukov, John Yates, Darij Zadnikar, Založba Sophia, and Howard Zinn. It is perhaps worth repeating that the responsibility for any shortcomings and imperfections you might discover in the book is solely mine.

The credit for preserving the spirit, sharpness, and liveliness of the translation goes to Nives Mahne Čehovin, Murray Bales, and Romy Ruukel. The translator and the language-editors not only performed the harder part of the work but did so with excellence. In the manner of colleagues from the past, I say: *Kudos!*

From the very beginning, this project has received full support from PM Press. Its staff's response to my requests demonstrated that a different work method is possible in times of monoculture of knowledge, capitalist production, and efficiency. In both theoretical and organizational terms, this entire project can be considered an experiment in recognizing and valuating other knowledge and validity criteria

---

9   Emma Goldman, *Anarchism and Other Essays* (Mineola, NY: Dover Publication, 1969), 63.

as well as those alternative production systems discredited by the hegemonic idea of productivity. Of course, this does not mean there would have been no book without its help, although clearly the book would have been very different.

Last but not least, I would like to thank my family. The weeks and months I spent writing this book took their toll. It is a heavy burden if, on the way to producing a manuscript, you lose one of your nearest and dearest. The doubts about whether it was worth it, the questions about what I missed, the reproach that I was not there when I really should have been, linger on. This book carries this very burden to justify that the self-isolation needed to accomplish it was not a complete waste of time. Although the judgment is solely yours, these doubts and reproaches will forever be mine.

Ž.V.
Ljubljana, January 2013

1

Lectori Benevolo Salutem!

> *"Die Anarchie ist nicht die Sache der Zukunft, sondern der Gegenwart; nicht der Forderungen, sondern des Lebens."* (Anarchy is not a matter of the future; it is a matter of the present. It is not a matter of making demands; it is a matter of how one lives.)
> —*Gustav Landauer, "Anarchische Gedanken über Anarchismus," 1901*

> *"The choice between libertarian and authoritarian solutions occurs every day and in every way, and the extent to which we choose, or accept, or are fobbed off with, or lack the imagination and inventiveness to discover alternatives to, the authoritarian solutions to small problems is the extent to which we are their powerless victims in big affairs."*
> —*Colin Ward, "The Unwritten Handbook," 1958*

IN A CITY OF NEARLY HALF A MILLION PEOPLE, THERE HAVE BEEN no police on the streets ever since the onset of the public uprising three months ago. All government agencies have been closed and are now populated by women's delegations of the new people's assembly. Improvised clinics have been set up in different parts of the city where doctors, nurses, and medical students offer medical care and medicines for free. The occupied radio and television stations have opened up their studios to anyone wishing to take part in the creation of their programs. Façades of city houses have turned into "canvasses" and are freely used by both men and women working jointly under the auspices of the Assembly of Revolutionary Artists. Many shops are giving out free food and water. All across the neighborhoods, people are consulting each other and coordinating activities that are helping them to defend and strengthen their newly gained autonomy. Despite, or perhaps because of, the absence of the police and government agencies, the crime rate in the city has fallen substantially and any violations and offenses are only being sanctioned with a day of community service.

Nearly all the streets are packed with heaps of stones, abandoned trucks, buses, burning containers, or simple banners protecting the city against attacks by paramilitary groups, and the police attempts to reestablish "order and discipline" through killings and bomb attacks. The paradox that people must protect their experiment in the prefiguration of direct democracy from the police is not the only one that can be seen on the streets of this city. People at the city square are saying that the attacks at the barricades and the explosions right across the city become worse during the night. The masked attackers are heavily armed, while the women, men, and children at the barricades only have stones to defend themselves. Only the *topiles*—groups of young men and women in charge of public order and safety in the city—are better armed and carry slings, petards, and rockets that were probably purchased for the upcoming Independence Day.

As a token of solidarity, most students and professors from the local university have suspended lectures and joined groups committed to setting up new barricades or rebuilding the old ones. The central square is the headquarters of the People's Assembly, which brings together over three hundred different groups from feminist collectives, agricultural cooperatives, indigenous organizations, anarchist affinity groups, trade unions, and artistic collectives to students' societies, district communities, nongovernmental organizations, and parties from the left side of the political spectrum.

This is not Barcelona in 1936, as a friend erroneously describes my report, but Oaxaca, the capital of the State of Oaxaca in southern Mexico, in 2006. There are countless reasons for discontent and revolt—poverty, corruption, the systematic violation of human rights, racism, cultural imperialism. One could easily overlook any one of them, or paint an oversimplified picture of the entire political and economic situation, but the cause of the uprising is well known.

In the early morning hours of June 14, Governor Ulises Ruiz Ortiz ordered the police to remove more than twenty thousand teachers of Section 22 of the National Union of Education Workers (Sindicato Nacional de los Trabajadores en la Educación, SNTE) occupying the *zócalo*. As a result of the brutal raid, the strike suffered a high number of casualties among the teachers, their children, and pupils who joined them in occupation of the city square; the shelters the teachers had prepared for their *plantón* (encampment) were destroyed. And the people of Oaxaca revolted, for the first time viewing this annual, nearly traditional protest by teachers calling for higher salaries, better working conditions, and free school supplies for all pupils as their own battle, a capacitor of all other social struggles.

With every passing hour, the teachers' strike was joined by more individuals and collectives who had together coordinated the Zapatista Other Campaign (la Otra Campaña) stop in Oaxaca only a few months before. The main aim of the Other Campaign was to intertwine the (so far) separate revolts by marginalized groups and build a new political force to connect "from below and to the left" (*abajo y a la izquierda*) those subjects that had either been unnoticed or disregarded by political leaders.

In response to the police repression of the teachers' strike, the people of Oaxaca not only liberated the square and rebuilt the *plantón* for the teachers but set the entire city free in a few hours. After three days, the Popular Assembly of the Peoples of Oaxaca (Asamblea Popular de los Pueblos de Oaxaca, APPO) represented a revolutionary decision-making body that faithfully followed the Zapatista principle *mandar obedeciendo* (to rule by obeying) for the next five months, until the "Federal Preventive Police" broke in and brutally suppressed the uprising.

The APPO united over three hundred different collectives and initiatives with different visions of the future society, internal decision-making structures and organizational forms that, according to Gustavo Esteva, were characterized by "one no and many yeses." Namely, they were all critical of the status quo but professed different aspirations. In its collectivity, Oaxacan community once again showed the creative potential of people during the "orgasms of history."[1] Their efforts showed and proved that real, participative or direct democracy is not a matter of a specific type of production or consumption but a matter of freedom.

The APPO was first established as a coordinating body with no formal structure, for the purposes of discussion and reflection. However, the need soon arose for a new political form to offer those involved—as heterogeneous as they may be in their form and content—a suitable place for collective work. The Assembly discovered many solutions for building a fluid and dynamic political structure in the political practices and traditions of the indigenous communities whose *usos y costumbres*, fused with anarchist and autonomist thought, resulted in a new and unique formation of direct

---

1   Yves Fremion, *Orgasms of History: 3000 Years of Spontaneous Insurrection* (Oakland: AK Press, 2002), xi.

democracy leading to people's power (*poder popular*). The Assembly rejected the idea of majority voting at all levels, inevitably requiring a new center of power to be established for sanctioning failures to follow the adopted solutions. It rather embraced the radical concepts of consensual decision-making, communal labor (*tequios*), and mutual help (*guelaguetza*).

Even though the "commune" was crushed bloodily after five months of the prefiguration of radical democracy, the movement was far from dead. The Oaxacan movements not only pursued the project of democratization from below, but the popular assemblies in other parts of Mexico took over and adjusted the APPO model to their needs. They also adopted and built on the ideas and experience of the Zapatista movement which, despite the geographical limits of its "other democracy" and autonomous organization, was able to stir the imaginations of progressive movements all over the world.

In the early morning hours of January 1, 1994—the day of the foretold "end of history" when the North American Free Trade Agreement (NAFTA) entered into force—in the Mexican province of Chiapas, the Maya peoples of Tzeltal, Tzotzil, Tojolabal, Ch'ol, Zoque, and Mam emerged from the Lacandon rainforest and historical oblivion. The slim figures of these indigenous people—wearing traditional Maya clothing, faces covered with black masks or red scarves (so that the world would finally "see" them), armed with obsolete (and, in most cases, fake wooden) rifles and waving black-and-red flags—disrupted the festive atmosphere by declaring war on neoliberal capitalism. They had come to realize that Mexico's entry to the "free-trade" union was a fatal blow for Maya culture that would lead to the extermination of the entire indigenous population of the region. Subcomandante Marcos, the strategist and voice of the Zapatista Army of National Liberation (Ejército Zapatista de Liberación Nacional, EZLN), offered the perplexed European tourists on their Christmas and New Year's holidays in Chiapas only a brief explanation: "I apologize for the inconvenience, but this is a revolution!"

In the years marked by the global predominance of neo-liberalism, even the most optimistic were forced to believe in the illusion of the perpetuity of the existing regulation. Then, just when it seemed that the "capitalist magicians" had succeeded in their intention, the collective hypnosis was disrupted by the story of the Maya indigenous peoples who, in the face of hundreds of years of injustice and oppression, showed courage by again sending their oppressors the message *¡Ya Basta!*. *Zapatismo* is dangerous for the opponents on one side and attractive to the sympathizers on the other mainly because of its "humble" claim: to change the world. To create a different world or a world of many worlds (*un mundo donde quepan muchos mundos*) where the enormous wealth on Planet Earth would (will) be allotted to people and these would finally be given what they need. As Gustavo Esteva has pointed out, this unhumble goal of the Zapatista uprising is not the upshot of romantic dreams and illusions, but a very pragmatic attitude in a world of cynics and hypocrites.[2]

Why is it both reasonable and necessary to start this work on anarchism and its forgotten currents with a description of the uprising of the peoples of Oaxaca and Chiapas in southern Mexico? If we understand anarchist thought and practice as a flexible, ever-changing set of ideas and practices open to modifications in the light of new findings, we can see that anarchism has never been a result of individual anarchist thinkers. It was "born *among the people*; and it will continue to be full of life and creative power only as long as it remains a thing of the people."[3] All around the world, people will

2   Gustavo Esteva, "The Other Campaign, APPO and the Left: Reclaiming an Alternative" in *Teaching Rebellion: Stories from the Grassroots Mobilization in Oaxaca*, eds. Diana Denham and C.A.S.A. Collective (Oakland: PM Press, 2008), 336.

3   Peter Kropotkin, *Anarchism: A Collection of Revolutionary Writings* (Mineola, NY: Dover Publications, 2002), 146.

continue to evolve and enrich anarchism with their theoretical and practical contributions.

According to Stuart Christie, the anarchist movement owes very little to "theorists" and "intellectuals." Rather, "professional writers have dipped into the achievements of anarchist workers to enlighten themselves on social theory or to formulate other theories."[4] Similarly, Albert Meltzer reckoned that for every Kropotkin there were a thousand like Facerias, a thousand Jack Kieltys for every Rudolf Rocker.[5] While the extraordinary contribution of the "classics" of anarchism should not be underrated, they are usually the results of many anonymous individuals who played active roles in the workers' movement of the nineteenth century and, with their common sense and activism, contributed, as Mikhail Bakunin says, "not only the ideas, but also the facts of the future itself."[6]

Throughout history, anarchism has been an idea and practice not only of self-proclaimed anarchists but also of common people practicing anarchism without being aware of it or with no previous knowledge of the word *anarchism*. The anarchist principles of nonauthoritarian organization have spread around to such an extent, that many social movements could be classified as anarchist even without assuming this identity. By contrast, many anarchists intentionally refuse to declare themselves anarchists, probably due to their extreme adherence to the anarchist ideas of an anti-cult attitude, openness, and flexibility, whereby complete emancipation also encompasses emancipation from the rigidity of identity.

Accordingly, the following movements came close to an anarchist milieu and some could even be placed in it: the labor

---

4   Stuart Christie and Albert Meltzer, *The Floodgates of Anarchy* (Oakland: PM Press, 2010), 9.

5   Albert Meltzer, *Anarchism: Arguments For and Against* (San Francisco: AK Press, 1996), 18.

6   Bakunin, *Bakunin on Anarchy*, trans. Sam Dolgoff (London: Allen and Unwin, 1973) 255.

unrests in Great Britain (1910–1914), Germany (1919–1921) and Portugal (1974); the Mexican Revolution (1910–1919); the German Socialist Students' Union (Sozialistische Deutsche Studentenbund, SDS) in the then Western Germany (1950s and 1960s); the Japanese student movement Zengakuren (1950s and 1960s); the Italian "Hot Autumn" (1969); the broad coalition of radical antimilitarist groups called "The Committee of 100" in Great Britain (1960s and 1970s); the Provos and Kabouters in the Netherlands (1960s and 1970s); the "March 22" movement and Situationist International in France (1960s and 1970s); the strike by British miners (1984–1985); the radical unionist movement Cobas (Comitati di Base) in Italy (1980s and 1990s); the alterglobalization movement (since 1994); and a series of other "carnivals of resistance."

Colin Ward wrote that "an anarchist society, a society which organizes itself without authority, is always in existence. Like a seed beneath the snow, buried under the weight of the state and its bureaucracy, capitalism and its waste, privilege and its injustices, nationalism and its suicidal loyalties, religious differences and their superstitious separatism."[7] Darij Zadnikar postulates that the seeds of resistance are to be sought in the everyday resistance of life against the imperatives of the system; in the joy of living and the buffoonery of ordinary people; in the dance of the ignored; in the moving of nomads; in the settling of migrants and the struggle of peasants for land; in the love between homosexuals; in the piercing of punks; and, last but not least, in the smile of an overworked shop-assistant.[8] One should not forget the squatters; people without documents (the "Erased" in Slovenia and the

---

7   Colin Ward, *Anarchy in Action* (London: Freedom Press, 1982), 14.
8   Zadnikar, "Que se vayan todos!" *Časopis za kritiko znanosti, domišljijo in novo antropologijo* 31, no. 212 (2003): 5–8; Zadnikar, "Kronika radostnega uporništva" in John Holloway, *Spreminjamo svet brez boja za oblast: pomen revolucije danes* (Ljubljana: Študentska založba, 2004), 207.

sans-papiers in France) and the "illegal dwellers" in the global Babylon; adbusters and culturejammers; women working in *maquiladoras*; the unemployed, precarious workers, *piqueteros* and *cacerolazos*; the activists of social centers; the pacifists in the streets; the feminist groups; the antifascist organizations; Reclaim the Streets; Food not Bombs; the No Borders network; the gardening guerrillas; the No-to-War and No-to-NATO activists; Black Cross; the graffitists and hackers or hacktivists on the Internet; the Earth Liberation Front (ELF), the Animal Liberation Front (ALF), and Earth First!; Indymedia activists; the open-source code and copyleft advocates; the producers of healthy food; and the explorers of spiritual dimensions.

Still, many still argue that anarchism has long been over. While this thesis (like the pronouncement of "end of history,") is premature, it points to a perennial problem. Through theoretical purism, stubborn adherence to principles and the absolute rejection of compromises and reformism, anarchism has preserved its ontological radicalism. Along the way, however, it has lost some of its value and topicality, since "anachronist" anarchism is torn "between tragic Past and impossible Future, and it seems to lack a Present."[9] In 1847, Alexander Herzen issued his comrades a similar warning:

> If progress is the goal, for whom then are we working? Who is this Moloch who, as the toilers approach him, instead of rewarding them . . . can only give the mocking answer that after their death all will be beautiful on earth? Do you really wish to condemn human beings alive today to the mere sad role of caryatids supporting a floor for others one day to dance upon? . . . A goal which is infinitely remote is not a goal at all, it is a deception. A goal must be closer—at the very

---

9 Bey, *T.A.Z.*, 61.

least the laborer's wage or pleasure in the work performed. Each epoch, each generation, each life has had, and has, its own experience, and en route new demands grow, new methods.[10]

According to Paul Goodman, anarchism is simply a continuous process of facing future situations, while ensuring that already won freedoms do not disappear or degenerate into their opposites, as the free economy degenerated into neoliberal capitalism and voluntary slavery became disguised as wage labor.[11] By overcoming the rigid adherence to a specific doctrine and paying attention to the concrete consequences for people's lives, anarchism can remain one of the most important and topical intellectual streams in the modern world and a springboard for future social changes.

To do so, anarchism must first overcome the negative "fetishization" of the state, because today's struggle for a better world involves antistatism but should be much more encompassing. It would be useful here to imagine the struggle as the fight against the mythological many-headed monster Hydra, wherein the state represents only one of the threats (i.e., heads) to be "severed" while others (capitalism, racism, sexism, militarism, homophobia, nationalism, etc.) remain to be fought. The state should be understood not as a monolithic external structure, but rather, as German anarcho-socialist Gustav Landauer explained it, "a social relationship; a certain way of people relating to one another." As such, it should be addressed as soon as possible, rather than rejected it for the sake of theoretical purity or an ontological high-principled attitude.

Landauer contended that the state was not something that could be destroyed by a one-off revolution, which is why

---

10   Herzen quoted in Colin Ward, *Anarchism: A Very Short Introduction* (Oxford: Oxford University Press, 2004), 32.

11   Paul Goodman, *Drawing the Line Once Again: Paul Goodman's Anarchist Writings* (Oakland: PM Press, 2010), 56.

a free society cannot be achieved by simply replacing the old regulation with a new one; this can only be accomplished by broadening the spheres of freedom to the extent that they eventually triumph in all social life:

> A table can be overturned and a window can be smashed. However, those who believe that the state is also a thing or a fetish that can be overturned or smashed are sophists and believers in the Word. The state is a social relationship; a certain way of people relating to one another. It can be destroyed by creating new social relationships; i.e., by people relating to one another differently. . . .
>
> We, who have imprisoned ourselves in the absolute state, must realize the truth: *we* are the state! And we will be the state as long as we are nothing different; as long as we have not yet created the institutions necessary for a true community and a true society of human beings.[12]

The solution, therefore, lies in the prefigurative adventure into new political practices and structures which, already in the here and now, are drawing the contours of the world we are striving to achieve some day. I evoke here, too, Bey's conception of the spontaneous and subversive tactics of creating Temporary Autonomous Zones (TAZ) which "liberate a part (of land, of time, of imagination) and then dissolve themselves to re-form elsewhere/elsewhen, before the State can crush them."[13] In his excellent reading of Bey, Nikolai Jeffs emphasizes that "subversion must be deterritorialized, decentralized and delinealized in all political, economic,

---

12   Gustav Landauer, *Revolution and Other Writings: A Political Reader* (Oakland: PM Press, 2010), 214.
13   Bey, *T.A.Z.*, 99.

social, libidinal and, last but not least, narrative levels, and that small and nomadic types of resistance must be launched also because there is no place in the world that would not be territorialized by a national state.... [TAZ] is invisible to the state and sufficiently flexible to disappear the very moment it is identified, defined, fixed."[14]

In view of the above, the TAZ concept can be termed "a revolution doomed to fail" but only because its success would represent the complete failure and negation of the future TAZ.[15] This kind of emancipation project does not need to wait until the objective circumstances are ripe or an appropriate revolutionary subject is formed; rather, it assumes that all individuals are capable of changing and co-creating the present world with their own gestures, however small they may be. As Landauer assessed, revolution "concerns every aspect of human life—not just the State, the class-structure, industry and commerce, arts and letters, education and learning, but a combination of all these social factors.... The way to a new, higher form of human society leads from the dark, fateful gate of our instincts and *terra abscondita* of our soul, which is our world. Only from within to without can the world be transformed."[16]

When we allow experimentation and imagination to flourish, anarchist praxis is especially helpful in searching for new methods of social change. For Howard Zinn, the subversiveness of anarchism is rooted in its holistic approach to political change, uncharacterized by narrow economic reductionism, fetishization of economic exploitation, and class antagonism. In the words of Murray Bookchin, anarchism has confronted concepts and practices of hierarchy

---

14 Nikolai Jeffs, "Intelektualci, novi razredi, anarhizmi" in *Somrak demokracije*, Noam Chomsky (Ljubljana: Studia humanitatis, 1997), 368–69.
15 Truscello in Giorel Curran, *21st Century Dissent: Anarchism, Anti-Globalization and Environmentalism* (New York: Palgrave, 2006), 43.
16 Landauer quoted in Peter Marshall, *Demanding the Impossible: A History of Anarchism* (Oakland: PM Press, 2010), 412.

and domination that have little or no economic meaning at all, thus raising the broader and more important questions not only of class antagonism, but of hierarchy and domination themselves. Thus, anarchists do not perceive revolutionary change as something that concerns only an alternation in hegemonic economic and political arrangements but as something that changes or transcends the ways we live, work, make love, collaborate, etc.

Such broader and deeper understanding of anarchist theory and practice allows us to conceive of it as the kind of "infrapolitics" that, according to James C. Scott, "provides much of the cultural and structural underpinning of the more visible political action on which our attention has generally been focused."[17] The infrapolitics of the seemingly nonpolitical are as much a product of political necessity as of political choice: not only a form of political resistance in the circumstances of tyranny, but also as "the silent partner of a loud form of public resistance" within modern democracies. While the infrapolitics of the seemingly nonpolitical are not part of the mainstream, and detecting the "immense political terrain that lies between quiescence and revolt," is occasionally difficult, they are "in many respects conducted in more earnest, for higher stakes, and against greater odds than political life in liberal democracies."[18] The political struggles of the *sans-papiers* in France, the Erased in Slovenia, and the "illegal" immigrants in the United States demonstrate this.

These forms of struggle are, nevertheless, still marginalized and trivialized, from the political Right and Left advocating *real* political action meaning action via political parties, as: (a) unorganized, unsystematic, and individual; (b) opportunistic and self-indulgent; (c) having no revolutionary potential/consequences; and (d) implying accommodation

---

17 James C. Scott, *Domination and the Arts of Resistance: Hidden Transcripts* (New Haven, CT: Yale University Press, 1990), 184.
18 Ibid., 200.

with the system of domination.[19] It is true that in case of "the unwritten history of resistance," the prosaic but constant, or even Brechtian forms of struggle—Paul Goodman might even call them Schweikian forms of struggle that result from the realization that "to make a frontal attack is to play according to the enemy's rules, where one doesn't have a chance, and the victory would be a drag anyway"[20]—often merely result in marginal gains that ease forms of their exploitation. It is also true that instead of targeting the main source of exploitation or the immediate source of exploitation, everyday forms of resistance, as Scott also chooses to call them, rather follow the line of least resistance.

Although we should never overly romanticize the "weapons of the weak," conversely, these forms of infrapolitical actions—such as passive noncompliance, evasion, desertion, deception, foot-dragging, pilfering, arson, subtle sabotage—are also not trivial. Needless to say, the advantage of such resistance is that it results in concrete and immediate advantages. As Scott observes, even failed petty acts of resistance may achieve some gains: "A few concessions from the state or landlords, a brief respite from new and painful relations of production and, not least, a memory of resistance and courage that may lie in wait for the future."[21] Moreover, when multiplied by thousands and millions of people such individual acts of quiet resistance "may in the end make an utter shambles of policies dreamed up by their would-be superiors."[22]

It is ironic that in times of "fluid modernity" (Bauman), infrapolitical action that in the past characterized peasant resistance in settings where open political activity was restricted is once again becoming the most convenient form of struggle for "social movements with no formal organization,

---

19   James C. Scott, *Weapons of the Weak: Everyday Forms of Peasant Resistance* (New Haven, CT: Yale University Press, 1985), 292.

20   Goodman, *Drawing the Line Once Again*, 97.

21   Scott, *Weapons of the Weak*, 29.

22   Ibid., 36.

no formal leaders, no manifestoes, no dues, no name, and no banner."[23] What we therefore need, says Zinn, are "political guerrilla tactics in the face of mass society—in which enclaves of freedom are created here and there in the midst of the orthodox way of life, to become centers of protest, and examples to others. It is in techniques of organization, pressure, change, community-building—that the New Radicals need the most thought, and the most action. It may take an ingenious combination of energy and wit to carry through a new kind of revolution."[24] This would indeed be an anarchy of everyday life.

☾ ☾

I want to begin with some theoretical, epistemological, methodological, and technical instructions.

First, the British writer Alan Alexander Milne once wrote that it is practical to quote others because it saves one from the trouble of thinking. This work also includes—sometimes more, sometimes less ample—quotes, especially from literary works. This is not a consequence of Milne's conclusion that we can spare ourselves many troubles nor an attempt to prove he was right, but more the result of our sensibility so that no one is deprived of their own findings and interpretation of literary works. Namely, the "metaphysical" nature of the latter leaves plenty of space for one's own interpretation.

Second, the work follows Howard Zinn's epistemological position that objectivity in the social sciences is impossible and even undesirable. If objectivity means to pretend that ideas play no particular role in social struggles and that we should adopt specific positions within them, then this work will be far from "objective."

---

23 Ibid., 35.
24 Howard Zinn, *The Zinn Reader: Writings on Disobedience and Democracy* (New York: Seven Stories Press, 2009), 685.

The contemporary world is a world of conflicting interests—war against peace, selfishness against equality, nationalism against internationalism, elitism against democracy—therefore, it is both impossible and unwelcome to remain neutral. Objectivity is impracticable also for the methodological fact: every analysis encompasses a subjective and limited range of relevant data taken from a myriad (i.e., market) of available information. Every analysis is defined with one's own subjective belief of what is relevant and what is not, and is thus already contradicting the requisite "myth" of objectivity.[25]

Even if "objectivity"—understood as passivity and non-engagement—were possible, it would be undesirable. That is to say, science should never serve only its own purpose but should contribute to the broadening of human values such as freedom, equality, fairness, and brotherhood, and to solving the fundamental problems faced by humanity such as famine, warfare, and poverty. Too many of today's scientists and academics are merely passive reporters of more or less absurd, trivial, and esoteric subjects, while outside their offices and lecture rooms social struggles—crucially important for humankind—are taking place. Despite our privileged position, we have still not realized that we are first humans and only then, or for this very reason, "objective" scientists. Their work must rather be "consciously activist on behalf of the kind of world which history has not yet disclosed, but perhaps hinted at."[26]

Of course, the "impartiality" of this work does not suggest that some specific (historical) facts have been ignored or modified, let alone invented. Moreover, this "nonobjectivity" does not mean that the analysis of the subject-matter has failed to follow scientific standards (cognitive and

25 Objectivity could thus only be achieved by encapsulating all individual subjectivities or partial objectivities.
26 Howard Zinn, *The Politics of History* (Chicago: University of Illinois Press, 1990 [1970]), 3.

argumentative procedures). It merely means that the analysis of a mass of data was not underpinned by predefined (desired) answers but with predefined (useful) objectives and questions, particularly the consideration of "How to achieve a better world?" But becoming an activist-scholar should not, Zinn says, result from our partial and egotistic aims, but from our immersion in the struggles of "the etceteras of history": "We will be doing this, not in the interests of the rich and powerful, or in behalf of our own careers, but for those who . . . so far have had to strive alone just to stay warm in winter, to stay alive through the calls for war."[27]

By now it should be obvious that we are not trying to hide that this work has a subjective position and, frankly, there is no need to do so. It will be evident from the work itself that in the name of fundamental human values we have a (personal) wish and a (social) responsibility to take part in the social struggles of our time. As Zinn put it, "You can't be neutral on a moving train." Things are already happening; absurd wars are taking place, children are dying of hunger. In a world moving in the wrong direction, to be neutral and passive means to accept or even approve of the existing injustices. Such passivity cannot and must not be tolerated by us as activist-scholars, and even less by us as people who believe in the universality and inseparability of human rights and fundamental freedoms. For scholars, being in a position of having knowledge entails additional responsibility; instead of using their privilege to "advance careers, but hardy anything else," they should become catalysts for change:

> Let the economists work out a plan for free food, instead of advising the Federal Reserve Board on interest rates. Let the political scientists work out insurgency tactics for the poor, rather than counter-insurgency tactics for the military. Let

---

27   Ibid., 14.

the historians instruct us or inspire us, from the
data of the past, rather than amusing us, boring
us, or deceiving us. Let the scientists figure out
and lay before the public plans on how to make
autos safe, cities beautiful, air pure. Let all social
scientists work on modes of change instead of
merely describing the world that is, so that we
can make the necessary revolutionary alterations
with the least pain.[28]

Third, unlike most other studies which have focused
solely on classical "thinkers" of anarchism while neglecting
the creative potential of "ordinary" people, this study builds
on the assumption that the most important theoretical contributions inside anarchism have for some time been made
by authors who have in one way or another been involved
in the critical and reflective practice of social movements.
The involvement of anarchist activists/theoreticians in contemporary social struggles through "co-research," "militant
investigation," and "research in action" also results in a "collective theoretizing" about the most pressing and sensitive issues as well as in a search for realistic and, in particular, credible analyses which are then offered as a gift to movements so
as to partake in the success of their shared struggle.[29]

According to Zinn, the epistemological transformation
must always also include a methodological transformation.
In his essay titled "Historian as Citizen," Zinn urges that "in
a world hungry for solutions, we ought to welcome the emergence of the historian—if this is really what we are seeing—
as an activist-scholar, who thrusts himself and his work into
the crazy mechanism of history, on behalf of values in which

---

28   Ibid.
29   For more about the potential of "co-research," "militant investigation" and "research in action," see Stevphen Shukaitis, David Graeber
and Erika Biddle, eds., *Constituent Imagination: Militant Investigations—
Collective Theoretization* (Oakland: AK Press, 2007).

he deeply believes. This makes of him more than a scholar; it makes him a citizen in the ancient Athenian sense of the word."[30] This is also evident in Zinn's book on the Student Nonviolent Coordinating Committee, *SNCC: The New Abolitionists*, in which he demonstrates that the benefits of the work are that it is not "a comprehensive scholarly book on the SNCC, but a work of on-the-spot reportage."[31]

Unlike the majority of scholars who neglect the creative potential of "ordinary" people, Zinnian epistemology and methodology is based on the assumption that activists often apprehend the processes of social change and the relations of power within society more accurately than unengaged academics. For Zinn, there are two benefits of activist research:

- An ethnographic approach can transform scholars and enable them to "transcend their immediate circumstances by leaps of emotion and imagination."[32]

- Engagement in social struggles can enrich the scholarship of the activist-scholars, enabling them to uncover subaltern infrapolitics of the hidden or seemingly nonpolitical. "Contact with the underground of society, in addition to spurring the historian to act out his value-system, might also open him to new data: the experiences, thoughts, feeling of the invisible folk around us. This is the kind of data so often missed in official histories, manuscript collections of famous personalities, diaries of the literate, newspaper accounts, government documents."[33]

Fourth, to understand the relevance of anarchism, both the justification of its criticism and the reasonableness of its

---

30 Zinn, *Zinn Reader*, 543.
31 Howard Zinn, *SNCC: The New Abolitionists* (Cambridge, MA: South End Press, 2002 [1964]), i.
32 Zinn, *The Politics of History*, 33.
33 Ibid.

vision, we need a cognitive transformation that Boaventura de Sousa Santos perceives also as a prerequisite for any social justice. According to Arjun Appadurai, research in the era of globalization is a peculiar optical challenge. Nowadays many concepts and categories are too elusive for traditional disciplines, classical theories, and Western epistemologies, therefore the analysis must be founded on a new, more flexible epistemology.[34] On the other hand, we are witnessing epistemological ignorance and the suppression of knowledge, a form of *epistemicide*, that strengthens the status quo and at the same time dismisses, discredits, and trivializes arguments and solutions not in line with the hegemonic epistemological position—a hegemonic notion of truth, objectivity, and rationality.[35]

In the past decades many disciplines went through radical transformation or are today facing the greatest turbulence. Within historiography a new generation of young scholars of the New Left enabled the discipline no earlier than the 1960s and 1970s to overcome inner limitations, best summed up by Henry Kissinger's thesis that history is the memory of states, everything else is of minor importance. Authors such as E.P. Thompson, Howard Zinn, Staughton Lynd, and Jesse Lemisch initiated *history from the bottom-up* or *people's history* which, figuratively speaking, moved its focus from those in the White House to those picketing the White House. With this very shift, epitomized by the 1968 publication of Barton J. Bernstein's edited volume *Towards a New Past: Dissenting Essays in American History*, the discipline was able to detect new questions and offer new answers.

---

34 Arjun Appadurai, "Grassroots Globalization and the Research Imagination" in *The Anthropology of Politics: A Reader in Ethnography, Theory, and a Critique*, ed. Joan Vincent (Malden, MA: Blackwell Publishers), 273.

35 See Boaventura de Sousa Santos, *The Rise of the Global Left: The World Social Forum and Beyond* (London: Zed Books, 2006); Boaventura de Sousa Santos (ed.), *Cognitive Justice in a Global World: Prudent Knowledges for a Decent Life* (Lanham, MD: Lexington Books, 2007).

For Staughton Lynd, by far the most influential piece of radical historiography is Zinn's *A People's History of the United States*, a book that alone "has probably done more good, and influenced more people (especially young people), than everything the rest of us [radical historians] have written put together."[36] In *A People's History*, Zinn explains that in the inevitable taking of sides he prefers

> to try to tell the story of the discovery of America from the viewpoint of the Arawaks, of the Constitution from the standpoint of the slaves, of Andrew Jackson as seen by the Cherokees, of the Civil War as seen by the New York Irish, of the Mexican war as seen by the deserting soldiers of Scott's army, of the rise of industrialism as seen by the young women in the Lowell textile mills, of the Spanish-American war as seen by the Cubans, the conquest of the Philippines as seen by black soldiers on Luzon, the Gilded Age as seen by southern farmers, the First World War as seen by socialists, the Second World War as seen by pacifists, the New Deal as seen by blacks in Harlem, the postwar American empire as seen by peons in Latin America. And so on, to the limited extent that any one person, however he or she strains, can "see" history from the standpoint of others.[37]

In this reversal of perspective, Zinnian epistemology anticipates the idea of "diatopical hermeneutics" as developed by Raimon Panikkar. Diatopical hermeneutics, as we will see later, can be understood as a *détournement* of perspective that,

36   Lynd in *From Here to There: The Staughton Lynd Reader*, ed. Andrej Grubačić (Oakland: PM Press, 2010), 120.

37   Howard Zinn, *A People's History of the United States: 1492–Present* (New York: Harper-Perennial, 2005 [1980]), 10.

instead of one (hegemonic) position from which "research," proposes a plethora of such perspectives and "dialogical dialogue" between them.

It is obvious that for Zinn exclusion, oppression, and discrimination not only have economic, social, and political dimensions but also an epistemological one. As opposed to past practices, political control and domination are today not grounded solely on economic and political power, but foremost on knowledge or the hierachization of knowledge. They also do not aim at the exclusion of others, but at specific ways of their inclusion that result in a certain constellation of a political community and the asymmetry of power within it. According to Zinn, in this process knowledge plays the crucial role: "True, force is the most direct form of power, and government has a monopoly of that (as Max Weber once pointed out). But in modern times, when social control rests on 'the consent of the governed,' force is kept in abeyance for emergencies, and everyday control is exercised by a set of rules, a fabric of values passed from one generation to another by the priests and the teachers of the society."[38] Hence, we can understand why the knowledge industry, which these days directly reaches millions of young people in colleges and universities around the world, is becoming a vital locus of power. That is also why the traditional centers of power, which already control obvious forms of power, are trying to monopolize it.

Particularly beneficial directions for the epistemological transformation within the social sciences, closely resembling Zinnian epistemology, can be found in Boavantura de Sousa Santos's theory of "the sociology of absences." For Santos, the solution is "the sociology of absences" which transforms impossible into possible, absent into present, or irrelevant into relevant. If the production of the nonexistence, *ergo* the hegemonic conception of social sciences, is founded on:

---

38 Zinn, *The Politics of History*, 6.

- *a monoculture of science* that turns modern science and high culture into the sole criteria of truth and aesthetic quality, respectively;

- *a monoculture of linear time* that dismisses as "backward" whatever is asymmetrical and contrary to whatever is declared "forward";

- *a monoculture of* classification that attempts to naturalize social differences and hierarchies;

- *a monoculture of the universal and the global* that trivializes all particular and local practices and ideas, and renders them incapable of being credible alternatives to what exists globally and universally; and

- *a monoculture of capitalist production and efficiency* that privileges growth through market forces and dismisses other systems of production as nonproductive;

then "the sociology of absences" should be founded on the following:

- *an ecology of knowledges* that recognizes other knowledge and criteria of rigor;

- *an ecology of temporalities* that understands linear time as only one of many conceptions of time: the rejection of linear time places other and different political and social practices on the same level as political and social practices of the West since now they become another form of contemporaneity;

- *an ecology of recognition* that tries to articulate a new nexus between the principles of equality and of difference, thus allowing for the possibility of equal differences: the differences remaining after the elimination of hierarchy would thus become an important criticism of the differences requested and needed by hierarchy so as to subsist;

- *an ecology of trans-scale* that rejects the logic of the global scale and recuperates particular and local practices and ideas as relevant alternatives;

- *an ecology of productiveness* that refutes the hegemonic paradigm of development and infinite economic growth: it recuperates and validates alternative systems of production, popular economic organizations, cooperatives, and enterprises, which have been trivialized by the hegemonic orthodoxy of productivity.[39]

"The sociology of absences" thus reveals social and political solutions, initiatives and concepts which were suppressed, coopted or trivialized by the dominant political or epistemological position, since according to Santos "what does not exist is, in fact, actively produced as non-existent, that is, as a non-credible alternative to what exists."[40]

To completely understand anarchism, a relevant example of the epistemological transformation can also be found within anthropology. With their conceptualization of "other anthropologies/anthropology otherwise," Eduardo Restrepo

---

39　For more about the "sociology of absence" and the "sociology of potentiality," see Boaventura de Sousa Santos, "The World Social Forum: Toward a Counter-Hegemonic Globalisation (Part I)" in *World Social Forum: Challenging Empires*, eds. Jai Sen and Peter Waterman (New Delhi: The Viveka Foundation, 2004); Boaventura de Sousa Santos, *The Rise of the Global Left: The World Social Forum and Beyond* (London: Zed Books, 2006); Boaventura de Sousa Santos (ed.), *Cognitive Justice in a Global World: Prudent Knowledges for a Decent Life* (Lanham, MD: Lexington Books, 2007); Boaventura de Sousa Santos (ed.), *Another Knowledge Is Possible: Beyond Northern Epistemologies* (New York: Verso, 2008).

40　Santos, *The World Social Forum*, 238.

and Arturo Escobar call for a critical awareness of both the larger epistemic and political field in which disciplines emerged and continue to function, and of the micropractices and relations of power within and across different locations and traditions of individual disciplines.[41]

By analogy to Restrepo and Escobar, "other social sciences/social science otherwise" would consequently have to analyze subalternized forms of knowledge, modalities of writing, political and intellectual practices, etc. The solution is once again an epistemological and methodological transformation that will overcome the "asymmetrical ignorance" and "parochial mentality" that still characterizes the disciplines of social sciences and humanities. Such epistemological and methodological transformation would result in new styles of thinking and new forms of knowledge organization. It can also be added that the result would be an assumption of political practices and ideas which in the past were too often marginalized and trivialized, and would at the same time represent the first step to pluralization and decentralization of social sciences. Even more, it would also be the first step to cognitive justice that, as mentioned earlier, a prerequisite for social justice.[42]

Fifth, bearing in mind that this is a theoretical discussion of specific political theory and practice, one would expect that, methodologically speaking, our analysis would be less diversified. Considering that narrow disciplinary approaches to formulating big theories are impossible nowadays and that, similarly, interdisciplinary approaches which implicitly insist on dividing and separately discussing specific aspects of political, social, and economic realities are also completely inappropriate, we decided to also deal with the subject of analysis epistemology-wise.

---

41   Eduardo Restrepo and Arturo Escobar, "Other Anthropologies and Anthropology Otherwise: Steps to a World Anthropologies Framework," *Critique of Anthropology* 25, no. 2 (2005): 99–129.

42   Ibid.

The book is thus underpinned by an undisciplinary or counterdisciplinary approach which rejects all pretentious objectives to formulate or consolidate a universal theory. It offers a radical criticism of the canon of authority/authorization which reproduces the dominant political theory and simultaneously discards the notion of inter- and transdisciplinarity as well as implicitly builds on and advocates the separation of disciplines and fields of research. It understands theory as a starting point and not as a goal of a multidimensional—"equally philosophical and historical, cultural and economic, political and anthropological"—study of anarchism as a practice-based theory.[43]

🌙 🌙

Armed with these findings, we can embark on the road to study anarchism and its forgotten currents.

The first part of the book offers an overview of anarchism where the reader will find a condensed yet still broad reading of anarchist theory, ontology, and genealogy. Those already familiar with anarchist theory and praxis might skip over this part, although in doing so they might lose some reflections on a much neglected question within the anarchist milieu—such as, what can anarchist theory and praxis offer to a new understanding of democracy and political membership? In the past many intellectual currents (not excluding anarchism) still subsumed *politics* under *statecraft*. This has resulted in a theoretical purism that has rejected every in-depth reflection on key political concepts such as political power or even citizenship. The first part of the book is thus meant to make up for this deficit since there are few books to consult on the anarchist understanding of democracy, citizenship, political power, etc. These are questions we should

---

43 Michael Hardt and Antonio Negri, *Empire* (Cambridge, MA: Harvard University Press, 2001), xvi.

address as soon as possible instead of ignoring them for the sake of our theoretical purity.

What follows the introductory chapters is a much more demanding task—a bold attempt to refresh anarchist social thought with new contributions which will be looked for in one of the forgotten currents, New England Transcendentalism as promoted by Ralph Waldo Emerson, Henry David Thoreau, Walt Whitman, and others. We will explore Gerald Runkle's thesis that the new generations of American anarchists did not arrive at their aspirations and views by delving into Godwin, Bakunin, or Tucker but rather by reading the works of Thoreau, Emerson, and Whitman.[44] We will therefore ascertain that Transcendentalism should not be treated as a literary movement only, but also as a philosophical and even a political one. After all, the principal works of Transcendentalism—including Thoreau's *Walden*, Emerson's "Nature," and Whitman's *Leaves of Grass*—are today part of the American literary canon not so much for their aesthetic value as for their political implications and social criticism. What is surprising, of course, is the fact that the Transcendentalists' contribution to the creation of a better, more just social system is still overlooked or ignored.

That is why many might consider it senseless, if not illogical, to look for parallels between Transcendentalism and anarchism in the United States. There is political theory and praxis on one side and literary direction on the other which, in the last few decades, has for the first time attracted serious research attention. The reason for such reservation or skepticism, as we will see, stems from the separation of the spheres in which both concepts are discussed. While anarchism is discussed in the sphere of politics, Transcendentalism is chiefly discussed within literature. The interpretative blindness is therefore a result of an erroneous classification of

---

44 Gerald Runkle, *Anarchism: Old and New* (New York: Delacorte Press, 1972), 199.

New England Transcendentalism exclusively in the milieu of American literary renaissance and the failure to link it to European (and, of course, American) political developments.

What, then, is anarchism?

2
PERCEPTIONS AND CONCEPTIONS OF ANARCHISM

About the (Mis)Understanding of Anarchism

IN ANSWER TO THE QUESTION OF WHAT ANARCHISM REPRESENTS to the average citizen, Uwe Timm conclusively wrote that in it they mostly see chaos, violence, destruction—in short, everything that has unjustly been imputed to anarchism.[1] Even those with better knowledge still tend to repeat the usual criticism that drifts from the utopia of the elimination of authority to some kind of chimera, and views anarchists as scholars, moralists, and idealists who are worthy of praise yet unable to produce a concept that can change the economic, social, and political reality.

Timm's considerations highlight the main problem that has loomed large over anarchist thought throughout history and strongly curbed its potential—namely, an erroneous interpretation of the concept, and its leveling. Many entertain the hope that anarchism will only begin to live when it rids itself of its stigma and when people and society cease to

---

1   Uwe Timm, "Lernziel Anarchie" in *Antologija anarhizma*, ed. Rudi Rizman (Ljubljana: Knjižnica revolucionarne teorije, 1986), 634.

view anarchism solely through the distorting lens of prejudices. Yet, there is also the fear that this will not be enough if the true essence of anarchism remains misunderstood; anarchism, after all, is not a monolithic block but a flow that can accommodate a host of ideas. This can give anarchist thought the appearance of contradiction; on the other hand, it adds to its flexibility.

Nowadays, an even greater problem related to understanding and thus writing about anarchism has been observed in environments where the history of anarchism has been distorted or completely overlooked. For instance, even though one can find some valuable attempts to delve into the history of anarchism in the Balkans—for example Kristan (1927), Kesić (1976), Fischer (1979 and 1986), Rozman (1979), Maserati (1982), Indjić (n.d.), Grubačić (2011)—the general perception of anarchism and its (pre)history remains problematic. According to Darij Zadnikar, "When the political theory and practice of anarchism thrived in the youth subcultures of the West and filled up the new-left or Bolshevik void, the 'punks' in Slovenia understood anarchism at the level of bourgeois semantics: as chaos. They were not influenced by the Dead Kennedys and eventually they stuck to a derivative image of punk and a bottle of cheap booze."[2]

Even though anarchism is amorphic, paradox-ridden, and full of contradictions, a loose working definition would

---

2   Zadnikar, "Kronika radostnega uporništva," 209. The absence of an in-depth analysis of anarchism in the region is also reflected in some attempts of reflection over its own history, where among others the following can be observed: "Anarchism and anarchist movement in the territory of former Yugoslavia have no real tradition and history, save some bright exceptions. The first genuine anarchist initiatives were launched only in the 1990s, after the fall of the Communist regime and the disintegration of the SFR Yugoslavia" (an invitation to the first Balkan Anarchist Book Fair). If we take the task of writing our own history seriously, as we are required to do by the political and academic values of the task, then superficial knowledge of the subject would suffice to realize that such an attempt should draw a completely different picture.

understand it as a political theory and practice aimed at (according to Proudhon) achieving a society without a ruler.[3] Anarchism as a praxis is geared toward a society founded on justice and equality. As such, it opposes all types of hierarchy, exploitation, and authority along with their main two manifestations: capitalism and the state.

At this point, it is worth noting the much broader definition of anarchism by John Clark, who defines it concurrently as:

1. a view of an ideal, noncoercive, nonauthoritarian society;

2. a criticism of existing society and its institutions, based on this antiauthoritarian ideal;

3. a view of human nature that justifies the hope for significant progress toward the ideal;

4. a strategy for change, involving institutions of noncoercive, nonauthoritarian, and decentralist alternatives.[4]

Etymologically, the words *anarchy* and *anarchism*, which are today synonyms of *chaos* and *disorder*, originate from the Greek word ἀρχός (*archos*, Greek: "ruler, leader, superior") with a prefix ἀν (*an*, Greek: "without"), meaning a society without rule and authority. As the Italian anarchist Errico Malatesta put it, in this place,

---

3　Anarchists advocate that anarchism should be discussed as a theory and not an ideology: a set of flexible ideas open to modifications in the light of new findings, rather than a closed set of ideas which, instead of offering a clear insight into the social and political reality, veil this reality or only offer a distorted picture where *camera obscura* additionally strengthens and justifies this ideology.

4　John Clark, "What Is Anarchism?" in *Anarchism: Nomos xix*, eds. Roland J. Pennock and John W. Chapman (New York: New York University Press, 1978), 13.

we will not enter into a philological discussion, since the question is historical and not philological. The common interpretation of the word recognizes its true and etymological meaning; but it is a derivative of that meaning due to the prejudiced view that government was a necessary organ of social life, and that consequently a society without government would be at the mercy of disorder, and fluctuate between unbridled arrogance of some, and the blind vengeance of others.[5]

The association of anarchism with violence and chaos stems from at least two related erroneous assumptions: first, that lack of rulers and authority leads to disorder; second, that freedom and order prevail under strong rulership and strict authority. History has proven both assumptions wrong, as authority, states, governments, and laws have hitherto not been a steady remedy for disorder, inequality, and injustices, but often the cause of them.

In their discussions of anarchism, many authors have reached a conclusion that anarchism's complexity and internal fragmentation facilitate its historical adaptability but also offer other ideological practices an opportunity to make accusations against it.[6] This may be one reason why today's discussions on anarchism, the same as various conceptions

---

5   Errico Malatesta, *Anarchy* (London: Freedom Press, 2001), 16–17. Malatesta refutes the reproaches of those who think that anarchists chose a wrong name for themselves because the masses misunderstand it and this leads to its misinterpretation: "The error does not come from the word but from the thing; and the difficulties anarchists face in their propaganda do not depend on the name they have taken, but from the fact that their concept clashes with all the public's long established prejudices on the function of government, or the 'state' as it is also called."

6   Rudi Rizman, ed., *Antologija anarhizma* (Ljubljana: Knjižnica revolucionarne teorije, 1986), xxiii.

of anarchism within modern political theory, too often stem from misunderstanding and biased judgments.

Most people still associate anarchism and anarchy with violence, disorder, and chaos. This association is naturally absurd and ill-founded, whereas the fear is justified and understandable given that these people have been living for quite some time in a world of violence, disorder, and chaos. Of course, they do not live in anarchies but in modern nation-states in which a handful of people enjoy unimaginable wealth and power while the majority live in poverty, famine, misery, prisons, fear, and are angry about the widespread liberal egoism and pragmatism in the international community.

Murray Bookchin sees the value of anarchism in that it

> has raised to the foreground those ecological, sexist, and community issues, the problems of self-empowerment, the available concepts of self-administration, namely the themes that are now at the foreground of a famous "social issue." And it has raised these issues from within its very substance as a theory and practice directed against hierarchy and domination. . . . The anarchist theories today do not involve a mystical return to a "natural man," a simple antistatism, a denial of the need for organization, a conception of direct action as violence and terrorism, a mindless rejection of sophisticated theory.[7]

It is ironic that this seems to have been forgotten and that anarchism is depicted as a "poor cousin" of Marxism: "theoretically a bit flat-footed but making up for brains, perhaps,

---

7 Murray Bookchin, "Anarchism, Past and Present" in *Reinventing Anarchy, Again*, ed. Howard J. Ehrlich (San Francisco: AK Press, 1996), 29.

with passion and sincerity."[8] According to David Graeber, those considered as its founding figures are still often portrayed as agitators, pamphletists, and moralists and not as relevant theoreticians and philosophers, whereas contemporary anarchist are not regarded as authors of sophisticated theoretical analyses but more as sources of witty slogans, politically charged poetry, and readable science-fiction novels.[9]

To some extent, anarchist ideas have succeeded in infiltrating into progressive social thought or establishing themselves within it, particularly within the social sciences, even if the latter rarely refer to anarchism and more often than not conceal it. Even today, the bearers of social power are reluctant to give anarchism any credit, or continue to unduly incorporate its contributions in their own milieu of (post) Marxism, (neo)liberalism and all other "-isms." Anarchism, it seems, is one of the most, if not the most, plundered political philosophies.

The beginning of ("authentic") anarchist ideas dates back to the seventeenth and eighteenth centuries when two main forms of hierarchy and exploitation are gaining ground—the modern state and capitalism. The works of Gerrard Winstanley and William Godwin are considered a pioneering works in this field. Nevertheless, the ideas and practices geared toward building an alternative to the almighty entity and monolithic structure of authority can already be traced to many "primitive" nomadic tribes of prehistory, Ancient Greek philosophers and other "pioneers" of personal freedom, regardless of whether their motives for these ideas were of a philosophical or religious nature.

Ideas opposing hierarchy and dominance (in society, at school, at the workplace and in the family) should not be

---

8   David Graeber and Andrej Grubačić, "Anarchism; or, The Revolutionary Movement of the Twenty-First Century," http://www. zcommunications.org/znet/viewArticle/9258.

9   David Graeber, *Direct Action: An Ethnography* (Oakland: AK Press, 2009), 211.

limited and ascribed only to anarchism only as they have roots also in the liberalism of the Enlightenment. Given the theoretical backdrop of anarchism, it is unsurprising that some ideas of liberal thinkers may be considered protoanarchist. The entire opus of Adam Smith is often reduced to only the first few pages of his famous work, *An Inquiry Into the Nature and Causes of the Wealth of Nations*, and thus only to the idea of an "invisible hand," even though his work has five volumes and the concept of the invisible hand of the market is mentioned just once. Nowadays, many keep quiet that the key message of Smith's work is to rebuff the "brutal" and "wicked attempts" of the "masters of mankind" who want to follow the "repulsive principle": "All for ourselves and nothing for other people." Contrary to such pathological thinking, Smith set up the free market concept that should lead the way to the ideal of freedom and equality and guarantee every man their right to creative and self-fulfilling work. A couple hundred pages later, in the chapter "The Expenses of the Sovereign or Commonwealth," Smith writes:

> The understandings of the greater part of men are necessarily formed by their ordinary employments. The man whose whole life is spent in performing a few simple operations, of which the effects, too, are perhaps always the same, has no occasion to exert his understanding . . . and generally becomes as stupid and ignorant as it is possible for a human creature to become. He is completely incapable of forming judgments, much to the enjoyment of the state. His skills at workplace develop at the expense of his intellectual and social traits. But in every "progressive" and "civilized" society, only the poor working class is forced into this position, namely a great body of people.

It is otherwise in the barbarous societies, as they are commonly called. In such societies, the varied occupations of every man oblige every man to exert his capacity and the mind is not suffered to fall into that drowsy stupidity, which, in a "civilized" society, seems to benumb the understanding of almost all the inferior ranks of people. In those barbarous societies, as they are called, every man, it has already been observed, is a warrior.[10]

Other liberal thinkers also came to conclude that governments and states, despite their underlying mission to prevent injustice, inequality and violence, assume quite different roles in everyday life. Some have gone even further with the thesis that a society without a ruler (i.e., an "anarchist" society) would not result in a state of chaos and violence but would much likely develop into the most desired form of organized social life. Their position concurs with that of anarchism; namely it rejects Hobbes's thesis on the "state of nature" according to which in a governmentless society a permanent war of all people against all people would prevail. They emphasize that this would soon lead to a peaceful and productive social system where only full freedom would determine the acts of people. People, constrained only by the laws of nature, would live by their common sense, without a ruler above and an authority among them.[11]

---

10   Adam Smith, *An Inquiry into the Nature and Causes of the Wealth of Nations* (University Park, PA: Penn State University Press, 2005), 637–38.
11   The radical standpoint of the classics of liberalism should not come as a surprise, since liberalism is pre- and anticapitalist in its genesis. Smith's ideas deserve to be reinvestigated since there is a widespread trend of distorting and adapting his teachings, and used to ensure the legitimacy of the projects of privatization, liberalization, and fiscal discipline. The aureole of liberalism is a handy way of ensuring (political) support for nondemocratic and even antidemocratic projects.

About Anarchism and Violence

Division between the word and nitroglycerin within anarchism is not a historical constant but more of an exception and a characteristic of the anarchist movement at the end of the nineteenth century when a current focusing on so-called "propaganda by the deed" was formed. Even today, the centers of authority and power reduce anarchism to chaos, violence, and disorder, although by definition it only opposes hierarchy and domination, not order, rules, and an organized social system. Anarchism is regarded as a stand-in for terrorism, nihilism, and the abandonment of all moral values; anarchists are equated with terrorists, vandals, brutes, madmen, murderers, and extremists.

In *The Principles of Revolution*, Mikhail Bakunin defined the destructive orientation of anarchism as a creative force generating a new start. The destruction of the state does not mean only the destruction of the physical manifestations of the state (i.e., buildings, symbols) because a state is not only a physical structure, but a relation and idea that can be destroyed metaphysically. New interpretations of Bakunin's texts revolve around the elusive dilemma of whether he meant "destruction with construction" or "construction with destruction."

In his reply to the reproach that revolution and anarchism are destructive and not constructive, Alexander Berkman said:

> What, really, is there to destroy? The wealth of the rich? Nay, that is something we want the whole of society to enjoy. The land, the fields, the coal mines, the railroads, factories, mills, and shops? These we want not to destroy but to make useful to the entire people. The telegraphs, telephones, the means of communication and distribution—do we want to destroy them? No, we

> want them to serve the needs of all. What, then,
> is the social revolution to destroy? Not to destroy
> is the aim of the revolution, but to reconstruct
> and rebuild.[12]

Using the example of an American anarchist movement, Graeber assesses that today's anarchist movement is dangerous and subversive for those who rule precisely because its absence of violence, as "governments simply do not know how to deal with an overtly revolutionary movement that refuses to fall into familiar patterns of armed resistance."[13] The anarchist movement has already outclassed the futile discussions on the right and the appropriate method of political struggle. Since the 1999 WTO protests in Seattle, there has been a consensus within the movement that the best answer to the question of the means of political struggle is a diversity of tactics following the anarchist principles of direct action and prefigurative politics.

I will not discuss here at length the senseless yet relatively frequent discussions on the question of the destruction of private property. As the ACME collective rightfully replied in its communiqué written after the Seattle protests, however:

> We contend that property destruction is not a
> violent activity unless it destroys lives or causes
> pain in the process. By this definition, private
> property—especially corporate private prop-
> erty—is itself infinitely more violent than any
> action taken against it. . . . When we smash a
> window, we aim to destroy the thin veneer of

---

12   Alexander Berkman, *What Is Anarchism?* (Oakland: AK Press, 2003), 184.

13   David Graeber, "The New Anarchists" in *A Movement of Movements: Is Another World Really Possible?*, ed. Tom Mertes (New York: Verso, 2004), 207.

legitimacy that surrounds private property rights. At the same time, we exorcise that set of violent and destructive social relationships which has been imbued in almost everything around us. By "destroying" private property, we convert its limited exchange value into an expanded use value. A storefront window becomes a vent to let some fresh air into the oppressive atmosphere of a retail outlet (at least until the police decide to tear-gas a nearby road blockade). A newspaper box becomes a tool for creating such vents or a small blockade for the reclamation of public space or an object to improve one's vantage point by standing on it. A dumpster becomes an obstruction to a phalanx of rioting cops and a source of heat and light. A building facade becomes a message board to record brainstorm ideas for a better world. After N30 [protests], many people will never see a shop window or a hammer the same way again. . . . Broken windows can be boarded up and eventually replaced, but the shattering of assumptions will hopefully persist for some time to come.[14]

Militancy should indeed not be equated with violence, as anarchism should not be associated with destruction only; any destruction involved is destruction aimed at old and incorrect prejudices, which is essentially constructive task. Since one of the key features of anarchism is the link between political struggle and its objectives—"the means are the goals in the making"—it is not surprising that the theory and practice of prefigurative politics developed in an anarchist

14 ACME Collective, *N30 Black Bloc Communiqué*. http://the anarchistlibrary.org/HTML/ACME_Collective__N30_Black_Bloc_ Communique.html.

milieu. Prefiguration is an attempt to use methods of political organization and action to create the future in the present, or at least to some extent foresee and manifest the social changes we are striving for. As explained by Tim Jordan, it means acting in the present the ways we would want to act in the future, or acting as if the world in which we aspire to live has already materialized. It is a brief attempt to delegitimize the existing system and to build up its alternative from the bottom up.[15]

Noam Chomsky suggests that anarchism does not demand a life without rules, but rather is a socioeconomic, political theory and practice that aims to establish a highly organized society based on justice and equality in which all means of state and social restraint are abolished, and which cannot function without rules. This dilemma was highlighted by Errico Malatesta, who stated that "aspiration towards unlimited freedom, if not tempered by a love for mankind and by the desire that all should enjoy equal freedom, may well create rebels who, if they are strong enough, soon become exploiters and tyrants, but never anarchists."[16] The French anarchist Élisée Reclus further defines individual freedom as "the right of a person to act in accordance with their wishes while considering the welfare of all."[17] Others and care for others should not be understood as an obstacle since, according to William Godwin, a person takes the greatest pleasure from their work for the common good.

Anarchy is therefore a state without a ruler, which is why anarchism has a tendency to introduce a social state with no

---

15   Tim Jordan, *Activism! Direct Action, Hacktivism and the Future of Society* (London: Reaktion Books, 2002), 73.
16   Marshall, *Demanding the Impossible*, 38. There is also much truth in the warning that those who have not lost their children due to famine and curable diseases, their wives due to accidents at work, their relatives due to bombs dropped in the name of democracy, and so on, have no right to judge and condemn acts of despair.
17   Ibid.

room for humans exploiting and dominating each other, so it is no longer possible to speak about the state, the government and legal or other means of restraint. In the society of the future, the role of a social regulator would (will) be played by free agreements, the power (dissent) of public opinion, the laws of nature (restrictions), morals, and human nature itself. In the words of Alexander Berkman,

> Anarchism is not bombs, disorder, or chaos. It is not robbery and murder. It is not a war of each against all. It is not a return to barbarism or to the wild state of man. Anarchism is *the very opposite of all that*. Anarchism means you are free, nobody is allowed to enslave you, rule over you, steal from you or give you orders. . . . In short, anarchism means a condition or society where all men and women are free, and where all enjoy equally the benefits of an ordered and sensible life.[18]

Anarchism certainly has no monopoly on political violence, since violent political acts have been committed not only by anarchists, socialists and other revolutionaries, but also by patriots, nationalists, democrats and republicans, conservatives, monarchists, and even fervent Christians. Political extremism is a relational concept always conditioned by time and space and stemming from the prevailing asymmetry of power and the related labeling practices.[19] Millions of innocent people,

18 Berkman, *What Is Anarchism?*, xv.
19 The irony of the "extreme" can also be read in the personal tragedies of protagonists of the anarchist movement at the start of the "short twentieth century" (Hobsbawm) when many were deported or sentenced to jail for a number of years for "obstructing the war effort." The Mexican anarchist Ricardo Flores Magón received a twenty-year sentence for his antiwar activities and for violating the Espionage Act and did not live to its end. Alexander Berkman and Emma Goldman

after all, have been killed, maimed, or raped in the name of liberal democracy. Liberal democracy, however, continues to be seen as an untarnished ideal, whereas anarchism is portrayed as a pathological craving for destruction.

It should be added that skyrocketing profit margins in Western democracies have depended on corporations moving their production to third world countries and prisons. Along the way, corporations have avoided other nuisances such as transport costs, the threat of trade unions, and the possibility of strikes.

Although crime rates in the United States have declined over the past few decades, the number of prisoners in American "golden gulags" has risen nearly 500 percent from 1980 until the present day.[20] Considering the well-known facts—that the Thirteenth Amendment to the U.S. Constitution abolishing and prohibiting slavery does not apply to convicts; that sentences (even for obscure felonies) are constantly prolonged; the racism of law enforcement bodies (there are more African Americans in U.S. jails than in U.S. colleges and universities); the privatization of prisons that sell "their" prison labor force to external corporations (such as Victoria's Secret, Toys "R" Us, and Microsoft); that prisoners are charged for their accommodation and care in prisons and thus coerced into forced labor—it is easy to draw the conclusion that such bonded work is nothing but a socioeconomic system also known as slavery.

About Anarchism and Political Power

Throughout history, anarchism as a practice-based theory has been able to detect many more problems and offer

---

were deported from the United States for the same reason, without any possibility of return.

20 Ruth Wilson Gilmore, *Golden Gulag: Prisons, Surplus, Crisis, and Opposition in Globalizing California* (Berkeley: University of California Press, 2007), 7–8.

many more solutions than other intellectual traditions. Its persistent prefigurative political praxis, however, has led to unwarranted reduction. This primarily applies to concepts and categories rejected by anarchism as anomalies of the past and requiring no detailed theoretical reflection as they have no place in the anarchist project of horizontal organization and consensus decision-making. In the past, this collection often included the concept of political power which, in recent years, has been discussed in all its complexity and all its manifestations, primarily by merging classical anarchism with poststructuralism.

Unlike "diamat" Marxism, anarchism has never been defined by a short-sighted criticism of power, as it has been capable of identifying and addressing domination as a power that must and can be eliminated. Nevertheless, the demands for the immediate abolition of all monopolies of power have occasionally given rise to anarchism's theoretical purism which has frustrated profound discussion and reflection on political power as a crucial aspect of political struggle and the reality of every anarchist political community of the future.[21]

An interesting breakdown of political power within anarchist political theory has been proposed by Uri Gordon, referencing anarcho-pagan activist Starhawk and her innovative typology of power.[22] Gordon distinguishes between the following:

1. power-to: the basic sense of power as the capacity to affect reality;

2. power-over: power-to wielded as domination in hierarchical and coercive settings; and

---

21 Todd May, "Jacques Rancière and the Ethics of Equality," *SubStance* 36, no. 2 (2007): 20–21.
22 See Starhawk, *Truth or Dare: Encounters with Power, Authority, and Mystery* (New York: HarperCollins Publishers, 1987).

3. power-with: power-to wielded as noncoercive influence and initiative among people who view themselves as equals.[23]

Such a categorization usefully upgrades Holloway's binary conception of good and bad power or power-to and power-over, as there are cases when power-to realizes leads to power-over, and there are cases when power-to realizes itself but not through power-over.[24] Moreover, Gordon claims that power-over must not be reduced solely to force or coercion, as in modern societies, power-over frequently realizes itself through the manipulation and power of social roles or authority.

In his ethnography of the American anarchist movement, Graeber accepts the above tripartite scheme of power by detecting and unveiling the seemingly hidden aspects of the issue of power within egalitarian collectives and exposing the problem of the uneven distribution of power-to and lack of transparency in the implementation of power-with within collectives.[25] The issue of power concerns not only power-over (as was the case with classical anarchism that for several decades has constantly fetishized it) but primarily other manifestations of power. After all, power-over is not static and does not exist *in vacuo*, but always results from a dynamic redistribution of power-to and consequently also power-with. Power-over can only be limited through a redistribution of power-to and this, of course, shifts the focus of struggle and criticism from institutions and politics beyond movements to the movements themselves and their internal asymmetry of political resources.

Hence the perennial question arises about the (in)adequacy of decision-making and communication structures within egalitarian collectives that can reinforce the abovementioned

---

23 Gordon, *Anarchy Alive!*, 48.
24 See John Holloway, *Change the World Without Taking Power: The Meaning of Revolution Today* (London: Pluto Press, 2002).
25 For more, see Graeber, *Direct Action*, 239–85.

inequalities and, by rejecting formal solutions and delegating responsibility, lead to informal hierarchies and the "tyranny of structurelessness."[26]

Over the past few decades, when anarchism experienced many bifurcations, an important revision of the concept of political power took place within it. In his book *The Political Philosophy of Poststructuralist Anarchism*, Todd May emphasized: if in the past anarchism often assumed a deterministic and reductionist perception of power which, as a rule, was located only within the state, it is capable—by hybridizing and incorporating poststructuralism—of also detecting microtechnologies of power not only inside but also and mostly beyond the state.[27] According to May, anarchism must continue to broaden the scope of its criticism beyond the state and capitalism, to other places of political contestation and address the question of revolutionary power: "While [anarchists] have two-part distinction: power (bad) vs. nature (good), I have a four-part one: power as creative/power as repressive and good/bad. I do not take creative power as necessarily good, nor repressive power as necessarily bad. It all depends on what is being created or repressed."[28]

Similar simplifications and distortions likewise take place through (mis)understanding anarchist conceptions of authority. Anarchism, after all, does not oppose authority (technical competence and expert knowledge) but unjustified, imposed authority, which is to say authoritarianism. Authority as understood by anarchism must be justified, free, nonimposed, optional, functionally specific, and underpinned by competence and approval.

Chomsky suggests that structures of authority, hierarchy, and domination should be searched for, identified, and then

---

26   For more about this concept, see Jo Freeman, "The Tyranny of Structurelessness," http://www.jofreeman.com/joreen/tyranny.htm.

27   Todd May, *The Political Philosophy of Poststructuralist Anarchism* (University Park: The Pennsylvania State University Press, 1994).

28   May quoted in Curran, *21st Century Dissent*, 36.

challenged in all aspects of life. If it is impossible to find an excuse for them, then these structures are illegitimate and should be abolished to broaden the extent of people's freedom. This also includes political power, property, and management in the sense of the relationship between men and women, parents and children, our control over the destiny of future generations and many more. "That is what I have always understood to be the essence of anarchism: the conviction that the burden of proof has to be placed on authority and that it should be dismantled if that burden cannot be met."[29] Of course, Chomsky submits to such scrutiny all institutions that at first glance appear neutral and independent, including institutions that were perhaps useful and purposeful in the past, but are now only remnants of the period in which their existence was justified for ensuring security, survival, or economic development, and today contribute only to material and cultural impoverishment.

About Anarchism and the State

Since much has been written on anarchism and the state, this section will be rather short but still not redundant. Anarchism perceives the state as a conservative force that authorizes, regulates, and organizes the denial and restriction of progress (including the expansion of freedom) or uses progress to its own benefit and the benefit of the privileged class but does not encourage it. The state is not based on a social agreement as many "liberal theologians" claim, but on a social conflict. The state is therefore an anomaly, which is corroborated by Harold Barclay in his work *People Without Government: An Anthropology of Anarchy*, where he reflects on a plethora of anthropological studies suggesting that anarchies are not only utopian wishes but a necessity and even a

---

29 Noam Chomsky, *Chomsky on Anarchism*, ed. Barry Pateman (Oakland: AK Press, 2005), 178.

rule in human history: "Anarchy is by no means unusual; it is a perfectly common form of polity or political organization. Not only is it common, but it is probably the oldest type of polity and one which has characterized most of human history."[30]

Todd May has found that, in the past, the narrow understanding of power as repressive and never productive was often the only seamy side of the anarchist political philosophy.[31] This simplified discussion does not necessarily concern only its perception but also its localization, as many currents of anarchism equated power—that is, power-over—solely with the state. Anarchism does not distinguish itself from other revolutionary currents only for its criticism of the state, since its epistemological position and the resulting criticism are much broader in scope. The state and capitalism are perhaps the most striking sources of domination but are far from being the only ones. This is particularly true for the postmodern globalized world where, for some time, nation-states have been losing their political independence and economic sovereignty.

In his communiqué "Siete piezas sueltas del rompecabezas mundial," Subcomandante Marcos ascertains that the end of the Cold War brought with it a new framework of international relations in which the new struggle for those new markets and territories produced a new world war, the Fourth World War. This required, as do all wars, a redefinition of the

---

30 Harold Barclay, *People Without Government: An Anthropology of Anarchy* (London: Kahn & Averill, 1996), 12.

31 May, *The Political Philosophy*. In the twentieth century, anarchists were responsible for certain sophisticated analyses and criticisms of the state. Landauer, for example, understood the state as *a* state or specific relationship between people that can be surpassed by creating different relationships and different behavior. Murray Bookchin also revived the classical definition of the state as a "constellation of all bureaucratic and coercive institutions," a specific mentality or "implanted state of perceiving reality."

nation-states. In this "strange modernity that moves forward by going backward" the nation-states went from being directors of the economy to those who were directed. With the current processes of economic globalization, the nation-state is being forced to redefine its position and purpose. The structure of the global economy, which has up till now been leaning against the system of sovereign nation-states, is today in an irreversible crisis. World capitalism sacrificed without mercy that which gave it a future and a historic project, national capitalism: "Companies and states fell apart in minutes, not due to the torments of proletarian revolutions but the stalemates of financial hurricanes. The child (neoliberalism) ate the father (national capitalism) and in passing destroyed all of the discursive fallacies of capitalist ideology: in the new world order there is no democracy, liberty, equality, nor fraternity."[32]

According to Marcos, in the "cabaret of globalization," with the construction of a de-territorialized Empire, the nation-state shows itself as a "table dancer that strips off everything until it is left with only the minimum indispensable garments: the repressive force. With its material base destroyed, its possibilities of sovereignty annulled, its political classes blurred, the nation-states become nothing more than a 'security apparatus' of the megacorporations."[33]

According to Marcos, politics thus cease to exist as organizers of nation-states. Rather, politicians are administrators of companies while "national" governments are responsible for the administration of business in different regions of the Empire. "Nations are department stores with CEOs dressed as governments, and the new regional alliances, economic and political, come closer to being a modern commercial

---

32 Subcomandante Marcos quoted in Žiga Vodovnik, ed., *Ya Basta! Ten Years of the Zapatista Uprising: Writings of Subcomandante Insurgente Marcos* (Oakland: AK Press, 2004), 259.

33 Ibid., 271.

'mall' than a political federation."[34] This type of political architecture is not a *novum*, but merely a continuation and perfection of the hegemonic logic in a new form.

According to Marcos's description of contemporary political and economic architecture, with more multinational corporations than national economies in the top one hundred largest economic entities, the nation-state ceases to exist as the only center of sovereignty and arena in which key political decisions are made. Anarchism, then, must not offer only a criticism of the state, but continue to oppose all forms of political, social, and economic exploitation that curtail freedom, equality, and solidarity and render impossible "the full development of all the material, intellectual, and moral capacities latent in everyone of us."[35]

Within contemporary anarchism, the loudest opponent of negative fetishization of the state—in particular all-or-nothing demands that one should "fast" completely until the "main course"—is Noam Chomsky. Chomsky advocates an ostensibly paradoxical stance that the protection or even consolidation of the state is the first step to its abolition as it preserves public space where people can participate, organize themselves, and influence public politicians, even if in limited ways and within a limited scope. He simultaneously remains loyal to the anarchist belief that the state is an illegitimate institution while concluding that without opposition to the neoliberal agenda the state could become even more illegitimate, violent, and unfair. To pursue ideals such as freedom and equality, today's anarchism should defend the state against the attacks of multinational corporations that are eager to ruin the democratic and social institutions of the state, regardless of the limits of their influence. As Chomsky warns, radical slogans are attractive but do not help us when

---

34   Ibid., 261.
35   Bakunin in Sam Dolgoff, ed., *Bakunin on Anarchy* (New York: Alfred A. Knopf, 1972), 261.

crucial decisions and actions are taken that have very serious consequences.[36]

About Anarchism and Political Membership

According to James C. Scott, political membership beyond the state is the regularity of history, despite an inscription on the political map with nation-state and consequently with the sedentarization or administrative, economic, and cultural standardization of fluid political entities.[37] In the past, many intellectual currents, including anarchism, subsumed *politics* under *statecraft*, a mistake that has resulted in a theoretical purism and anti-intellectualism and tended to reject in-depth reflection on key political concepts such as political power or citizenship.

But, according to Murray Bookchin and James C. Scott, politics and statecraft are not only significantly different, they are in opposition to each other.[38] Historically, politics has not and could not be developed within the state, since it has always been closer to a philosophical concept of praxis as a free and creative activity of individuals within fluid polities. Only in our present time has politics been integrated by the state and strengthened the belief that there is no distinction between the political realm and the statist realm, even though the modern state was born as a reactionary response to Renaissance humanism, and has always been an obstacle to global democracy.[39] Moreover, for Richard J.F. Day, the

36 Chomsky, *Chomsky on Anarchism*, 212, 223.

37 James C. Scott, *Seeing Like a State: How Certain Schemes to Improve the Human Condition Have Failed* (New Haven, CT: Yale University Press, 1999), 3–4.

38 Murray Bookchin, *Social Ecology and Communalism* (Oakland: AK Press, 2007), 93–94; James C. Scott, *The Art of Not Being Governed: An Anarchist History of Upland Southeast Asia* (New Haven, CT: Yale University Press, 2010), ix–x and 1–39.

39 Tom Mertes, "Grass-roots Globalism," *New Left Review* 17 (September–October 2002): 101–10.

struggle to dismantle community through demutualization, a struggle that is waged between the newest social movements on one hand, and state and corporate forms on the other, is the struggle of the (post)modern condition.[40]

Although the etymological origin of the word *citizenship*—from *civitas*, *civitatus*, to the modern *citoyen*—always linked political membership to smaller and more fluid polities, we still find it difficult to understand the relationship between citizenship and the state in settings where the leveling of political membership to national or even ethnical identity results from a linguistic or semantic similarity between both concepts. We often forget that at the very beginning, citizenship was not related to the state but meant a specific urban relationship between rights and duties in the city. *Citizenship*, therefore, meant political membership in a *city*. It is thus erroneous to talk only about a "citizen of the state," since we can also identify other types of citizenship that are built on different—such as territorial or functional—criteria.[41]

A new imagining of citizenship and its constitution under different criteria necessarily leads us to an enquiry about the relationship between the nation-state and citizenship, and the relationship between democracy and citizenship. It therefore leads to a familiar question that does not allow unambiguous answers: is representative democracy within nation-states in an era of globalization and unprecedented mobility of the *demos* still a proper framework for "full membership of a community"?

If we bare in mind acceleration in the rate of international migration, we can agree with Ruth Lister when she writes that to avoid a partial integration of a new political

---

40 Richard J.F. Day, *Gramsci Is Dead: Anarchist Currents in the Newest Social Movements* (London: Pluto Press, 2005), 38.

41 For more about the genealogy of citizenship, see Bryan Turner, "Outline of a Theory of Citizenship" in *Citizenship: Critical Concepts*, eds. Bryan Turner and Peter Hamilton (London: Routledge, 2002), 199–226.

subject into the polity—and therefore rising numbers of *denizens* or *margizens*—we should once again understand citizenship not only as a legal status, but rather as a practice.[42] Here, a reconfiguration of the relationship between equality and difference is one of the most important aspects of a new citizenship. Citizenship is nowadays perhaps the most important point of contest about the identity and recognition of (group) differences that cannot be resolved by the current model of multiculturalism, or rather can only be resolved in times of economic growth. Today it is obvious that the multicultural project in its hegemonic form did not succeed. New citizenship rejects the paradigm of universalism, since it only results in the homogenization and uniformity of polities, not in social justice and the inclusion of their members. Universal citizenship and the related enlargement of the scope of the political subjects have certainly represented an important political achievement. We should still understand this process within its historical context since it has not been initiated to empower new political subjects, but to reflect a deep concern about the fate of the new political innovation, the modern nation-state.

The concept of a uniform, homogeneous citizenship emerged as a political tool and—like the invention of meter, kilogram, and other units of measurement, standards, and reforms—is a poor abstraction needed for the administrative, economic, and cultural standardization of heterogeneous and fluid political entities.[43] Universal citizenship can, in fact be seen as a political equivalent to the meter that was introduced with a revolutionary decree: "The centuries old dream of the masses of only one measure has come true! The Revolution has given the people the meter."[44] If the universal meter swept away differences in the units that it measures, then universal

---

42 Ruth Lister, *Citizenship: Feminist Perspectives* (New York: New York University Press, 1998).

43 Scott, *Seeing Like a State*, 32.

44 Ibid.

citizenship swept away and denaturalized differences among "unmarked" and "one-dimensional" citizens. On the other hand, new citizenship should be understood as an objection to the republican interpretation of citizenship as a universal office, conscripting rather than mobilizing the *demos* to participate in the *res publica*, and which is best epitomized in the *levée en masse* (1793) and *La Marseillaise* ("Aux armes, citoyens!").[45]

The affirmation of equality and universalism does not mean emancipation, since it can result in a loss of identity. Affirmation of differences and relativism can, conversely, result in another anomaly: in the justification of discrimination and subjugation. The question remains: Is there any solution to the so-called "politics of difference"? The errors and limitations of universalism and relativism can be eliminated with a use of diatopical hermeneutics, a *détournement* of perspective that, instead of one (hegemonic) position from which to determine the relationship between equality and difference, proposes a plethora of such perspectives and "dialogical dialogue" between them.[46] It builds on the thesis that *topoi*—places of (self)understanding within a certain culture and tradition or, to put it differently, forms through which we think, although we do not think about them—cannot be understood with tools and categories of other topoi, but at least we can gain a better understanding of them by traversing between various topoi. In moving between topoi (dia-topoi), Boaventura de Sousa Santos identifies the meta-right of equal difference.[47] The meta-right of equal difference is based on two axioms that transcend the old relationship of equality *vs.* difference in a genuinely new relationship of equality *and* difference: first, it stresses difference when

45   Michael Walzer, "Citizenship" in *Political Innovation and Conceptual Change*, eds. Terence Ball, James Farr, and Russell L. Hanson (New York: Cambridge University Press, 1995), 211–12.

46   Raimon Panikkar, *The Intrareligious Dialogue* (Mahwah, NJ: Paulist Press, 1999).

47   Santos, *Another Knowledge Is Possible*, 28.

equality would threaten our identity and, second, it stresses equality whenever diversity would result in inferiority and discrimination. The differences that would remain when inequalities and hierarchy vanish thus become a powerful denunciation of the differences that the status quo reclaims in order not to disappear.

Yet the reconfiguration of equality and difference is not the only key characteristic of a new citizenship. The new understanding of citizenship also loosens the mechanical link between rights and duties and the constitution of citizenship beyond this link. Different theories of citizenship propose various understandings of the link between rights and duties—for example, the preponderance of duties within the republican tradition and the preponderance of rights within the liberal one—but it is always established and perceived entirely mechanically. Citizenship as a special status is thus impossible without a burden of corresponding duties. Although such a definition of citizenship may seem logical and reasonable, it is highly problematic in many aspects.

The process of economic globalization that redefines the position and purpose of the nation-state also transforms the arena of political participation. What is left from T.H. Marshall's triad of citizenship rights are largely only political rights and a legal status without a performative dimension. Since citizenship and citizenship rights are allocated only to subjects able to accept corresponding duties, a national citizenship is not open to subjects who are unable to be bearers of duties. This logic of reciprocity ensures, *inter alia*, that children, future generations, or nature cannot become full members of a community. Identifying an individual as a subject with rights and duties furthermore prevents the identification of group rights and group identity, and results in the exclusion of all indigenous communities that do not want to enter into a polity without their particular group identities.

The new concept of citizenship moves away from the nation-state as its territorial reference point and simultaneously

rejects its continuation within some new supranational entities. It rejects the very notion of permanence and continu-
ity and therefore builds on municipalized political praxes of
the "newest social movements."[48] Many important innovations on both political and theoretical levels have occurred
within a network of urban or rural local initiatives that have
gradually developed ties of mutual recognition and interaction.[49] For Santos, this network represents the beginning of a
translocal, yet truly global network of direct democracy that,
in its fight against social exclusion and the "trivialization of
citizenship," has recuperated an idea of alterglobalization, direct democracy, and subaltern cosmopolitanism.

One of the common denominators of the various collectives that comprise the alterglobalization movement and
one of its most interesting contributions on the political
and theoretical level is the new understanding of political
community and political membership, the idea of translocal
citizenship. The altered local-regional-global nexus makes it
possible to finally separate political membership from the
nation and its constitution according to entirely new criteria.
It is an attempt to overcome current limitations with a construction of alternatives from the bottom up, as it foresees
a renewal of the political power of local communities, and
their federation into a global nonstatist network as a coun-
terbalance to nation-states and corporate power.

The concept of translocal citizenship thus represents a
significant departure from classical theories of citizenship as
it builds on *inclusion* and *participation* rather than on *identity*;
instead of *equality*, it accentuates *equal differences*. Yet, translocal citizenship is not just another postmodern conception of
political membership characterized by relativism and particu-
larism that, according to Rudi Rizman, only detects diversity,
difference, fragmentation, conflict, and opposition, but not

---

48 Day, *Gramsci Is Dead.*
49 Santos, *Cognitive Justice in a Global World*, xv.

commonality, equality, integration, consensus, and integration.[50] As Darren O'Byrne argues, it rather "embraces plurality without being relativistic, universality without being deterministic, and identity without being unduly subjectivistic."[51]

Translocal citizenship thus represents a critique of the universalistic assumptions within the liberal tradition, or their upgrade with differentiated universalism that draws close to Habermas's idea of "constitutional patriotism." As translocal citizenship offers a different understanding of political community and stresses its constant reinvention, however, it represents a form of "unconstitutional patriotism" that in its replacement of *ethnos* with *demos* follows a significantly more radical definition of democracy than that of Habermas. It does not equate democracy with a particular constitutional system or with a particular constellation of centers of power within a society but instead understands "democracy" as a verb, and never as a noun.[52]

Although our epistemological position is not like a sweater that we can simply take off to be replaced by another, the difficult task of changing "a skin, not a sweater" is a prerequisite for a new imagining of citizenship.[53] On the margins of the political map, various "subterranean" collectives and movements are developing a genuinely new political alternative, and with it also a new understanding of political membership that can be and needs to be worked out first on a more manageable scale within local communities. A new citizenship is not a legal status, but a performative status that is constituted

---

50   Rudi Rizman, *Globalizacija in avtonomija: Prispevki za sociologijo globalizacije* (Ljubljana: Znanstvena založba Filozofske fakultete, 2008), 37.
51   Darren J. O'Byrne, *The Dimensions of Global Citizenship: Political Identity Beyond the Nation-State* (London: Taylor & Francis, 2003), 227.
52   Cornel West, *Democracy Matters* (New York: Penguin Books, 2005), 68.
53   Paul Furlong and David Marsh, "A Skin not a Sweater: Ontology and Epistemology" in *Political Science: Theory and Methods in Political Science*, eds. David Marsh and Gerry Stoker (New York: Palgrave Macmillan, 2002).

beyond the nation-state and sometimes in opposition to it, as it surpasses the parochial types of political communities which ignore or even impede global connectedness.

About Anarchism and Democracy

Contemporary discussions on democracy are informed largely by two main discourses: the first understands democracy as a word whose roots lie in Ancient Greece and whose etymological origin poses dilemmas; the second examines democracy as an egalitarian decision-making procedure and everyday practice which in antiquity were gradually labeled "democratic."[54] Theoretical "radicalism," then, renounces the simplified treatment of democracy as an invention, and instead of a legal dimension, analyses the genealogical dimension or the roots (lat. *Radix*) of democratic praxis. The results of this dualism are diachronous discussions on democracy and a series of debates on the level of democracy of institutions and institutes that by their very essence counterpoise democratic practices.

Democracy cannot be merely delimited to the sphere of politics (an achievement of the eighteenth century), as it must necessarily encompass all social and economic life. Namely, democracy is not a matter of "political agoraphobia" (Dupuis-Déri) and exclusion that define and are the result of representative democracy within states; it is a matter of integration and practice within transcultural communities.[55]

---

54   David Graeber, *Possibilities: Essays on Hierarchy, Rebellion, and Desire* (Oakland: AK Press, 2007), 340. The etymological origin of the word *democracy* reveals its pejorative beginnings as it first denoted a convenient warning of the elites against the people (*demos kratos*) and only much later, when it substituted republicanism, assumed the current meaning equivalent to the "rule of the people" (*demos archos*).

55   Francis Dupuis-Déri, "Qui a peur du peuple? Le débat entre l'agoraphobie politique et l'agoraphilie politique," *Variations: Revue internationale de théorie critique* 15 (2011): 49–74.

These and similar misconceptions have given rise to a hegemonic notion of democracy that has recuperated the word while rejecting its contents.

Despite the rise and reinforcement of (participatory) democracy over the last few years, the perception of the crisis of the existing economic project and statism as the crisis of democracy per se is the best proof of a (mis)conception of the essence of democracy and the main reason why we are searching for it in places where the possibility of actually finding it is the smallest.[56] When David Graeber suggests that modern liberal democracies feature nothing similar to the Athenian *agora* but offer a number of parallels with the Roman *circus*, he surely means something beyond architecture.[57]

Within anarchism, democracy is interpreted as a praxis and a free and creative activity in everyday life, not as a prefabricated institutional design. Anarchism stresses that democracy is not a matter of a specific type of production or consumption but first and foremost a matter of freedom. If "majoritarian democracy" advocates the sovereignty of people, then participatory democracy advocates the sovereignty of an individual; anarchism thus rejects the form of representative democracy as well as the conception of nation as an entity separate from the individuals composing it.[58]

If the main manifestation or proof of the level of democracy within representative democracy is (passive) voting or a

---

56   A number of emergent studies within anthropology (e.g., Barclay 1990; Graeber 2007) and history (e.g., Zinn 2005; Rediker 2004) suggest that democracy and (centralized) power per se are incompatible; therefore, democracy cannot be found within the statist frameworks and centers of power, but rather in the "pockets of rebellion" on the periphery of the map of institutionalized political power.

57   Graeber, *Possibilities*, 366.

58   Democracy is understood in such a radical way within anarchism, that some have suggested that it is a unique type of aristocracy: a "universalized and purified aristocracy. If anarchism called for the freedom of noble men, anarchism has always declared the nobility of free men" (Woodcock, *Anarchism*, 31).

choice between the offered options then, within anarchism, "democracy on steroids" means the active (co)creation of these options through which every form of majority *voting* is replaced by the genuinely democratic procedure of consensus *decision-making*. There is probably no need to list the many episodes in modern history warning about the fatal consequences of leveling democracy to the concept of representative democracy with majority decision-making where "democracy" resulted in the undemocratic or antidemocratic treatment of minorities. Majority voting is not only an inherently oppressive anomaly resulting in a tyranny of the majority, but (paradoxically) also an extremely disuniting and homogenizing institute leading to unstable and one-dimensional societies.

Representative democracy in all of its derivations seems to be rare in the history of political communities, as it is based on two rarely coinciding preconditions:

1. belief that people should have an equal say in the decision-making;

2. a coercive apparatus capable of enforcing those decisions.[59]

Both preconditions have coincided only for a few periods in human history, since in egalitarian communities such systems of restraint are usually perceived as unnecessary and irrational anomalies, and in those entities with established mechanisms of control and coercion, the political elites and the rulers have had little desire to follow and realize the popular will.

If we return to the anarchist conception of democracy as a creative and free activity, a more accurate understanding of the praxis philosophy is required as well. The philosophy of praxis represents an important hybridization of Left

---

59   Graeber, *Possibilities*, 342.

intellectual thought that restored humans in Marxism as a historical subject and a moral and ethical dimension as an important factor of political action.[60] This is an extremely innovative synthesis of Marxism and anarchism, especially if Marxism is understood as "a theoretical or analytical discourse about revolutionary strategy" and anarchism as "an ethical discourse about revolutionary practice."[61]

Even though the word *practice* occurs frequently in everyday life and seems relatively clear and easy to understand—it is mainly used as a synonym for action, creation, work, habit, experience, and training—its meaning in the sphere of philosophy, particularly in praxis philosophy, is much more clear-cut.[62] *Praxis* can be defined as a free, universal, creative activity with which one creates and changes the world and therefore oneself. Such an understanding of praxis differs substantially from the epistemological category of practice

---

60 Thanks to a radical reinterpretation of the young Marx, the praxis philosophy has closely approached the anarchist position. The Praxis group included Trivo Indjić, who explicitly intervened in the field of anarchist political thought, and the *Praxis* journal also included the French anarchist Daniel Guérin. Praxis philosophy met with the reproach that it was not authentic Marxism but "anarcho-liberalism." Such criticisms were somewhat justified as the praxis philosophy has never been characterized by a narrow economic reductionism that would result in the fetishization of economic exploitation and class antagonism only.

61 David Graeber, *Fragments of an Anarchist Anthropology* (Chicago: Prickly Paradigm Press, 2004), 6.

62 Despite a clear-cut demarcation between practice and alienated labor, Marx does not consistently stick to his analytical classification and terminology. In his *Economic and Philosophical Manuscripts* (1844), he sometimes equates practice with a general notion of labor, whereas other discrepancies are found in his later works where he abandons the concept of *practice* and introduces the concept of *self-activity* (*Selbstbetätigung*) as the opposite of *labor*. It can nevertheless be concluded that, despite all inconsistencies and changes in the terminology, the objective of Marx's transphilosophy or his mind-set remained the same: to transform labor into what he termed "practice" or "self-activity" (*der Verwandlung der Arbeit in Selbstbetätigung*).

that can mean the changing of an object, even if this activity can still be completely alienated.

The key characteristic of praxis as a normative concept is that this activity per se represents the objective and aim; it is an activity inherent to humans, distinguishing them from other creatures.[63] It must therefore be separated from *alienated labor* as an activity which prevents people from realizing their potential and satisfying their needs, as well as from *labor* which is a neutral concept and concerns instrumental activities of vital importance for human survival and development. If praxis is a matter of one's desire, self-realization, and the "kingdom of freedom," then (alienated) labor is a matter of necessity, alienation and the "kingdom of needs."

The bastardization of Marx, especially of his earlier works, resulted in the discovery of humanist philosophy that until then had largely been ignored or dismissed as an unimportant (Hegelian) deviation of the immature, idealist Marx before he arrived at the "true" findings—that is, the theory of surplus value and historical materialism. In his detailed study of praxis philosophy, Gerson Sher legitimately establishes that it "returned philosophy back to Marx and Marx back to philosophy" by identifying praxis as a key concept of his (meta)philosophy.[64] However, this rediscovery did not end with Marx nor the Marxist classics, as a change in the reading of Marx—stemming from the germs of his humanist philosophy and through them—revealed all the deficiencies and seamy sides of his (meta)philosophy and orthodox Marxism per se.

---

63 A philosophical analysis of praxis was first suggested by Aristotle, who attempted to give the term a clearer and more solid meaning. Aristotle emphasized that praxis, in a narrow sense, should only refer to humans and their activity. For more about historical development of the term, see Gajo Petrović, *Praksa/istina* (Zagreb: Kulturno-prosvjetni sabor Hrvatske, 1986), 14–43.

64 Gerson S. Sher, *Praxis: Marxist Criticism and Dissent in Socialist Yugoslavia* (Bloomington: Indiana University Press, 1977), 26.

Consequently, praxis philosophy made a complete turn-around with the dogmatism of the "diamat" Marxism and the acceptance of anarchist analysis through the understanding of the role of revolutionary philosophy, which has to lead to prefiguration for immediate broadening of praxis. This can only be achieved by moving beyond abstract critical theory with concrete, practically oriented social criticism which will not be limited to capitalist society as many types of alienation can be found in postrevolutionary society—for example, commodity fetishism, nationalism, appropriation of surplus value by political elites, division of work which broadens the gap between the creative activity of the minority and the monotonous and degrading work of the majority. Therefore, the criticism of praxis philosophy does not lead to an "abstract negation" which aims at the absolute cancelation of the criticized object, but is a "concrete negation" as it anticipates the *Aufhebung* or sublation of only those characteristics and elements of the criticized object that represent its substantial internal limitations.[65]

The "relentless criticism of all existing conditions," if we borrow passage from Marx's letter to Arnold Ruge, which underpins both anarchism and the praxis philosophy should not be understood as sheer nihilism and the destruction of everything that exists, but only as its transcendence through social revolution. According to Gajo Petrović, revolution should not be equated with the use of force, overthrow of governments or economic collapse of the system only, because revolution "is not merely the passage from one form of Being to another, higher one, . . . it is the highest form of Being, the Being itself in its fullness. Revolution is the most developed form of creativity and the most authentic form of freedom. It is the very 'essence' of Being, the Being in its 'essence.'"[66]

---

65   Cf. Gajo Petrović, Čemu Praxis (Zagreb: Praxis, 1972), 162.

66   Gajo Petrović, *Mišljenje revolucije: Od ontologije do "filozofije politike"* (Zagreb: Naprijed, 1978), 64.

3
ONTOLOGY OF ANARCHISM

About Human Nature

IN VIEW OF THE ASSESSMENT THAT ANARCHISM IS BOTH A BELIEF and a rational philosophy, it is not surprising that anarchist conceptions of human nature also build on very mixed assumptions.[1] Given that critics still reproach anarchism for having built on a completely utopian, simplified, and naively optimistic understanding of humanity, this chapter will attempt to demonstrate that, throughout history, anarchism has been aware of and recognized the danger of the ahistorical treatment of human nature which neglects the social conditionality of a person's characteristics. The anarchist conception of human nature has never been presocial and essentialist, but it has been contextualist at least in part because its determinants have never been searched, as people are always situated in a broader social and cultural environment.

Why partly contextualist? Anarchism rejects behaviorism as an extreme that reduces a person to a sort of *tabula rasa* or modeling dough, merely conforming to the current social, economic, and political system. Rather, it offers a completely different, dialectical understanding of human nature

---

1   James Joll, *The Anarchists* (London: Routledge, 1979), x.

that considers the social conditionality of people, while also searching for and confirming its eternal inclination to voluntary decision-making for solidarity, benevolence, and mutual aid. According to Bakunin, people are entirely products of the environment that fed and raised them and these environments are a result of individuals who not only compose them, but also form and change them.

In current debates on the value of anarchism, its critics still object that the ontological perception of man within anarchism is completely unrealistic or, at best, normative or prescriptive, as history offers more proof of lack of freedom and noncreativity than freedom and creativity. These objections are groundless, because the definition of men and women as free and creative creatures does not fall only within the scope of so-called descriptive or normative treatment, but within the scope of expressive and potential treatment, in the sense that it highlights human potential—something that is separate from what it is and separate from what it should be. Of course, the ontological position of anarchism cannot be understood as a naive and simplified apotheosis of human nature, dealing only with a person's potential for good and creativity. Along with the descriptive concept of human nature, which can be confirmed by historical evidence, anarchism also introduces a normative concept stemming from a consideration of the possibilities beyond the existing reality.

The ontological position of anarchism also involves drawing a distance from the reductionism of orthodox Marxism, arguing that the question of human freedom here and now is not essential because humans are kneadable material, freely determined by the socioeconomic formation of society and its internal limitations. The theory of human nature and philosophical anthropology found within anarchism are essentially more complex in this respect. In contrast to (dogmatic) Marxism, anarchism detects and poses the complex question of the appropriate form of social, economic, and political system that will enable the individual, as a person of practice with specific intrinsic potentials, the highest level of self-realization. It therefore asks under what terms and conditions a human activity can become the realization of one's most creative capacities and a means for satisfying authentic individual and common needs.

Kropotkin and Mutual Aid

When discussing anarchist concepts of human nature, it is reasonable to start with Kropotkin's *Mutual Aid: A Factor of Evolution*, in which he offers a lucid criticism of T.H. Huxley's and Herbert Spencer's explanation of Darwin's theory. While Huxley and Spencer reduce life to a sheer struggle for survival, Kropotkin proclaims the law of cooperation and mutual aid a law of nature. Huxley's and Spencer's explanation—producing excuses for the "natural selection" among individuals, nations, and races—is the first attempt of a "socio-Darwinist" and pseudoscientific apology for the status quo, hence capitalism, imperialism, patriarchy, and racism.

Kropotkin's standpoints were largely influenced by the work of Russian zoologist Karl Kessler, whose research supported the conclusion that mutual aid can be considered a natural law at least to the same extent as mutual struggle, though mutual aid is a much more important factor of species' evolution. Kropotkin's work reported similar results, namely that nature reveals more evidence of mutual aid within a species than of mutual struggle and that in the struggle for survival, mutual aid is followed by the most successful species. Kropotkin points out that the struggle for survival is foremost a struggle against unfavorable or even hostile circumstances and not a struggle among members of the same species: "We maintain that under any circumstances sociability is the greatest advantage in the struggle for life. Those species which willingly or unwillingly abandon it are doomed to decay; while those animals which know best how to combine have the greatest chances of survival and of further evolution."[2]

While Darwinist fundamentalists—the former socio-Darwinists are in today's world played by sociobiologists and evolutionary psychologists—emphasize that the struggle between members of the same species results in the survival of the most successful ones, Kropotkin defines an animal species as a whole as the basic unit of this struggle. Thus, the most successful and the most thriving are those species practicing the highest level of cooperation and aid between their individual members:

> The animal species, in which individual struggle has been reduced to its narrowest limits and the practice of mutual aid has attained the greatest development, are invariably the most numerous, the most prosperous, and the most open to further progress. The mutual protection which is obtained in this case, the possibility of attaining old age and of accumulation of experience, the higher intellectual development, and the further growth of sociable habits, secure the maintenance of the species, its extension, and its further progressive evolution. The unsociable species, on the contrary, are doomed to decay.[3]

Though many authors have objected to and expressed doubts about the appropriateness of Kropotkin's methodology, contemporary anthropological studies increasingly support his findings and the contention that mutual aid and cooperation are the key characteristics of the human and animal world. That mutual aid between members of an animal species is a

---

2   Peter Kropotkin, *Mutual Aid: A Factor in Evolution* (London: Freedom Press, 1998), 60–61.
3   Ibid., 230.

main factor of evolution has had revolutionary consequences, as it follows that biological and social progress (including within a society) can only be achieved by practicing mutual aid and cooperation and not at all by force and coercion.

According to Kropotkin, these primal instincts can be revived in two ways, namely by appropriate means of economic organization based on cooperation and by a new approach to moral systems which should stem from the principle of mutual aid. Consequently, evolutionary theory cannot (any longer) serve to justify racism, imperialism, capitalism, or even claims for a strong state, but may only serve as proof of the potential of and need for anarchy. Anarchy may thus be understood as the highest form of our biological needs for cooperative and peaceful social groups.

This aspiration should not be discussed as the idealism of a handful of utopianists from the nineteenth century whose ideas were finally decomposed by the liberal logics of egoism and pragmatism in the twentieth and twenty-first centuries; it can be seen also in the famous 1962 Port Huron Statement by Students for a Democratic Society, which declared:

> We regard men as infinitely precious and possessed of unfulfilled capacities for reason, freedom, and love. In affirming these principles we are aware of countering perhaps the dominant conceptions of man in the twentieth century: that he is a thing to be manipulated, and that he is inherently incapable of directing his own affairs. We oppose the depersonalization that reduces human beings to the status of things. . . . We oppose, too, the doctrine of human incompetence because it rests essentially on the modern fact that men have been "competently" manipulated into incompetence—we see little reason why men cannot meet with increasing skill the complexities and responsibilities of their situation, if society is

organized not for minority, but for majority, participation in decision-making. Men have unrealized potential for self-cultivation, self-direction, self-understanding, and creativity. It is this potential that we regard as crucial and to which we appeal, not to the human potentiality for violence, unreason, and submission to authority.[4]

Cartesianism and Biolinguistics

Another source of today's anarchist optimism is Cartesian philosophy and the related ideas of the uniqueness of human nature; increasingly, contemporary anarchism recognizes also those studies that relativize the unique distinction between human and other animal species. Compared to animal species in which all individuals do exactly the same (guided by the same mind and inspired by the same will), according to anarchism, human nature (intelligence) pushes these instincts to the background.

Similarly, Pierre-Joseph Proudhon maintains that "a society of beasts is a collection of atoms, round, hooked, cubical, or triangular, but always perfectly identical. These personalities do not vary, and we might say that a single ego governs them all."[5] In contrast to instinct-driven animals with a constant and unique will, human nature is "the thing" which facilitates freedom, individuality, development, and mostly progress. Human society is a kaleidoscope because the individuality of its members always transforms it into something fresh, newly constituting.

Using the example of language that serves as a "mirror of the mind," Chomsky succeeded in confirming the nativist

---

4   Tom Hayden, *The Port Huron Statement: The Visionary Call of the 1960s Revolution* (New York: Thunder's Mouth Press, 2005), 51–52.

5   Pierre-Joseph Proudhon, "What Is Property?: or, An Inquiry into the Principle of Right and of Government" in *Antologija anarhizma*, ed. Rudi Rizman (Ljubljana: Knjižnica revolucionarne teorije, 1986), 101.

hypothesis that the nature of *Homo loquens* has specific intrinsic intellectual and cognitive forms. Human nature must not be understood as a *tabula rasa* waiting for social shaping because it is to a large extent prestructured. In his research of autonomous universal grammar, Chomsky concluded that all human languages (about six thousand of them) have a common internal structure despite their obvious differences. It is worth noting that only the structure of the language is internalized, not the language itself; accordingly, a child will not learn any external language if they are not exposed to it.

Chomsky assumes that humans have a language-acquisition device which, when the condition of a suitable stimulus at the right time is met, enables a child to learn a language easily. A child does not acquire a language (only) by imitation; already at an early age he or she has an insight into the structure of the language and does not only compose sentences acquired from other people but also sentences and forms nobody has ever said before.[6]

In many works, Chomsky presents possible or potential links between linguistics and political philosophy, which are only abstract. From the eighteenth century onward, different considerations and theories have emerged on possible links between the main characteristic of natural language, often termed the creative aspect of language, and the instinct for

---

6   Rudi Rizman ascertains that linguistics strongly supports the argument that boundless freedom is the key identifying characteristic of human nature, as opposed to the animal world. "According to Chomsky, generative grammar must be capable of producing an indefinite number of sentences while relying on only a specific, fairly limited number of rules. The majority of such sentences are new and it is possible, even though the words are familiar and reproduced time and again, that these sentences were uttered or written for the first time in human history. The limited number of rules thus (paradoxically) opens up a wide, nearly boundless space of freedom which allows the indefinite production of sentences." ("Semantika nasilja—družbena misel Noama Chomskega" in *Somrak demokracije*, Noam Chomsky [Ljubljana: Studia humanitatis, 1997], 348).

freedom which in one way or another is assumed and dealt with in the libertarian tradition of thought (including classical liberalism and its different versions). According to Chomsky, the greatest respect and attention within this tradition should be paid to some forms of anticapitalist anarchism.[7]

Nevertheless, Chomsky warns that

> this is really a hope, it is not a scientific result. So little is understood about human nature that you cannot draw any serious conclusions. We cannot even answer questions about the nature of insects. We draw conclusions through a combination of our intuitions, hopes, some experiences that humans have an instinct for freedom. But we should not pretend that it is derived from scientific knowledge or understanding. It is not and cannot be. There is no science of human beings and their interactions, or even of simpler organisms, that reaches anywhere near that far.[8]

Chomsky's linguistic work importantly discloses how the structures of authority and control restrict and distort human capacities and needs and attempts to formulate a social theory that would result in practical ideas for overcoming these structures and abolishing them.[9] With his biolinguistic

---

7   For more about the "links" between linguistics and political philosophy, see Noam Chomsky, *Language and Problems of Knowledge* (Cambridge, MA: The MIT Press, 1988); Chomsky, *New Horizons in the Study of Language and Mind* (New York: Cambridge University Press, 2004); Chomsky, *Language and Politics* (Oakland: AK Press, 2004); Raphael Salkie, *The Chomsky Update: Linguistics and Politics* (London: Unwin Hyman, 1990); Neil Smith, *Chomsky: Ideas and Ideals* (Cambridge: Cambridge University Press, 2004); James McGilvray, ed., *The Cambridge Companion to Chomsky* (Cambridge: Cambridge University Press, 2005).

8   Chomsky, *Chomsky on Anarchism*, 240.

9   Marshall, *Demanding the Impossible*, 579.

theory, Chomsky refutes the (hegemonic) behaviorist position according to which a human being is nothing more than modeling dough adapting to the demands and desires of the rulers. This finding is revolutionary not only from the linguistic point of view, but carries important sociopolitical consequences.

Based on linguistics (already the most apposite insight to human nature for Cartesian philosophers), Chomsky shows that man has specific internal cognitive structures. The most appropriate social, economic, and political system is one that enables these intrinsic forms, and thus people, the highest degree of self-realization and maximization of internal creative abilities. Due to the current level of the (un)development of science, one can only guess what this ideal system would be. Here, anarchist anthropology can serve us only as a constant reminder of the influence of external circumstances that can drive human potential in one direction or another. Namely, human nature is a structure of conflicting dispositions that develop with time and, in appropriate historical conditions, can become stronger, fade out, or change in a number of ways.

The above considerations lead us to conclude that human nature per se has some intrinsic forms; which of the characteristics will be brought to light or become dominant largely depends on the external environment or external stimuli. Undoubtedly, individuals are capable of evil, but they are also capable of many other things. There are various ways for human nature to realize itself and there are various abilities a human being can have. Which of these ways will develop largely depends on institutional structures.

Civil Obedience

It is pointless to pretend that human nature is deprived of any potential for violence; our nature and abilities enable us the unique capacity of engaging in wars and organized crime, in a form unparalleled by any other animal species.

However, human nature also has an infinite desire and need for good and freedom, for rejecting violence, killing, and authority. Naturally, the question of the use and abuse of science springs to mind here. Why is it that history and science so scrupulously record all acts of despair and violence yet remain silent about the countless courageous acts of individuals who defied rulers and their orders when they were to result in new injustices for their fellow humans?

The reasons for our proclivity to warfare, violence, competition, and selfishness should not be searched for (only) in human nature. It would probably be more reasonable to look for them elsewhere—outside an individual person. The English writer and scientist Charles P. Snow rightfully commented that if one more attentively considers the long and murky history of humankind, one soon realizes that more hideous crimes have been committed because of obedience and submission than in the name of revolt. According to Zinn, what is often explained as "sick" human nature is actually civil obedience:

> Civil disobedience is not our problem. . . . Our problem is civil *obedience*. Our problem is the numbers of people all over the world who have obeyed the dictates of the leaders of their government and have gone to war, and millions have been killed because of this obedience. . . . Our problem is that people are obedient all over the world, in the face of poverty and starvation and stupidity, and war and cruelty. Our problem is that people are obedient while the jails are full of petty thieves, and all the while the grand thieves are running the country. That's our problem.[10]

The thesis that authorities have an influence on the voluntary committing of violence without a feeling of guilt was

---

10   Zinn, *Zinn Reader*, 438.

eventually empirically confirmed in the famous Milgram experiments conducted in the 1960s at Yale University.[11] In the original version of the experiment, project leader Stanley Milgram published a newspaper ad inviting people from all walks of life to participate in an experiment on the effect of punishment on learning. The selected participants, forty men aged between twenty and fifty years of age, were informed that the experiment dealt with learning and memory. Every participant was assigned one "pupil"—Milgram's colleague—and the couple was seated in a special laboratory. The participant ("teacher") began by reading one word from a pair of words that the pupil had previously memorized, and the pupil had to say the other word of the pair.

For each mistake, the teacher could administer a shock to the pupil using an electro-shock generator. The generator featured different voltage levels (from 15 V to 450 V); each button was labeled with an indication of how dangerous the respective shock was (for the pupil): a slight shock (15–60 V), a moderate shock (75–120 V), a strong shock (135–180 V), a very strong shock (195–240 V), an intense shock (255–300 V), an extremely intense shock (315–360 V) and "danger: a severe shock" (375–450 V). The shocks were not real but a planned illusion that the tested persons were supposed to believe in. The teacher was ordered to punish the pupil's first mistake with a 15 V shock, the second with 30 V, all the way to the "deadly shock" of 450 V. When receiving the punishment, the pupil acted as if they were in more or less severe pain: when shocks exceeding 75 V were administered the pupil started screaming and waving their hands; at 150 V they started trembling and asked the teacher to stop the experiment; when the voltage exceeded 330 V the pupil ceased answering the questions.

---

11   For more about the experiment, see Stanley Milgram, "Behavioral Study of Obedience," *Journal of Abnormal and Social Psychology* 67, no. 4 (1963): 371–78.

If at first Milgram had any doubts about finding enough people who would be willing to participate in this experiment and his colleagues thought that the punishment would end at 150 V in most cases, the results of the experiment came as a surprise for all. Of forty tested persons, five refused to obey the experimenter when the shocks reached 300 V, four at 315 V, two at 330 V, and one at 345 V, 360 V and 375 V, respectively. However, twenty-six research subjects, 65 percent, continued with the experiment until the very end—until the "deadly" intensity of 450 V.

Even though the result of the experiment is often interpreted as more proof confirming the "historically proven" conclusion about human cruelty and violent nature, the findings of the research group conducting the experiment were completely different. Milgram wrote the following about the results: "I observed a mature and initially poised businessman enter the laboratory smiling and confident. Within 20 minutes he was reduced to a wreck, rapidly approaching a point of nervous collapse. He constantly pulled on his earlobe and twisted his hands. At one point he pushed his fist into his forehead and muttered, 'Oh, God, let's stop it.' And yet he continued to respond to every word of the experimenter and obeyed to the end."[12]

Milgram found the results shocking because they demonstrated that one cannot count on human nature in similar situations. A great number of people did what they were asked to, without thinking about the meaning of the act or examining their conscience as long as they believed that the order came from a legitimate authority. Milgram thus rightly poses a much broader question which is more relevant to our analysis: if an anonymous leader of an experiment, wearing a white coat and holding a notepad, can successfully order people to meekly follow orders with which they would normally disagree, then what else can a state force its subjects to do?

---

12   Ibid., 377.

The experiments showed people's willingness to simply "perform their duty" and become collaborators in destructive processes that run against their personal convictions. The loss of the sense of responsibility and the mass abandonment of one's moral convictions are the most fatal consequences of blind obedience. Violence is not a consequence of human nature as such, but of conformism, pragmatism, and the power of social roles. Similar findings on the pernicious power of conformism and social roles were reported already by Henry David Thoreau in his essay "Civil Disobedience":

> A common and natural result of an undue respect for law is, that you may see a file of soldiers . . . marching in admirable order . . . to the wars, against their wills, ay, against their common sense and consciences, which makes it very steep marching indeed, and produces a palpitation of the heart. They have no doubt that it is a damnable business in which they are concerned; they are all peaceably inclined. Now, what are they? Men at all?[13]

Subsequent modifications of the Milgram experiments—aiming to define the factors influencing the intensity of blind submission to authority—revealed that the degree of conformism is influenced by: the degree of legitimacy of the authority; the proximity of the authority; the personal traits of the tested person; the presence of other people; and the proximity of the victim. The last finding is particularly important as it shows that when the tested person was in the proximity of the victim their obedience to the authority decreased considerably: the closer the victim, the less likely the obedience. Should we look for the reasons for this behavior

---

13 Henry David Thoreau, *Walden and Other Writings* (New York: Modern Library, 2000), 669.

in the fact that listening to or watching the suffering of another person—even a total stranger—aroused in the tested persons a natural feeling of empathy and sympathy that was stronger than the apparently legitimate orders of the experts?

Anarchists then, consider individuals, human nature, and society based on the concept of *natura naturans* (in the philosophical sense of "what things can become") and not *natura naturata* (in the historical sense of "what things are or have become"). Like Heraclitus, they do not consider human nature as an unchanging thing or state, but as a dynamic process that is compatible with their faith in social and moral progress. It is therefore understandable that anarchists build this community (of the free and the equal) on the assumption that people cooperate most successfully on an equal and free footing.

4

A BRIEF GENEALOGY OF ANARCHIST THOUGHT

The Prehistory of Anarchism

TO ATTEMPT TO REVIEW THE HISTORY OF ANARCHIST THOUGHT is to embark on a risky journey since, according to Irwing L. Horowitz, anarchism is not a completed ideology but a sentiment.[1] By analogy with Subcomandante Marcos's definition of Zapatismo, one could also say that anarchism "is not a doctrine. It is an intuition. Something so open and flexible that it really occurs in all places. *Anarchism* poses the question: 'What is it that has excluded me?', 'What is it that has isolated me?' In each place the response is different. *Anarchism* simply states the simple question and stipulates that the response is plural, that the response is inclusive."[2]

Andrej Grubačić, one of the most prominent anarchist historians of the new generation, has also established that anarchism should only be understood as a tendency in the history of human thought and practice, a tendency which

---

1   Irving L. Horowitz, ed., *The Anarchists* (New Brunswick, NJ: Aldine Transaction Publishers, 2005), xi.
2   Marcos in Vodovnik, *Ya Basta!*, 45.

cannot be encompassed by a general theory of ideology, since its contents as well as manifestations in political activity change with time.[3]

But the creation of an accurate genealogy of anarchism is not my objective at any rate. Rather, as I am mainly interested in an in-depth discussion of one of its forgotten chapters or, it will be more than enough to make a broad-brush outline of anarchism and discuss various fragments which bear witness to the (dis)continuity of its development. Several excellent historical reviews and anthologies have emerged over the past few years on the topic, and these should be read as appendices to fill in the gaps of what you might find missing here.[4]

Even though the beginnings of authentic anarchist ideas date back to as late as the eighteenth century (along with the intensification of the main forms of hierarchy and exploitation—the modern state and capitalism), ideas about finding an alternative to the almighty and monolithic structure of authority can be traced to the Ancient Greek philosophers and other "pioneers" of the ideas of personal freedom, irrespective of whether their motives were philosophical or religious.

Anarchist inspirations and aspirations can already be found among Taoists and (Zen) Buddhists of the sixth and

3   Andrej Grubačić, "Towards Another Anarchism" in *World Social Forum: Challenging Empires*, eds. Jai Sen and Peter Waterman (New Delhi: The Viveka Foundation, 2004), 35.

4   For historical reviews of anarchism, see: Peter Marshall, *Demanding the Impossible*; George Woodcock, *Anarchism*; and Max Nettlau, *A Short History of Anarchism* (Freedom Press, 1996). For anthologies of original texts which also draw the contours of the development of anarchism, see: Rizman, *Antologija anarhizma*; Daniel Guérin, ed., *No Gods, No Masters: An Anthology of Anarchism* (Oakland: AK Press, 2005); Robert Graham, ed., *Anarchism: A Documentary History of Libertarian Ideas, Vol. 1: From Anarchy to Anarchism (300 CE to 1939)* (Montreal: Black Rose Books, 2004); Graham, *Anarchism: A Documentary History of Libertarian Ideas, Vol. 2: The Emergence of the New Anarchism (1939–1977)* (Montreal: Black Rose Books, 2009).

fifth centuries BC. The rationale of Taoism is the concept of *wu-wei* which is usually translated as nonaction. An in-depth analysis soon reveals (philological) similarities between "anarchy" and "*wu-wei*." If ἀναρχός means the absence of ἀρχός (ruler), then *wu-wei* means the absence of *wei*, with *wei* referring to "artificial, contrived activity that interferes with natural and spontaneous development."[5] In political terms, *wei* can be defined as an imposed authority that, for example, Confucianism accepts as unquestionable. Acting in accordance with *wu-wei* is considered natural and correct as it leads toward an unforced and spontaneous order.[6]

The libertarian spirit of Taoism and Buddhism rejects any hierarchy and domination. It highlights the power of self-discipline, liberation, and the ability of every person to reach enlightenment. Every individual is treated as part of not only society but also organic nature, and this is also typical of many contemporary anarchist currents. The compassion for others and love for life and beauty which Taoism and Buddhism most strongly underscore constitute a moral foundation of a free(r) society. Their vision of social freedom today represents one of the most important sources of the anarchist sensibility and one of the more justified threats to modern states and churches.

Antiquity should not just be seen as a cradle of the words *anarchy* and *anarchism* but also as a period of the first serious—both theoretical and practical—consideration of anarchy and anarchism in their positive and also negative lights. The bulk of the antique political philosophy comprehended a state as the only possible space for justice, freedom, and a civilized life. It is not surprising that democracy was considered an unjust and inappropriate order that is always

---

5   Ames in Marshall, *Demanding the Impossible*, 55.
6   The key text of Taoism, *Dao de jing* (The Way and Its Power), allegedly by Lao Zi, defines an ideal order as a classless society where individuals live a simple and honest life in harmony with nature, without any government or (enforced) authority.

"anarchic" (Plato) and that "people without states are wild and dangerous beasts" (Aristotle).

Naturally, there were some out-of-the-box thinkers who thought that an ideal social order is not a hierarchical state that uses mainly strict laws to preserve social order. In his famous work *Antigone*, Sophocles presents a lucid criticism of human laws and outlines the difference between human laws on one hand and divine or natural laws on the other. Heraclitus, who is considered by many to be the most important pre-Socratic philosopher, defined movement or change as the motive power of nature and humankind. Since "everything flows," including "the eternal mountains and hills," the only constant is change. With his ideas and acts that encourage people to question all authority, Socrates was one of the first and most famous defenders of the freedom of thought and speech. His greatest so-called crime—for which he was eventually sentenced to death—was his unshakeable belief in the power of the human mind. After his death, the relative freedom of thought and public debate fueled the development of a variety of philosophical schools. The Epicureans, the Cynics, and the Stoics thus advocated extreme individualism, with no room for the state. If the theories of Plato and Aristotle envisaged progress only for a thin stratum of people—that is, for free men—the Epicureans, in their reflections the Cynics and the Stoics embraced all people—"brothers and sisters," "citizens of the world." We should not forget that Aristippus and Zeno are usually considered the first protoanarchist thinkers.

From the eleventh century onward, Europe was subject to continuous economic and social changes. The feudal fetters that bonded thralls or free peasants to feudal lords or the Catholic Church slowly started to yield, yet their exploitation continued or even intensified. Many peasants found their "exodus" from feudalism by moving to towns where "the air frees people"; others sought a solution in rebellion and the establishment of God's Kingdom on Earth. It is not surprising that elements of anarchist thought can be traced

as far back as the Middle Ages, followed by Christian movements such as the early Hussites, Taborites, and Anabaptists,
and especially with Thomas Müntzer, who broadened his
conception of religious revolution to also include social revolution—the destruction of the existing order and its replacement with God's Kingdom on Earth.[7]

The first explicitly anarchist movement appeared at the
end of the twelfth century in the Muslim part of Spain, particularly in Seville and gained momentum a century later
when they were accepted by the Paris intellectuals gathered
around William Aurifex. The movement was named "The
Heresy of the Free Spirit" and its cry "Bread for God's sake!"
became so popular that it eventually sprouted in practically
all parts of Europe.

The heretics, as they were often called, manifested their
hatred for totalitarian power and the hypocritical nature of
the Church by gate-crashing masses where they challenged
priests to join in polemical and heated discussions. They rejected the promises of a kingdom in the afterlife and demand-
ed a paradise on Earth, in the here and now. Even though the
Church soon suppressed the "heresy" with mass executions,
the ideas of so-called liberals were rapidly disseminated to
other countries along with the growing trade connections.
Forced into clandestine activities, the "brothers and sisters"
spread their ideas to Spain, Germany, and Italy. They never
evolved into a church with a uniform dogma, but remained
a movement of similarly thinking groups whose message was
spread by word of mouth:

> God was free and created all things in com-
> mon. . . . Theft is lawful. Eat in an inn and refuse
> to pay. If the landlord asks for money he should

---

7   In this duality of anarchism, the confluence of apocalyptic and
humanist, religious and rationalist ideas or amalgamations, many see
the contradiction of anarchism per se; however, this duality of anarchist thought broadens the scope of its flexibility.

be beaten. . . . The free person is right to do
whatever givest them pleasure. I belong to the
liberty of nature, and all that my nature desires I
satisfy. . . . Sex is the delight of Paradise; and the
delight of Paradise cannot be sinful.[8]

These ideas reached England in the fourteenth century and
sparked the interest of Oxford students. Together with radical priests they spread the so-called free spirit ideas among
beggars, soldiers, deserters, and unemployed and unskilled
workers of the urban underground. In 1381, the increase in
taxes that came as a consequence of the long and exhaust-
ing war with France triggered a mass uprising of commoners.
The peasant army arrived at the outskirts of London on June
12. The itinerant preacher John Ball, who was sometimes
called also the "mad priest of Kent," encouraged the rebels
with the following sermon:

Things cannot go well in England, nor ever will,
until all goods are held in common, and until
there will be neither serfs nor gentlemen, and we
shall be equal. For what reason have they, whom
we call lords, got the best of us? How did they deserve it? Why do they keep us in bondage? If we
all descended from one father and one mother,
Adam and Eve, how can they assert or prove that
they are more masters than ourselves? Except
perhaps that they make us work and produce for
them to spend.[9]

The next morning, the Londoners opened up the town gate to
the rebels and greeted them enthusiastically. The peasants first

---

8   Quoted in Clifford Harper, *Anarchy: A Graphic Guide* (London:
Camden Press, 1987), 4.
9   Ball quoted in Woodcock, *Anarchism*, 38.

burned down some palaces, then they demolished prisons and set prisoners free. The promises to grant the rebels' demands were not fulfilled, but were followed by deception and revenge.

Even though the "free spirit" ideas were bloodily suppressed, the movement was resurrected four decades later, this time in what today is Czech and Slovak territory, under the name of Taborites. In response to their persecution by the Church and the nobility, the Taborites publicly proclaimed that anyone who failed to join them by February 10, 1420, in the hills of southern Bohemia would be punished: "All lords, nobles and knights shall be cut down and exterminated in the forests like outlaws."[10] After the victory over the local rulers, the Taborites declared the end of feudal relations, taxes, annuities, and private property in the liberated territory and, instead, the establishment of egalitarian communities: "All shall live together as brothers, none shall be subject to another. The kingdom shall be handed over to the people of the Earth, who will know nothing of 'mine and thine.'"[11]

The so-called anarchism of the "free spirit" returned in its most perfect form—as both practical organization and a theoretical justification—in seventeenth-century England. In 1649, Gerrard Winstanley launched a utopian experiment by simply inviting people to join them in the St. George's Hill community in an exchange of food, drinks, and clothes. Although this community never had more than fifty members (also called Diggers), its significance is inestimable since it represents the start of utopian experimenting with alternative social systems. The community was so successful that it soon posed a serious threat to the local nobility—not only for spreading around and proving the idea that people can be free but also for the experiment's economic success. The demolition of the community's tools, produce, and buildings was soon followed by an escalation of physical violence

---

10   Marshall, *Demanding the Impossible*, 92.
11   Harper, *Anarchy*, 6.

on its members, ultimately leading to the nobility's desired goal—abolition of the community. Based on his experience in the St. George's Hill community, Winstanley wrote *The Law of Freedom*, considered the first theoretical justification of anarcho-communism.

From Anarchy to Anarchism

It should be noted that the abovementioned cases belong to protoanarchism because the germs of the original anarchist thought were only planted at the end of feudalism by intertwining the growing sense of individuality (the Renaissance) and the belief in progress (the Enlightenment). Therefore, anarchism sprouted at the end of the eighteenth century as a reaction to the development of centralized nation-states on the one hand and the thriving industrialization and capitalism on the other.

Anarchist thought and organization already existed during the French Revolution but were limited to specific areas and municipalities. The pejorative connotation of the word *anarchy* was already in use—first by the Girondists and later by the Jacobins and the Directorate—to attack the so-called extremist *Sans-coulottes* and *Enragés* who advocated federalism and the abolition of government. The deep-rooted conviction that a strong government is the only assurance of order resulted in those who resisted the new government being labeled disorder-seeking anarchists.

The new authority found the radicalism of rebellious workers even more undesirable and subversive, since they warned that social revolution did not necessarily mean liberation but could also mean a new form of despotism. In 1792, the French priest Jacques Roux warned about the "despotism of senators" which was just as "terrible as royal rule." The only real solution was to "abolish all governments." In his early anarchist manifesto titled *L'explosion*, Roux's friend Jean Varlet wrote, "What a social monstrosity, what a masterpiece of Machiavellism is this revolutionary government.

Government and revolution are incompatible unless the people is willing to have new bodies of power—which is absurd. . . . We cannot pretend ourselves being distrustful even of those who have won our votes. Kings' palaces are not the only homes of despots."[12]

Considering the plethora of excellent works and anthologies written over the past century, we will deliberately avoid listing out the ideas of the "classics of anarchism" whose theoretical contributions enriched anarchist thought in the nineteenth century. Suffice it to say that the beginning of authentic anarchist thoughts dates back to the seventeenth and eighteenth centuries in the works of Gerrard Winstanley and particularly in the *Enquiry concerning Political Justice* by William Godwin, considered a pioneering work in this field. In his work, Godwin offered the first explicit criticism of capitalism and statism and thus a clear definition of the anarchist demands to do away with the "crude machine" of political (pre)dominance. A few decades later, the first self-proclaimed anarchist Pierre-Joseph Proudhon wrote, "Anarchy is order!" This idea has continued to echo strongly until today; the rulers and manipulated masses have fearfully perceived it as nonsense, whereas the downtrodden have embraced it as offering hope for a better and freer world. Stirner's "association of egoists," Proudhon's "mutualism," Bakunin's "romantic rebelliousness," Kropotkin's "scientific anarchism," Tolstoy's "religious pacifism" and so on were complemented in the twentieth century by some new contributions to anarchist theory and practice. Emma Goldman endowed anarchism with an important feminist dimension, and Murray Bookchin derived a logical correlation between anarchism and social ecology. The Paris Commune, the October Revolution, and the Spanish Civil War were all important manifestations and confirmations of the anarchist vision of social organization in practice.

---

12   Marshall, *Demanding the Impossible*, 433; Harper, *Anarchy*, 20.

In his book, *Under Three Flags: Anarchism and the Anti-colonial Imagination*, Benedict Anderson establishes that the network of anarchist collectives at the end of the nineteenth century was the first global antisystem movement and, at the same time, the center of the revolutionary tumult.[13] The idea and practice of anarchism were flexible enough to proliferate outside Europe, particularly in Latin America and Asia. At the turn of the century, it seemed that humankind would witness a "century of anarchism," yet political developments again showed that the "contest of ideas" throughout history has never been a fair one. Many protagonists of the anarchist movement were murdered for their ideas and ideals (e.g., Landauer, Ferrer, Spies, Parsons, and Mühsam), others died in prisons or met a premature death after having been imprisoned for many years (e.g., Bakunin, Most, Magón, and Makhno), whereas some found a way out of the emerging (political) situation through suicide (e.g., Lingg and Berkman). Over three decades, the movement became a pale shadow of the global network that had prefigured a completely new political alternative, but the ideas of direct action, mutual aid, and participative democracy survived and continued to spread.

From Dada to Situationism

During World War I, Switzerland was a sanctuary for many radicals, turncoats, artists, and pacifists seeking refuge from the madness of war. In Zürich, a young poet and theater headmaster, Hugo Ball, and a cabaret dancer and singer, Emmy Hennings, started a movement whose aim was to shake up and tear down the existing bourgeois social order through the destruction of art. A motley bunch of "anti-artists" gathered around Cabaret Voltaire, forming a radical (anti)artistic avant-garde. Dadaists saw the goal of art in revolution and

---

13 Benedict Anderson, *Under Three Flags: Anarchism and the Anti-Colonial Imagination* (New York: Verso, 2007).

vice versa. On the one hand, they wanted to destroy contemporary art as the key symbol of bourgeois culture; on the other, they strived to create a world in which the redefined art would become life and vice versa.

Liberation was understood not only as the abolition of the tyranny of the bourgeois order or spreading of political rights, but as absolute freedom from order itself, from the existing rationality and logics. As Hans Richter pointed out, art should strive for new functions that will only be known after everything that existed before has been completely negated; until then disorder, destruction, challenge, and chaos will prevail. The objective was not an expansion of the scope or spectrum of contemporary art, but its dissolution, anti-art. The Berlin uprising in 1918 was a fertile ground for Dadaists to also manifest their philosophical rebellion in practice. In April of 1918, Richard Huelsenbeck and Raoul Hausmann established the Dadaist Revolutionary Central Council in Berlin whose manifesto included the following demands:

> The international revolutionary union of all creative and intellectual men and women on the basis of radical communism.

> The introduction of progressive unemployment through comprehensive mechanization of every field of activity. Only through unemployment does it become possible for the individual to achieve certainty as to the truth of life and finally become accustomed to experience.

> The immediate expropriation of property—that is, its socialization—and the communal feeding of all.

> Further, the erection of cities of light, the gardens of which will belong to society as a whole and prepare humanity for a state of freedom.

The compulsory adherence of all priests and teachers to the "Dadaist Articles of Faith."

The adoption of a Dadaist poem as a state prayer.

The compulsory requisition of churches for performance of Dadaist music and poetry.

The creation of 150 circuses for the enlightenment of the proletariat.[14]

Invigorated by the idea of workers' councils, Lettrism, and Surrealism, Dadaism resurfaced in 1957 with the establishment of the Situationist International, whose ideas predominantly dynamized the subsequent student protests in France. At first, situationism restricted itself to moving beyond the (artificial) distinction between art and life as two separate spheres, or as the Dadaist Tristan Tzara put it four decades earlier: "The modern artist does not paint, he creates directly. . . . Life and art are One." The "cultural revolution" of situationism soon mushroomed in other aspects of capitalist society, namely in the revolution of everyday life. The Situationist analyses revealed that capitalism had transformed all social relations into transactional relations, while life in its entirety had been reduced to a spectacle.

The Situationist concept of spectacle is largely derived from Lefebvre's theory of moments and Marx's idea of alienation; what distinguishes it from Marx is the idea that in order to maintain economic growth, modern capitalism should fabricate "pseudo-needs" to guarantee a sufficient level of consumption. Instead of advancing a thesis that the mind is determined by production, they suggest it is shaped by

14 The Berlin revolutionary council responded to the Dadaist requests by appointing Richard Huelsenbeck as Commissioner for High Art. Harper, *Anarchy*, 127.

consumption. If within classical capitalist society the prevalence of the economy over social life had resulted in the degrading of "to be" into "to have," then the absolute predominance of a modern society of spectacle was leading to the degradation of "to have" into "to appear." Accordingly, humanity has become an observer (consumer) of the spectacle characterized by a one-way flow of communicated experience to which individuals cannot react because an active life is replaced by passive observation.

The arena of the revolutionary struggle, then, is no longer limited to the economic sphere (production) but now encompasses our everyday life. It follows that a revolutionary project must contain a *détournement* of the spectacle and reconstruction of life, given that the change in the perception of the world and the change in the social structure are one and the same. Instead of a society of spectacle, the Situationists proposed a communist society where money, wage labor, interest, rents, social classes, private property, and, of course, the state are abolished and genuine desires finally replace pseudo-needs.

Situationist theory, in which art is the tactics and the goal, was no longer solely a domain of the artistic and intellectual avant-garde but slowly met with broad support abroad, particularly among Provos and Kabouters in the Netherlands, and the emerging student movement.[15] In 1966, students close to the Situationist International elected five "situationists" to their student organization council in Strasbourg. After seizing power, the first step of the group was to spend all the funds of the student organization to print the famous Situationist International pamphlet *De la misère en milieu étudiant* (On the Poverty of Student Life); the next step was abolition of the student organization. The exasperated university authorities brought the group before court on

---

15 See Richard Kempton, *Provo: Amsterdam's Anarchist Revolt* (Brooklyn: Autonomedia, 2007).

the grounds of "unlawful seizure of student funds," and the judge delivered a judgment with the following explanation:

> The accused have never denied the charge of . . . having made the student union pay some 5,000 francs for the printing of 10,000 pamphlets, not to mention the cost of other literature inspired by the "Situationist International." These publications express aims and ideas which, to put it mildly, have nothing to do with the purposes of a student union. . . . These five students, scarcely more than adolescents, lacking any experience of real life, their minds confused by ill-digested philosophical, social, political and economic theories and bored by the drab monotony of their everyday life, have the pathetic arrogance to make sweeping denunciations of their fellow students, their professors, God, religion, the clergy, and the governments and political and social systems of the entire world. Rejecting all morality and legal restraint, these cynics do not shrink from advocating theft, the destruction of scholarship, the abolition of work, total subversion and a permanent worldwide proletarian revolution with "unrestrained pleasure" as its only goal.[16]

Post–World War II capitalism did not fall apart as a result of internal contradictions, as predicted by most Marxists. Rather, it increasingly gained approval and support among the working class in the context of overall prosperity. Consequently, the currents of anarchism started running dry, although they never disappeared. In 1960, George Woodcock justly wrote that anarchism as a movement was

---

16 Ken Knabb, *Situationist International Anthology: Revised and Expanded Edition* (Berkeley: Bureau of Public Secrets, 2006), 501.

dead. But his hypothesis was proven completely wrong after only a few years.

During the student protests of 1968, the black and red flags of anarchy—in all of their complexity (i.e., feminist, ecological, cultural, and pacifist dimensions)—again fluttered in London, Paris, Amsterdam, Berlin, Chicago, Mexico City, Buenos Aires, and Tokyo. The 1968 revolution was the beginning of the end of the postwar social peace. These protests debunked the myth that the oppositions within the capitalist system had been solved for good.

Despite the relative economic progress, the dissatisfaction with the authoritarian nature of the so-called society of spectacle only grew over the years. While it was true that thanks to the postwar material progress, people in the West lived in relative abundance and had the benefit of education and leisure time—that is, a comfortable economic subsistence—some still wanted more: liberation. Consequently, the new radicalism did not acquiesce to demands for a shorter working week or higher salaries, but questioned all aspects of modern society, such as education, work, culture, property, money, family, and sexuality. The all-embracing and multifaceted nature of the new social struggles came as surprise for all who, until then, had still underestimated the power and creativity of the "little" people. The overall social atmosphere or revolutionary tumult that led to revolts in nearly all corners of the world are perhaps best illustrated by graffiti which in Situationist spirit, decorated walls in Paris:[17]

---

17 For more about the Situationist International (SI), see: Tom McDonough, ed., *Guy Debord and the Situationist International: Texts and Documents* (Cambridge, MA: The MIT Press, 2002); Christopher Gray, *Leaving the 20th Century: The Incomplete Work of the Situationist International* (London: Rebel Press, 1998); Dark Star Collective, ed., *Beneath the Paving Stones: Situationists and the Beach, May 1968* (Oakland: AK Press, 2001); Ken Knabb, ed., *Situationist International Anthology* (Berkeley, CA: Bureau of Public Secrets, 2006).

Je prends mes désirs pour la réalité car je crois en la réalité de mes désirs.

I treat my desires as realities because I believe in the reality of my desires.

Depuis 1936 j'ai lutté pour les augmentations de salaire. Mon père avant moi a lutté pour les augmentations de salaire. Maintenant j'ai une télé, un frigo, une VW. Et cependant j'ai vécu toujours la vie d'un con. Ne négociez pas avec les patrons. Abolissez-les.

Since 1936 I have fought for wage increases. My father before me fought for wage increases. Now I have a TV, a fridge, a VW. Yet my whole life has been a drag. Don't negotiate with the bosses. Abolish them.

Je t'aime! Oh! dites-le avec des pavés!

I love you! Oh! Say it with paving stones!

Il est interdit d'interdire.

It is forbidden to forbid.

Métro, boulot, métro, dodo . . .

Commute, work, commute, sleep . . .

Sous les pavés, la plage!

Under the paving stones, the beach.

La révolution est incroyable parce que vraie.

The revolution is incredible because it's really happening.

Quand l'assemblée nationale devient un théâtre bourgeois, tous les théâtres bourgeois doivent devenir des assemblées nationales.

When the National Assembly becomes a bourgeois theater, all the bourgeois theaters should be turned into national assemblies.

Ne me libère pas, je m'en charge.

Don't liberate me, I'll take care of that.

La politique se passe dans la rue.	Politics is in the streets.
La barricade ferme la rue mais ouvre la voie.	Barricades close the streets but open the way.
Travailleurs de tous les pays, amusez-vous!	Workers of all countries, enjoy!
Je décrète l'état de bonheur permanent.	I declare a permanent state of happiness.
L'action ne doit pas être une réaction mais une création.	Action must not be a reaction but a creation.
La marchandise est l'opium du peuple.	Commodities are the opium of the people.
Millionnaires de tous les pays, unissez-vous, le vent tourne.	Millionaires of the world unite. The wind is turning.
J'aime pas écrire sur les murs.	I don't like to write on the walls.

In Western Europe (mainly in Great Britain), the campaign against the installation of nuclear weapons on European soil radicalized a new generation of activists. At the same time the civil rights movement, the Student Nonviolent Coordinating Committee (SNCC), Students for Democratic Society (SDS), and the peace movement raised awareness among the broadest public in the United States about the coercive and violent nature of the state.

In this context, the rapid development of the so-called New Left was observed in the United States and Western Europe, which had rediscovered and further developed the ideas of libertarian or libertine socialism. In its struggle

against capitalism, state socialism and the pyramidal structure (power) of the university, factory, state, and family, it
emphasized traditional anarchist principles such as mutual
aid, self-management, participative democracy, and decentralization. Like Bakunin, its followers identified the greatest revolutionary potential in the so-called lumpenproletariat or the marginalized and *declassé* elements of modern
society. By building alternative institutions, it faithfully followed Bakunin's idea that the seeds of future society should
be sown in the existing social system.

A more intense presence of anarchist ideas was also discerned within the student movement. That student movements drew their anarchist inspirations and aspirations deliberately and directly from the abundant history of anarchism
can be seen in a telegram sent in 1968 by the Occupation
Committee of the Sorbonne to the Communist Party of USSR:

> SHAKE IN YOUR SHOES BUREAUCRATS
> STOP THE INTERNATIONAL POWER OF THE
> WORKERS' COUNCILS WILL SOON WIPE YOU
> OUT STOP HUMANITY WILL NOT BE HAPPY UN-
> TIL THE LAST BUREAUCRAT IS HUNG WITH THE
> GUTS OF THE LAST CAPITALIST STOP LONG
> LIVE THE STRUGGLE OF THE KRONSTADT SAIL-
> ORS AND OF THE MAKHNOVSCHINA AGAINST
> TROTSKY AND LENIN STOP LONG LIVE THE
> 1956 COUNCILIST INSURRECTION OF BUDAPEST
> STOP DOWN WITH THE STATE STOP[18]

After a number of bloodily suppressed student protests in
Europe, the rebellious spirit evolved into an "autonomist
movement" (*Autonomia* in Italy, *Autonomen* in Germany)
uniting radical workers, students, urban youth, unemployed,
and other marginalized social groups. Experiences from the

---

18 Knabb, *Situationist International Anthology*, 437.

1960s only strengthened the distrust of trade unions and political parties, resulting in a new form of political organizing. The first infoshops, social centers, and squats were founded and the first mass protests broke out against the growing power of supranational financial institutions or the "unholy trinity" (the International Monetary Fund, the World Bank, and the predecessor of the World Trade Organization, the General Agreement on Tariffs and Trade). The protests against the International Monetary Fund—often also called "riots for bread"—heralded the birth of a new global justice movement.

The Movement of Movements and Anarchism as a Methodology

Many studies conclude that the alterglobalization movement was born amid the tear gas and rain that accompanied the anti-WTO protests in Seattle in 1999. But its broader understanding—as the umbrella term under which we can place many different political inspirations and aspirations—opens a new dilemma of where to start with its genealogy. Zahara Heckscher, for instance, traces its antecedents to the late eighteenth century, more precisely, in the Túpac Amaru II uprising between 1780 and 1781. Heckscher believes the uprising represents "a bridge between local anti-colonial rebellion and transnational social movements against exploitive economic integration."[19] On the other hand, Benedict Anderson concludes that the global anarchist movement at the end of the nineteenth century is not only the main ideological inspiration of the alterglobalization movement but also its very beginning.[20]

---

19   Zahara Heckscher, "Long before Seattle: Historical Resistance to Economic Globalization" in *Global Backlash: Citizen Initiatives for a Just World Economy*, ed. Robin Broad (Manham, MA: Rowman & Littlefield Publishers, 2002), 86–87.

20   Anderson, *Under Three Flags*.

However, if we focus solely on the second half of the "short twentieth century," then we can trace the beginnings of the so-called global movement of movements in the Zapatista uprising in the Mexican province of Chiapas in January 1994. The uprising and the subsequent *encuentro* for humanity and against neoliberalism (Encuentro Intercontinental por la Humanidad y contra el Neoliberalismo) mark the birth of the alterglobalization movement or the "intergalactic" movement against neoliberalism. The *encuentro*, organized in the Lacandon jungle in 1996 by the EZLN, resulted in an appeal for

> the intercontinental network of resistance, recognizing differences and acknowledging similarities, will strive to find itself in other resistances around the world. This intercontinental network of resistance will be the medium in which distant resistances may support one another. This intercontinental network of resistance is not on organizing structure; it has no central head or decision maker; it has no central command or hierarchies. We are the network, all of us who resist.[21]

An important outcome of the *encuentro*, one still often overlooked, was the global network the People's Global Action (PGA) that unites anarchist collectives in Europe and elsewhere with groups ranging from Maori activists in New Zealand to fisherfolk in Indonesia and the Canadian postal workers' union, and that has become one of the main organizers of the countersummits from Seattle and Prague to Quebec and Genoa.[22] The network includes many movements and collectives devoid of an anarchist identity, although its

---

21 Subcomandante Marcos in *Our Word Is Our Weapon: Selected Writings of Subcomandante Marcos*, ed. Juana Ponce de León (New York: Seven Stories Press, 2001), 125.
22 Graeber and Grubačić, *Anarchism*.

"hallmarks" or organizational principles are identical to the main anarchist ideas:

1. A very clear rejection of capitalism, imperialism and feudalism; all trade agreements, institutions and governments that promote destructive globalisation.

2. We reject all forms and systems of domination and discrimination including, but not limited to, patriarchy, racism and religious fundamentalism of all creeds. We embrace the full dignity of all human beings.

3. A confrontational attitude, since we do not think that lobbying can have a major impact in such biased and undemocratic organisations, in which transnational capital is the only real policy-maker.

4. A call to direct action and civil disobedience, support for social movements' struggles, advocating forms of resistance which maximize respect for life and oppressed peoples' rights, as well as the construction of local alternatives to global capitalism.

5. An organisational philosophy based on decentralization and autonomy.[23]

The story of the alterglobalization movement thus continues with the growing international recognition of the landless workers' movement (Movimento dos Trabalhadores Rurais Sem Terra, MST) and the Indian Karnataka State Farmers' Association (Karnataka Rajya Raitha Sangha, KRRS); the strengthening of the global coalition of small farmers Vía Campesina; the restoration of the international network for

---

23   People's Global Action (PGA), *What Is People's Global Action?* http://www.nadir.org/nadir/initiativ/agp/en/pgainfos/about.html#hallmarks.

the democratic supervision of financial markets and institutions ATTAC (Association pour la Taxation des Transactions por l'Aide aux Citoyens); revolts against privatization of the water system (and rainwater!) in Bolivia, privatization of the energy system in South Africa and the "Washington Consensus" policies in Argentina; the creation of an international research and education institution, the International Forum on Globalization; the organization of the World Social Forum (Fórum Social Mundial) in Porto Alegre that was followed by regional social forums in Europe and Asia; the biggest protests in human history when on February 15, 2003, over twenty million people all over the world protested against the war in Iraq; and the culmination of the global initiative *Occupy*, on October 15, 2011, in mass protests against the neoliberal "crisis of crises."

This new movement is not necessarily only anarchist. Rather, it constitutes a broad coalition of environmentalists, farmers, feminists, trade unionists, indigenous activists, nongovernmental organizations, and initiatives, as well as anarchists. It draws most of its creative energy from the (self-declared) anarchist groups or autonomist nuclei whose volition and inspiration are inseparably linked to anarchism. Inside this movement, the anarchist principles—not only the principles of nonhierarchical and nonauthoritarian organization—are so widespread that the movement could easily be marked as anarchist even when it doesn't proclaim itself to be so. Today, the alterglobalization movement has joined the anarchist struggle at least for its libertarian spirit, decentralized and nonhierarchical organization, dedication to direct action, and a vision of the future that will not be determined by the profit motive or the dictates of leftist avant-gardes. The target of the struggle is no longer an individual state but capitalism per se as the latter has usurped the role and power of nation-states.[24]

---

24 Marcos stated that Zapatistas had risen up against the national government only to find that it did not exist: "In reality we were up

According to Giorel Curran, "post-ideological anar-chism" is the best framing of the reconfigured political, eco-nomic and social landscape that renders more traditional currents of anarchism obsolete. "Post-ideological anarchism" flexibly adopts ideas and principles from the heritage of clas-sical anarchism while rejecting its traditional forms to con-struct genuinely new autonomous politics through eclectic collection and merging. The anarchist renaissance within the movement of movements is not only inspired by anar-chism but also dynamized ideas that have counterpoised in the past.[25] Is it possible, then, to talk about a new anarchism?

Dave Neal, in his essay "Anarchism: Ideology or Methodology?" distinguishes between capital-A and small-a anarchism. The former, according to Neal, can be equat-ed with ideologically pure positions within the traditional schools of anarchism and an ideology or "a set of rules and conventions to which you must abide"; the latter is charac-terized by nondogmatism, eclecticism, and fluidity and is un-derstood as a methodology or "a way of acting, or a historical tendency against illegitimate authority."[26]

A very detailed analysis of the duality of anarchism can be found in Nikolai Jeffs's conceptualization of latent and manifest anarchism. For Jeffs, manifest anarchism represents "a deliberate takeover of ideology and practices, and with this self-identification of the subject as an anarchist," whereas la-tent anarchism assumes all characteristics of Neal's concep-tualization of anarchism as a methodology. Latent anarchism thus "represents various practices that have been throughout history conceived past relations of power and submission.

---

against great financial capital, against speculation and investment, which made all decisions in Mexico, as well as in Europe, Asia, Africa, Oceania, the Americas—everywhere." Subcomandante Marcos quoted in Sean M. Sheehan's *Anarchism* (London: Reaktion Books, 2003), 116.

25 Curran, *21st Century Dissent*, 2.

26 Dave Neal, *Anarchism: Ideology or Methodology?*, http://www.con nexions.org/CxLibrary/Docs/CX6984-MethodologyAnarchism.htm.

For these, neither interpellation nor the constitution of an individual into a subject of some self-reflected anarchism is crucial."[27]

In an essay written before the boom of the new movement of movements, Neal estimated that "within the anarchist movement we can still find a plethora of Anarchists—ideologues—who focus endlessly on their dogma instead of organizing solidarity among workers." A decade later, David Graeber contemplates that it is small-a anarchism that represents the real locus of the most creative and most lucid radical turmoil. In his reflection on new anarchism, Graeber stresses that it still has an ideology but for the first time it is an entirely new one—a post-ideology:

> A constant complaint about the globalization movement in the progressive press is that, while tactically brilliant, it lacks any central theme or coherent ideology. . . . Yet this is a movement about reinventing democracy. It is not opposed to organization. It is about creating new forms of organization. It is not lacking in ideology. Those new forms of organization are its ideology. It is about creating and enacting horizontal networks instead of top-down structures like states, parties or corporations; networks based on principles of decentralized, non-hierarchical consensus democracy. Ultimately, it aspires to be much more than that, because ultimately it aspires to reinvent daily life as whole.[28]

Barbara Epstein also ascertains that, within the movement of movements, anarchism represents the main inspiration and

---

27   Nikolai Jeffs, "All You Need Is Love (nasilje, emancipacija, pa tudi nekaj uvodnih besed . . .)," *Časopis za kritiko znanosti, domišljijo in novo antropologijo* 26, no. 188 (1998): 23.

28   Graeber, "The New Anarchists," 212.

aspiration. The new generation of activists do not view anarchism as a narrow and dogmatic interpretation of the world, a set of prefabricated solutions, or an eternal truth that can only be interpreted, commented upon, or confirmed anew with new data and evidence. Finally, it seems, we have upgraded Marx's eleventh thesis on Feuerbach which, according to Maurice Brinton, states that revolutionaries have only interpreted Marx and Bakunin, in various ways; the point, however, is to change them.[29]

Capital-A anarchism or anarchism, then, emerges as an ideological tradition, and anarchist sensibilities overlap with Curran's conceptualization of "post-ideological" anarchism, and Neal's conceptualization of small-a anarchism. In this reinterpretation, anarchist thought cannot be reduced to one single dimension as, despite its unshakeable basic premises, it is full of internal contradictions, own criticism and, consequently, redefined positions. The new movements point out that anarchism is not a coherent and completed system, but a set of ideas which addresses important questions but leaves many of them unanswered; it is a set of inquiries and researches without final results. According to Epstein, for contemporary young activists, anarchism does not represent some abstract radical theory but instead means

> a decentralized organizational structure, based on affinity groups that work together on an ad hoc basis, and decision-making by consensus. It also means egalitarianism; opposition to all hierarchies; suspicion of authority, especially that of the state; and commitment to living according to one's values. . . . Many envision a stateless society based on small, egalitarian communities. For

---

29 Brinton in *For Workers' Power: The Selected Writings of Maurice Brinton*, ed. David Goodway (Oakland: AK Press, 2004), 3. Marx's eleventh thesis on Feuerbach says: "The philosophers have hitherto only interpreted the world in various ways; the point is to change it."

some, however, the society of the future remains
an open question. For them, anarchism is important mainly as an organizational structure and as
a commitment to egalitarianism.[30]

Small-a anarchism is much more open to modifications
through freely disposing ideas and practices, and randomly
assuming, revising, and dismissing them to achieve goals. It
can thus be regarded as a reconfigured, "Type 3" anarchism.
According to Bey, the radically nonideological position of
"Type-3" anarchism is a detour from social anarchism ("Type
1") and also from individualist anarchism ("Type 2") precisely
due to its eclectic inclusion of useful conceptions of all ideological orientations.[31]

Perhaps it would be reasonable to reiterate here that the
abovementioned bifurcation of anarchism into "new" and
"old" is merely an analytical tool serving to explain or mark
the innovations and (dis)continuities within the anarchist
current. It does not attempt to conceal important links between the old and new manifestations as practically all subsequent bifurcations of anarchism have largely built on the
epistemological and theoretical conceptions of classical anarchism. The use of these adjectives is primarily descriptive
and not normative or evaluative.

---

30 Barbara Epstein, "Anarchism and the Anti-Globalization
Movement," *Monthly Review* 53, no. 4 (September 2001): 1.
31 Bey, *T.A.Z.*, 62.

5
CURRENTS OF ANARCHISM

Confluence of Anarchist Currents

ALTHOUGH ANARCHISM IS TODAY MOSTLY ASSOCIATED WITH THE political left (socialism and communism), many anarchist theoreticians consider the libertarian (liberal) ideas of the eighteenth and nineteenth centuries as its main ideational background.[1] The anarcho-syndicalist Rudolf Rocker defined contemporary anarchism as a confluence of "the two great currents which before and since the French Revolution have found such characteristic expression in the intellectual life of Europe: Socialism and Liberalism."[2] This is understandable, as the two main objectives of anarchist theory and practice are equality and freedom.[3] This definition was corroborated by Nicolas Walter, who added that like liberals, anarchists want freedom, and like socialists, anarchists want equality:

---

1   Noam Chomsky, *Radical Priorities*, ed. Carlos-Peregrín Otero (Oakland: AK Press, 2003), 2.
2   Rudolf Rocker, *Anarcho-Syndicalism: Theory and Practice* (Oakland: AK Press, 2004), 9.
3   Realization of the objectives in an individual "current" is only partial—equality at the expense of freedom in socialism and vice versa in liberalism.

But we are not satisfied by liberalism alone or by socialism alone. Freedom without equality means that the poor and weak are less free than the rich and strong, and equality without freedom means that we are all slaves together. Freedom and equality are not contradictory, but complementary; in place of the old polarization of freedom versus equality—according to which we are told that more freedom equals less equality, and more equality equals less freedom—anarchists point out that in practice you cannot have one without the other. Freedom is not genuine if some people are too poor or too weak to enjoy it, and equality is not genuine if some people are ruled by others. The crucial contribution to political theory made by anarchists is this realization that freedom and equality are in the end the same thing.[4]

Rocker insisted that classical liberal ideals had collapsed when confronted with the reality of capitalism, whereas anarchism was essentially anticapitalist because it opposed exploitation and emphasized that socialism was either free or not socialism. Mikhail Bakunin further stated that freedom without socialism is unjust and that socialism without freedom is slavery and brutality. Anarchism, of course, is itself is a type of socialism (while many anarchists reject state socialism) or can be regarded as a libertarian wing of socialism. This has often spurred discord among the "socialists," as shown in Friedrich Engels's remark in a letter to Philipp Van Patten, dated April 18, 1883:

The anarchists put the thing upside down. They declare that the proletarian revolution must begin by doing away with the political organization of the state. . . . But to destroy it at such a moment would

---

Nicolas Walter, *About Anarchism* (London: Freedom Press, 2002), 29.

> be to destroy the only organism by means of which the victorious proletariat can assert its newly conquered power, hold down its capitalist adversaries, and carry out that economic revolution of society.[5]

In a letter to Theodore Cuno, dated January 24, 1872, there is a similar and much repeated rant over anarchists: "How these people propose to run a factory, work a railway or steer a ship without having in the last resort one deciding will, without a unified direction, they do not indeed tell us."[6] Is it really so?

Anarchism and Marxism

These clashes of opinion within the socialist camp culminated with the expulsion of Bakunin and other anarchists from the First International at the Hague Congress in 1872 on the grounds of their disapproval of Marx's views of the objectives and means of political struggle. Many other anarchists and anarchist organizations were also expelled or forced to resign on the grounds of their disapproval of Marx's view of the objectives and means of political struggle. As stressed by Rudolf Rocker, this dispute involved two different conceptions of socialism and, chiefly, the path to it. Though Marx and Bakunin were truly the protagonists of the rift, Rocker maintains that this conflict would have emerged without them as it arose not from a disagreement between two people but between two currents of thought. Daniel Guérin, however, assessed that the rift between Bakunin and Marx was much greater than the mere ideational discord between anarchism and Marxism.[7]

---

5   Friedrich Engels, "Engels to Philipp Van Patten in New York," http://www.marxists.org/archive/marx/works/1883/letters/83_04_18.htm.
6   Friedrich Engels, "Letter from Engels to Theodore Cuno," *Marx and Engels Correspondence*, http://www.marxists.org/archive/marx/works/1872/letters/72_01_24.htm.
7   Daniel Guérin, "Marxism and Anarchism," in *For Anarchism: History, Theory, and Practice*, ed. David Goodway (New York: Routledge,

To put it simply, Marxism can be understood as a "theoretical or analytical discourse on a revolutionary strategy" and anarchism as an "ethical discourse on a revolutionary practice." From this perspective, the demarcation line between anarchism and Marxism is much more porous than drawn by Rocker, and a bifurcation within anarchism or Marxism makes a more accurate delineation even more challenging.

Lest we conclude that the gulf between the two is insurmountable, it is important to reiterate that anarchism cannot be thought of without Marxism and vice versa. Below, I will attempt to outline the main differences between the two positions, focusing only on those that have not changed through time.

Let us start with the revolutionary subject. Within Marxism, the key factor of revolutionary changes is believed to be the urban, qualified proletariat. According to the prevailing interpretation of Marx, revolution is only possible in those places where the proletariat accounts for the bulk of society; therefore, a revolutionary project must be led because the party runs it top-down and centrifugally from the industrialized center to the periphery.

Anarchism, on the other hand, assesses that the working class is often the least revolutionary element of the society, since its objectives are frequently limited to better working conditions, higher wages, health care and safety at work, etc. The objective of a revolutionary movement should not be to merely replacing the authority, but rather to revolutionize the society. The main actor of revolutionary changes is thus the lumpenproletariat, composed of the unemployed,

---

1989), 109. Guérin warns that an assessment of the rifts between Marxism and anarchism raises doubts on how to define the authentic core of Marxism (does it comprise the works of the young or the old Marx?) and how to define the essence of anarchism (is it about social anarchism passing into communism or about individualist anarchism often approaching pure nihilism and solipsism?).

students, marginalized groups, and the unskilled and rural labor force. Anarchism criticizes not only the potential of the urban proletariat but also the Marxist framing that reduces the proletariat to a bourgeois concept of a class which does not perceive it as a heterogeneous, inclusive group of people. Bakunin warns that such a definition of proletariat creates fertile grounds for a new aristocracy, namely the aristocracy of industrial or urban workers, which excludes millions of people that are the rural proletariat. Since it is impossible to talk about a preconceived plan of revolution, it can only evolve spontaneously, from the bottom up, and centripetally, from the periphery to the center. According to Bakunin, revolution thus has to be always and everywhere independent of the central point which is its expression, its product and not its source and cause.

Another major point of disagreement between Marxism and anarchism is the definition of the causes of revolutionary changes. Within classical Marxism, the desire to tear down capitalism stems from alienation and economic exploitation. According to Marx, the radical social revolution is intrinsically linked to a specific historical phase of economic development; the latter is its precondition. In contrast, anarchism refuses to reduce the causes of revolutionary changes to only economic exploitation as a series of other exploitations can be important to or even key factors in the spurring of a revolt.

Anarchism emphasizes that people have the drive for freedom. The desire to abolish oppression (capitalism) is thus a universal characteristic of all people regardless of their class, which is why communism does not emerge from theory but from a natural instinct. Bakunin adds that Marx's analyses of only economic issues distorted his assessment that those who are the most progressive and capable of a social revolution are those who live in societies where modern capitalist production has achieved its peak level of development. According to Marx, these countries are the only civilized ones and are called upon to start and lead a revolution.

Important differences between Marxism and anarchism are also found in the role of scientific theory that according to Marx is essential for both justifying revolutionary changes and understanding the socioeconomic development of society. Namely, Marx suggests that a society is governed by scientific laws that can only be comprehended and interpreted by educated individuals. Anarchism, generally speaking, does not consider scientific theory to be vitally important, insisting instead that it is not essential for a revolution to teach people the theory, but to trigger a revolt that is in itself educative and formative. Revolution and scientific theory have nothing in common because a revolutionary process cannot be subjected to a scientific study. In this framing, Marx dooms workers by attempting to transform them into theoreticians, making possible the emergence of a class of "theoreticians"—separated from the people— would again cause the emergence of a new aristocracy. Before his expulsion from the First International, Bakunin had asked, "As soon as an official truth is pronounced—having been scientifically discovered by this great brainy head laboring all alone—a truth proclaimed and imposed on the whole world from the summit of the Marxist Sinai, why discuss anything?"[8]

Marxism and anarchism also have diametrically opposing perceptions of the role of the state in a revolutionary project. For Marxism, a strong, omnipresent state may be vital for a transition from capitalism to communism; anarchists, however, believe that the state can never be used for revolutionary purposes because the revolutionary power and authority can lure even the most fair and courageous. Bakunin's well-known warning that the worst thing that can

---

8   Bakunin quoted in David Miller, *Anarchism* (London: J.M. Dent & Sons, 1984), 80.

happen to socialism is for it to become entwined with some new absolutism unfortunately has been frequently confirmed in history. Every revolution, once it is in the hands of a particular party, loses its real purpose and degenerates into a counterrevolution.

All of the rifts between Marxism and anarchism mentioned above are implicitly linked to the question of the revolutionary avant-garde and specifically the role of a political party. According to the Marxist conception of social transformation, revolutionary changes are only feasible if led by a strong organization or party that controls the process of revolutionary changes and adopts key decisions for the transition to communism.

Anarchism rejects the understanding of revolution as a led process and a one-time breaking off from the previous system, claiming that this should be a free and creative invention and the prefiguration of the future society already in today's practices of organization and functioning. The establishment of a new political party, then, would only mean a new class of professional politicians, and their avant-gardism only a new authoritativeness. The "dictatorship of the proletariat" would lead to the "dictatorship over the proletariat," the emergence of "professional revolutionaries" and the "red bureaucracy" which Bakunin says is "the vilest and most fearful lie of our century." Anarchism thus maintains that dictatorship and revolution are incompatible.

Even though Marx emerged victorious in the personal, political and ideational clash within the First International, further historical developments justified Bakunin's warnings against the consequences of state socialism and the dictatorship of the proletariat, and proved them right. With his lucid analyses of authority, bureaucracy, state, and power he outlined the subsequent theoretical contributions to social sciences such as the theory of bureaucracy of Max Weber, the iron law of oligarchy of Robert Michels and, last but not least, the critical theory of society.

The Singularity of Anarchism?

Probably the best metaphor for both understanding and analyzing anarchism is provided by Peter Marshall, who argues that anarchism should be perceived as a river with many currents, constantly changing and being refreshed by new waves while always moving toward the ocean of freedom.[9] Despite this diversity of various currents, all anarchists are thought to share some basic presuppositions. By delving deeper into the anarchist philosophy, one finds a specific view of human nature, a criticism of the existing order, a vision of a free society and eventually the path to it. Collectively termed anarchism, all these ideas associate socialism with freedom, and democracy with the abolition of authority. While there are many schisms within the movements, all share a definition of the way to a new, better society and an outline of the nature of this new society and the individuals in it.

Some (sub)currents of anarchism can be identified based on their ideas (e.g., religious anarchism) and others on their strategies (e.g., pacifist anarchism) and so on. The line between many differences is fuzzy. Still, we can analytically distinguish between two main schools of anarchism: individualist anarchism and social anarchism.

Individualist Anarchism

Individualist anarchism, originally limited to the United States, emphasizes the acceptability of the evolution or evolutionary processes in finding the way to a new society. For this purpose, it highlights the importance of education and the creation of alternative economic structures (i.e., banks and cooperatives) but does not neglect the importance of trade unions, strikes, and other nonviolent types of protest. The "individualists" perceive the classical anarchist "solution" of a

---

9   Marshall, *Demanding the Impossible*, 3.

revolution as being contrary to anarchist principles, and use (its) formative characteristics to substantiate its uselessness:

1. a revolution always results in new relations of inequality, since it only involves the replacement of those who rule;

2. the idea of revolution is based on an authoritative approach, for example the dispossession of capital; and

3. a revolution is inappropriate for its violent moment itself.[10]

The "individualists" believe the result of the "apocalyptic" revolution and its radical policies and acts would be chaos and a general social collapse that would eventually lead to a new dictatorship. The dictatorship would guarantee its existence by merely restoring order and reinstating the feeling of social stability in people. Many individualist anarchists warn that violence-seeking revolutionary changes would only bring about an imaginary change—the oppressors would be punished and would thus become a segment of the society which experiences suffering and new injustice. The French geographer and anarchist Élisée Reclus, who does not belong to the individualist milieu, also points out the problem of the post-revolutionary mirroring of old exclusions and hierarchies:

> What boots it to those who truly love humanity and desire the happiness of all that the slave becomes master, that the master is reduced to servitude, that the whip changes hands, and that money passes from one pocket to another? It is not the rich and the powerful whom we devote

---

10 Max Stirner and Albert Camus, for example, distinguish between revolution and insurrection/rebellion. While the result of a revolution is only the replacement of the old rulers with new ones, an insurrection can cause a change in human nature by creating new morals and values.

to destruction, but the institutions which have favored the birth and growth of these malevolent beings. It is the medium which it behooves us to alter, and for this great work we must reserve all our strength; to waste it in personal vindications were merest puerility. "Vengeance is the pleasure of the gods," said the ancients; but it is not the pleasure of self-respecting mortals; for they know that to become their own avengers would be to lower themselves to the level of their former oppressors. If we would rise superior to our adversary, we must, after vanquishing them, make them bless their defeat. The revolutionary device, "For our liberty and for yours," must not be an empty word.[11]

For individualist anarchists, the regulatory mechanism in a new society should be a genuinely free market, but they reject any form of capitalism and argue that it hinders the development of the (free) market. They acknowledge private property, however, if it stems from one's own work and is not used as a means of exploiting and oppressing others; they claim that private property is so good that everyone should have it.

Chomsky legitimately warns that individualist anarchism, if limited only to the "minarchists" of the second half of the twentieth century, is a highway to an extremely distorted version of liberalism. It has no connection with the rest of the international anarchist movement, but only means total dedication to free-market capitalism: "U.S. and to some extent British libertarianism . . . has no objection to tyranny as long as it is private tyranny. That is as long as it is private tyranny. This is radically different from other forms of anarchism."[12]

---

11   Élisée Reclus, "Anarchy" in *Antologija anarhizma*, ed. Rudi Rizman (Ljubljana: Knjižnica revolucionarne teorije, 1986), 379.
12   Noam Chomsky, *Chomsky on Anarchism*, ed. Barry Pateman (Oakland: AK Press, 2005), 235.

The notion of human nature also distinguishes the "individualists" from social anarchists. Individualist anarchists emphasize that a society without conflict is impossible in the short term. Each and every individual should have the possibility to develop his/her personality, to practice a cooperative behavior, to learn to respect their own freedom and that of others, but "good" relationships between people in the extreme and most idealized meaning of the word are not feasible after all. Therefore, individualists advocate a regulatory framework strictly prohibiting any aggressive outburst and inevitably incorporating other safety measures.

In this respect, individualists do not strive to abolish the state as such but to abolish all of its (anachronistic) forms existing so far. Many of them even offer alternative formulas for creating a better state. These proposals have mainly been influenced by Nozick's concept of "the minimalist state" which is essentially analogous to Smith's concept of "the invisible hand."[13] The issue of state is also connected to the last point of disagreement between both currents as individualists recognize the right to private property, which can only be preserved and maintained through the power of the state.

Social Anarchism

The main characteristics of social anarchism can be found articulated in an 1894 letter from French anarchist Émile Henry to the director of the jail where Henry was on death row for a bomb attack:

---

13   The task of the state (government) would be reduced and limited to protecting individuals and private property, namely to the police, courts, the legal system, and national defense. The position which aims not to abolish government/state could be defined as minarchist. For more about the minarchist vision, see Robert Nozick, *Anarchy, State, and Utopia* (New York: Basic Books, 1977).

Monsieur, I am going to summarize for you my ideal of an anarchist society:

No more authority, which is far more contrary to human happiness than the few excesses that could occur at the beginning of a free society.

In place of the current authoritarian organization, the grouping of individuals by sympathies and affinities without laws or leaders.

No more private property; the gathering in common of products. Each one working and consuming according to his needs, which is to say, as he wishes!

No more family, selfish and bourgeois, making man the property of woman and woman the property of man; no more demanding of two beings who loved each other but a moment that they remain attached till the end of their days.

Nature is capricious: it always demands new sensations. It wants free love. This is why we want free unions.

No more fatherlands, no more hatred between brothers, pitting against each other men who have never set eyes on each other. Replacement of the narrow and petty attachment of the chauvinist for his country by the large and fruitful love of all of humanity, without distinction of race or color.

No more religions, forged by priests to degrade the masses and give them the hope of a better life, while they themselves enjoy life in the here and now.

On the contrary, the continual expansion of the sciences, put within the grasp of every being who will feel attached to their study . . .

In a word, absolutely no more hindrances to the free development of human nature. The free blossoming of physical, cerebral and mental faculties.[14]

This definition clearly shows that while all anarchists are to some extent individualists because they advocate personal freedom and diversity, social anarchists still emphasize that the solution to social problems cannot be arrived at on an individual level. In order to replace contemporary society with a better social system, it is crucial to connect and work with other people and develop solutions on a communitarian level. Social anarchism considers revolution as the main solution for achieving a better society, yet does not overlook the importance of other (nonviolent) methods of revolt. Accordingly, the need for revolution should arise from the fact that everything is interconnected in a society and thus the society cannot be radically reformed without jeopardizing the entire structure.

On one hand, social anarchism nurtures ideas that accentuate spontaneity (and a new society should form spontaneously), the importance of political and intellectual struggle and the self-organization. On the other hand, it equally appreciates ideas that stress and support the so-called propaganda by the deed, which is to say acts that demonstrate fallibilities and vulnerabilities of existing power structures. Historically, this has taken the form of bombings and assassinations of people who identify themselves with the organization of the establishment and regime.

The revolutionary violence of individual anarchists can be interpreted as insistence on the idea that no class waives its privileges and no government waives its power unless forced to do so. There is also much truth in the warning that those who have not lost their children due to famine and curable diseases, their wives due to accidents at work, their

---

14 Émile Henry, "Anarchy and Terror" in *Antologija anarhizma*, ed. Rudi Rizman (Ljubljana: Knjižnica revolucionarne teorije, 1986), 407–8.

relatives due to bombs dropped in the name of democracy, etc. have no right to judge and condemn acts of despair and revenge. Yet even Bakunin concludes that while bloody revolutions are often necessary "thanks to human stupidity . . . they are always an evil, a monstrous evil, and a great disaster, not only with regard to the victims, but also for the sake of the purity and perfection of the purpose in whose name they take place."[15]

The main deficiencies of social anarchism are generally considered to be its ideological (over)load and the kind of idealism that frequently leads to an underestimation of the power of social forces that struggle to keep their authority and privileges. Social anarchists view the state as a superstructure in the hands of the elite seeking to protect their interests and property. A better society of the future, however, should be organized as a community of voluntary associations. According to Chomsky, any interaction among human beings that is more than personal (in that it takes institutional forms of one kind or another) in community, or workplace, family, or larger society should be under direct control of its participants: "So that would mean workers' councils in industry, popular democracy in communities, interaction between them, free associations in larger groups, up to organization of international society."[16]

Social anarchists' concept of private property is somewhat vague. The smallest common denominator of their ideas can perhaps be found in Pierre-Joseph Proudhon's "What Is Property?; or, An Inquiry into the Principle of Right and of Government." The answer is simple: "Property is theft!":

> If I were asked to answer the following question:
> *What is slavery?* and I should answer in one word,
> *It is murder*, my meaning would be understood at

---

15   Paul Eltzbacher, *Anarchism* (London: A.C. Fifield, 1908), 123.
16   Chomsky, *Chomsky on Anarchism*, 238.

once. No extended argument would be required to show that the power to take from a man his thought, his will, his personality, is a power of life and death; and that to enslave a man is to kill him. Why, then, to this other question: *What is property?* may I not likewise answer, *It is robbery*, without the certainty of being misunderstood; the second proposition being no other than a transformation of the first? . . . Such an author teaches that property is a civil right, born of occupation and sanctioned by law; another maintains that it is a natural right, originating in labor—and both of these doctrines, totally opposed as they may seem, are encouraged and applauded. I contend that neither labor, nor occupation, nor law, can create property; that it is an effect without a cause: am I censurable?[17]

It should be noted that Proudhon's intention was not to provide a negation of private property in general, but only of property as understood under Roman law, namely *ius utendi et abutendi re sua, quatenus iuris ratio patitur* in the sense of absolute right to use and abuse/consume/destroy property as far as compatible with ratio, that is, the logic of the law. Moreover, he perceived private property and property rights as the best protection against state interference. Proudhon's economic system and attitude to private property, wherein all exchange services would be treated equally, is also called mutualism (*mutuallisme*). Proudhonism, which after 1840 was the first manifestation of anarchism as an organized social movement in Europe, set federalism (as a method of organization) and mutualism (as the basic economic principle) as

---

17 Pierre-Joseph Proudhon, "What Is Property?: or, An Inquiry into the Principle of Right and of Government" in *Antologija anarhizma*, ed. Rudi Rizman (Ljubljana: Knjižnica revolucionarne teorije, 1986), 70.

its main objectives. The core idea of mutualism was to organize society without any intervention from the state and with individuals who are capable of entering into mutual, free agreements:

> It is industrial organization that we will put in place of government. In place of laws, we will put contracts; no more laws voted by a majority, nor even unanimously. Each citizen, each town, each industrial union, makes its own laws. In place of political powers, we will put economic forces. . . . In place of public force, we will put collective force. In place of standing armies, we will put industrial associations. In place of police, we will put identity of interests.[18]

Mutualism would do away with social inequalities and polarization without requiring any expropriation of capital, land, and the means of production. He had in mind an "exchange bank" that should be founded on the mutual trust of all participants in the production process, prepared to exchange their products at their actual cost of production and the amount of labor time. A nominal means of payment would be workers' checks denominating the number of working hours required to produce each individual good.[19]

This theory suggests that free crediting, enabling everyone to borrow money interest-free, is the best economic system of a society without government. It leads to leveling of

18 Pierre-Joseph Proudhon, "General Idea of the Revolution in the Nineteenth Century" in *Antologija anarhizma*, ed. Rudi Rizman (Ljubljana: Knjižnica revolucionarne teorije, 1986), 141.

19 The abovementioned system—the idea of equivalence and a wage based on the number of working hours—received much criticism, including from within anarchist circles. Proudhon revised this idea in his later work *Théorie de la Propriété* with the idea of "equal pay for equal work," where the difficulty of the work performed is also considered.

income, minimization of profit margins, and thus the elimination of both wealth and poverty. Free crediting and compensation in a free market would hence lead to economic equality, but not the abolition of private property, as the abolition of government would lead to social equality. According to Walter, economic mutualism can also be defined as "co-operativism minus bureaucracy" or "capitalism minus profit."[20]

If Proudhon's attitude to private property and distribution is labeled mutualism, the economic system of Mikhail Bakunin can be termed collectivism, suggesting that economy and society should be organized by the (socialist) principle "from each according to his abilities, to each according to his contribution." By organizing the economy and society at the level of production that, along with distribution, would be organized as a free federation of different associations of producers, the basic cell of the future social system would be a collective. In this new social system, all land and means of production would be collectively owned, and the wage labor system and thus private ownership over the direct results of a person's work would be preserved.

Peter Kropotkin advocated an even more radical view of private property and distribution, as his ideas of communism suggested absolute abolition of the wage labor and private property, except for a person's personal belongings. He held the belief that if the work of every person is interconnected with the work or contributions of other people, it is in fact impossible to precisely define the contribution of every person or their work. The economy and society should thus be organized on the basis of the (communist) principle "from each according to his abilities, to each according to his needs." It follows, then, that not only the means of production but also the results of the work must be owned collectively. If the collectivists, by advocating the organization of society and economy at the level of production, consider a

---

20   Walter, *About Anarchism*, 56.

collective to be the basic cell of the future social system, the communists identify a commune as the basic cell, comprising both producers and consumers.

It is clear that all distribution systems—mutualism, collectivism, and communism—reach a specific level of economic inequality, since either people's abilities or needs differ. As Murray Bookchin has stated, the objective of anarchism is not to guarantee equal shares but fair shares: in an anarchist society, absolute equality is impossible and, above all, unnecessary to achieve, except for "equality of the unequal" that recognizes and considers the differences among individuals in a broader scope of social equality and economic communism.[21]

The praxis of anarcho-syndicalism within social anarchism to further stresses that revolutionary changes can only occur if the labor force duly organizes and liberates itself. In the opposite case, people can achieve liberation, but not freedom, or in the words of Max Stirner, "The man who is set free is nothing but a freed man, a libertinus, a dog dragging a piece of chain with him. He is an unfree man in the garment of freedom, like the ass in the lion's skin."[22] Anarcho-syndicalism emphasizes voluntary socialism through workers' councils or trade unions as the basic cells or nuclei of a forthcoming (highly organized) social system. Eugène Varlin, a French anarchist who was killed during the bloodily suppressed Paris Commune, wrote:

> Unions have the enormous advantage of making people accustomed to group life and thus preparing them for a more extended social organization. They accustom people not only to get along with one another and to understand one another,

---

21   Marshall, *Demanding the Impossible*, 49.

22   Max Stirner, *The Ego and Its Own* (Cambridge: Cambridge University Press, 1995), 168.

but also to organize themselves, to discuss, and to
reason from a collective perspective. . . . As well
as mitigating capitalist exploitation and oppression in the here and now, the unions also form
the natural elements of the social edifice of the
future. It is they who can be easily transformed
into producers associations; it is they who can
make the social ingredients and the organization
of production work.[23]

Chomsky suggests that anarcho-syndicalists are striving to
create "free associations of free producers" that would join
the struggle and take the helm of production on a democratic basis within the already existing social system. These
associations would serve as a "practical school of anarchism."
From this perspective, they follow Bakunin's idea that the
seeds of future society must be sown in the existing social
system and thus create "not only the ideas, but also the facts
of the future itself." Trade unions are not simply perceived
as a weapon in a revolutionary struggle but also as models of
the future social system. Anarcho-syndicalists thus reject the
need for a higher force above organized work, such as a party
that would establish a new order of things. In an economic
system in which private ownership of the means of production is abolished and in which there is no room for parasitism
and special privileges, the state would also be abolished.

During the Spanish Civil War, anarchists demonstrated
that the ideas of anarcho-syndicalism had true practical
value. After the outburst of the revolution on June 19, 1936,
in response to the Francoist *pronunciamiento*, most industri-
alists and large landowners abandoned their belongings and
fled abroad. Agricultural and industrial self-management

---

23   Varlin quoted in Julian P.W. Archer, *The First International in France,
1864–1872* (Lanham, MD: University Press of America/Rowman &
Littlefield, 1997), 196.

gained impetus after the abandoned land estates and factories had been taken over. When during Franco's *coup d'état*, the unrest exploded into a social revolution, Spain had already witnessed workers' organizations with a structure of their own, with experience and theoretical tools to be used in implementing the task of social reconstruction. Collectivization of the land and industry proved to be economically very successful as records were set in agriculture and industry.[24]

Anarquismo Sin Adjetivos

Anarchism as a socioeconomic and political philosophy and practice cannot be regarded as a monolithic, unique set of ideas leading to absolute uniformity and singular solutions with a universal value. Anarchism is not a (self-sufficient) dot but a mosaic composed of a variety of pieces whose common denominator is a readiness for democratic dialogue with others for purposes of harmony. Compared to many Marxist currents, the case of anarchism and its diverse currents is less about doctrinal differences than about relatively different views on the issue of political goals and means.

---

24 It is worth noting that the Spanish experiment was successful in economic terms as well as general social and cultural development. Literacy campaigns and expert education courses were organized for adults, along with compulsory schooling for children (and the prohibition of manual work) and many (free) lectures, concerts, and theatre plays. There was much solidarity among municipal communities in the form of industrial councils and agricultural collectives; joint funds for allowances and leveling off provided aid (and thus all benefits) to those units that for one reason or another found themselves in difficulty. For more about anarcho-syndicalism in Spain and the joint struggle of communists and Francoists against anarchists, see Daniel Guérin, *Anarchism: From Theory to Practice* (New York: Monthly Review Press, 1970), 114–43.

Chomsky stresses that "anarchism is a very broad category; it means a lot of different things to different people."[25] Hence, if a person defines herself as anarchist, this does not tell much about her impulses and motives, nor about her political goals and means of political struggle. Nevertheless, anarchists have always generally tried to pursue Bakunin's idea that future society has to be prefigured in the current political struggle. For Zinn, anarchism should not be anarchistic "just in wanting the ultimate abolition of the state, but in its immediate requirement that authority and coercion be banished in every sphere of existence that the end must be represented immediately in the means."[26] This means that the means of our political actions should always correspond to the ends or, to put it differently, that we should organize ourselves in such a way as to create that kind of human relationships that prefigure a future society.

Over years of the mutual transmission and fertilizing of ideas, the "margins" between individual currents of anarchism have become even more porous, resulting in a series of other anarchist positions. Therefore, someone can be an *individualist* in her private life, choosing her associations and occupation; a *mutualist* in her social life, freely conducting social agreements on mutual exchange; a *collectivist* in the workplace, cooperating with other people to produce a public good; an *anarcho-syndicalist* striving for self-management at work; and a *communist* in her political life, aspiring to and follow the vision of a communist social system. Likewise, in practice, different associations and neighborhoods (e.g., collectivist, communist, mutualist, individualist) can exist at the same time and in the same place, trying to experiment and in various ways satisfying their requirements and needs. In the current discussions on the construction of a broad anarchist coalition capable of coping with the challenges of a new

---

25 Chomsky, *Chomsky on Anarchism*, 234.
26 Zinn, *Zinn Reader*, 679.

millennium, the concept *anarquismo sin adjetivos*—anarchism without any adjective, prefix, or suffix—has thus unsurprisingly been once again gaining ground.[27]

27 Even though authorship of the phrase "anarchism without adjectives" is often ascribed to Malatesta, its author is Fernando Tarrida del Marmol, who introduced the concept in 1889 while trying to overcome the disagreements between the collectivists and communists in the Spanish anarchist movement. Compared to a common goal, i.e., the abolition of capitalism and state, the economic theories were thought to be of secondary importance.

6
THE FORGOTTEN CURRENT
OF ANARCHISM:
New England Transcendentalism

How to Read Transcendentalism?

THE PRINCIPAL WORKS OF TRANSCENDENTALISM—SUCH AS
Thoreau's *Walden*, Emerson's "Nature," and Whitman's
Leaves of Grass—are considered a part of American literary canon. According to Lawrence Buell, these works acquired this status less for their aesthetic value as for their
political implications and social criticism.[1] Surprisingly, then,
Transcendentalists' contribution to the creation of a better,
more just social system in the United States is still overlooked
or ignored.[2] Contemporary political theory and changes in

---

1   Lawrence Buell, "Henry Thoreau Enters the American Canon"
in *New Essays on Walden*, ed. Robert F. Sayre (Cambridge: Cambridge
University Press, 1992).
2   Nearly all Transcendentalists withdrew from Boston and
Cambridge to the countryside, bringing their books and ideas and
dedicating themselves, besides horticulture and social activism, to
literary creation. The center of Transcendentalism was not Boston
or Cambridge but a small village called Concord where the following, among others, led a creative life: Ralph Waldo Emerson, Henry
David Thoreau, the feminist Margaret Fuller, the philosopher Bronson
Alcott, the poet William Ellery Channing, and the novelist Nathaniel

literary course or direction, however, have merited this area more attention in the last decades.[3]

The reason for reservations or skepticism probably stems from the separation of the political and literary spheres in which anarchism and Transcendentalism are respectively discussed. In his excellent genealogy of American pragmatism, *The American Evasion of Philosophy*, Cornel West concludes that the abovementioned interpretative blindness has largely been due to an erroneous classification of Emerson exclusively in the milieu of American literary renaissance, rather than in the context of European political developments that produced Karl Marx, John Stuart Mill, and others.[4]

The same is true for other Transcendentalists and Transcendentalism as illustrated by Staughton Lynd's creative parallel reading of Thoreau and Marx in *Intellectual Origins of American Radicalism*. In this study, Lynd concludes that Thoreau and Marx were not only linked by their very similar vision of the political alternative but also by "a literary style that emphasized contradiction and drove conclusions to

---

Hawthorne. Here, the Transcendentalists also realized their ideals by establishing utopian communities such as Brook Farm and Fruitlands. For a description of Brook Farm (1841–1847), see Richard Francis, *Transcendental Utopias: Individual and Community at Brook Farm, Fruitlands, and Walden* (Ithaca, NY: Cornell University Press, 1997).

3   The influence of the Transcendentalists was not strong while they were living, and the broad public was not acquainted with their works. First and foremost, this is a consequence of the general social, political, and economic influence of their opponents. An important reason for the Transcendentalists' relative anonymousness is to some extent also the absence of an international copyright protection policy. Accordingly, up until the end of the nineteenth century, English books were copied and sold at "dumping prices," whereas American authors requested higher prices to at least cover their costs. The demand for American literature was thus much smaller. Naturally, it should be considered that for several years, even decades, American literature was only a poor imitation of the European models.

4   Cornel West, *The American Evasion of Philosophy: A Genealogy of Pragmatism* (Madison: The University of Wisconsin Press, 1989), 11.

extremes." By directly comparing the authors, Lynd reveals that at some points "parallelism is almost uncanny."[5]

For example, for both Thoreau and Marx freedom means more than a political democracy:[6]

America is said to be the arena on which the battle of freedom is to be fought; but surely it cannot be freedom in a merely political sense that is meant. Even if we grant that the American has freed himself from political tyrant, he is still the slave of an economical and moral tyrant.

Political emancipation certainly represents a great progress. It is not, indeed, the final form of human emancipation, but is the final form of human emancipation *within* the framework of the prevailing social order.

The reader surely needs some time to correctly identify the author of each quotation. Even more effort and time are required to correctly define the authorship of the next segments with an apparent resemblance of the authors' styles:[7]

In the large towns and cities, where civilization especially prevails, the number of those who own a shelter is a very small fraction of the whole. The rest pay an annual tax for this outside garment . . . which would buy a village of Indian wigwams, but now helps to keep them poor as long

Man is regressing to the cave dwelling, but in an alienated, malignant form. The savage in his cave (a natural element which is freely offered for his use and protection) does not feel himself a stranger; on the contrary he feels as much at home as a fish in water. But the cellar dwelling

---

5   Staughton Lynd, *Intellectual Origins of American Radicalism* (New York: Cambridge University Press, 2009), 94.
6   Left column: Thoreau; right column: Marx. Ibid., 92.
7   Left column: Thoreau; right column: Marx. Ibid., 95.

as they live. . . . The myriads who built the pyramids to be the tombs of the Pharaohs were fed on garlic, and it may be were not decently buried themselves. The mason who finishes the cornice of the palace returns at night perchance to a hut not so good as a wigwam. It is a mistake to suppose that, in a country where the usual evidences of civilization exist, the condition of a very large body of the inhabitants may not be as degraded as that of savages.

of the poor man is a hostile dwelling, "an alien, constricting power which only surrenders itself to him in exchange for blood and sweat." He cannot regard it as his home, as a place where he might at last say, "here I am at home." Instead, he finds himself in another person's house, the house of a stranger who lies in wait for him every day and evicts him if he does not pay the rent.

As is evident from Lynd's study, an attempt to read Transcendentalism in this light is more than an appropriate epistemological and methodological direction. American "literary circles" often tend to undermine the literary value of Transcendentalism for its pronounced didactical character, since it mainly comprises economic, political, philosophical, and theological works with social criticism as their common denominator. Transcendentalism must not be discussed only as a literary but also as a political movement.

In Search of Definition

There are as many definitions of Transcendentalism as there are attempts to define it. The main obstacle to a unique definition is surely its complexity and inconsistence, as Transcendentalism did not construct a logical intellectual system because such a system would negate its romantic belief in intuition and flexibility. We can define Transcendentalism as a movement of literary experimentation and theological invention that emerged from Unitarianism and flourished in New England between 1830 and 1850.[8] A more comprehensive definition is offered by Perry Miller, who defines it as "children of the Puritan past who, having been emancipated by Unitarianism from New England's original Calvinism, found a new religious expression in forms derived from romantic literature and from the philosophical idealism of Germany."[9]

The group of young Boston idealists who established a debating club called the Transcendental Club of Boston and started publishing *The Dial* magazine, advocated a free interpretation of the Bible, turned their back on Christian dogmatism and found their "exodus" in the idea of the spiritual potential of all living creatures, primarily people. They rejected the need for a priest as a mediator between God and man, and were committed to the idea that humans contain the germ of divinity giving them the right and duty to oppose forced tradition and authority in all forms. They emphasized the meaning of self-enthusiasm or self-reliance as prerequisites for everyone who strives to establish contact with the divinity or Over-Soul within themselves.

For the first time in the history of American literature, Transcendentalism created a desire to implement the idea that a writer is or should become the true demiurge of the world. A writer thus acquired a new role—the role of a priest or even a prophet. In the preface to the first edition of *Leaves of Grass*, Whitman wrote that a poet must not be satisfied merely with the artistic value of their verses, but become a prophet, a seer, a bard, a teacher, and a moralist in the sense of defending the future and democracy:

> A poet is a seer . . . he is individual . . . he is complete in himself . . . the others are as good as he

---

8   Wesley T. Mott, ed., *Encyclopedia of Transcendentalism* (Westport, CT: Greenwood Press, 1996), 224.

9   Perry Miller, ed., *The American Transcendentalists* (Garden City, NY: Doubleday Anchor Books, 1957), ix.

> is, only he sees it and they do not. He is not one
> of the chorus . . . he does not stop for any regula-
> tion . . . he is the president of regulation. What
> the eyesight does to the rest he does to the rest.[10]

The Transcendentalists drove self-enthusiasm, individualism, and optimism to such an extreme that every person was
perceived as an autonomous god. This idea was completely
contradictory to Puritanism, the leading religious philosophy
of the time.

Ontological and Epistemological Starting Point

Transcendentalism drew its name and impetus from
Immanuel Kant's *Critique of Pure Reason* (1788) and simultaneously rejected the empirical and materialistic philosophy
of John Locke.[11] In his *Essay concerning Human Understanding*,
Locke postulated that everything in the human intellect was
furnished by the senses. Kant's idealism rebuffed Locke's philosophy by elucidating ideas that cannot be arrived at through
experience but serve as a means of gaining experience in
themselves. Kant emphasizes that our behavior is based on
external experience but only if we already have specific abilities to recognize and remember them. All our knowledge is
thus an essential result of our innate abilities and our perception of the objects outside us is only subjective, whereas
the real thing is beyond human grasp. Kant termed these *a
priori* abilities transcendental forms. This contrast between

---

10   Walt Whitman, *Poetry and Prose* (New York: Library of America,
1982), 10.
11   While Transcendentalists mainly drew their inspirations and aspirations from Kant's principal work, authors such as Herder, Jacobi, and
Schelling also made their contributions. Their ideas also incorporated
insight from Eastern religions, Homer, Sophocles, Euripides, Plato,
Aristotle, Virgil, Shakespeare, Bacon, Goethe, Swedenborg, Coleridge,
Carlyle, Wordsworth, and others.

idealism and materialism is perhaps best elucidated by Ralph Waldo Emerson in his essay "The Transcendentalist":

> What is popularly called Transcendentalism among us, is Idealism; Idealism as it appears in 1842. As thinkers, mankind have ever divided into two sects, Materialists and Idealists; the first class founding on experience, the second on consciousness; the first class beginning to think from the data of the senses, the second class perceive that the senses are not final, and say: the senses give us representations of things, but what are the things themselves, they cannot tell. The materialist insists on facts, on history, on the force of circumstances, and the animal wants of man; the idealist on the power of Thought and of Will, on inspiration, on miracle, on individual culture.[12]

The Transcendentalists approved of Kant's explanation of human nature, while emphasizing that there must be something more in humans than merely subjective abilities of recognizing the environment.

Redefined Self

Emerson's "Nature" (1849) and Whitman's "Song of Myself" (1855) both surpass the dichotomy of self and no-self. In "Nature," Emerson writes about cosmic unity: "Standing on the bare ground—my head bathed by the blithe air and uplifted into infinite space—all mean egotism vanishes. I become a transparent eyeball; I am nothing; I see all; the currents of the Universal Being circulate through me; I am part or parcel of God!"[13]

---

12 Ralph W. Emerson, *The Essential Writings of Ralph Waldo Emerson* (New York: The Modern Library, 2000), 81.
13 Ibid., 6.

Whitman also puts the redefined romantic self at the core of *Leaves of Grass* (1855), in a complete rupture with the European liberal tradition that, drawing on the Copernican revolution of the sixteenth century, slowly but surely led to the atomization of the political community:

> I celebrate myself, and sing myself,
> And what I assume you shall assume,
> For every atom belonging to me as good belongs
>   to you![14]

Transcendentalists brought individualism to its extreme and on this basis defined the need to redefine the self as well as man's attitude to the Over-Soul.[15] This individuality differs from the one found in classical liberal doctrine, however, which suggests that every individual is a closed whole, whereas an "open" society is ruled by the principle *homo homini lupus* (Thomas Hobbes) or *homo homini felis* (Karl Popper). In Whitman's words, we find within New England Transcendentalism the beginnings of communal individualisms overcoming the old dichotomy individual versus society: "One's-Self I Sing, a simple separate person/Yet utter the word Democratic, the word En-Masse."[16]

Communal Individualism and Personal Freedom

Transcendentalists stressed that humans and nature are but one thing and the rest belongs to a common whole. Emerson wrote about the redefining of an individual and the self: "A leaf, a drop, a crystal, a moment of time, is related to the whole, and partakes of the perfection of the whole. Each

---

14 Whitman, *Poetry and Prose*, 27.
15 This relationship is personal and mostly direct, which is why a person needs no intermediation by the chosen representatives or any ritualized procedures.
16 Whitman, *Poetry and Prose*, 165.

particle is a microcosm, and faithfully renders the likeness of the world."[17]

With their thesis of human and cosmic unity, the Transcendentalists reached beyond liberal pragmatism and egoism and saw each person as morally committed to others and responsible for them. This is one of Transcendentalism's best theoretical endorsements of the anarchist conception of communal individualism (as articulated by Emma Goldman) and personal freedom. According to the (neo) liberal position, an individual's freedom is restricted by the freedom of others. Anarchists insist, however, that only in society and only by the joint activity of the entire society does a human being really become a human being since people's intellectual capacities can only be "acquired or activated in a society.

A person's freedom is not only a matter of isolation, but of universal recognition of freedom; it is not a matter of closeness, but a matter of combining. We are only truly free if everyone is equally free. We become truly free only with the freedom of others; the higher the number of free people surrounding us and the deeper and larger their freedom, and the deeper, larger, and wider our freedom becomes. Hence, freedom of others does not mean a restriction or denial of our freedom; what is more, it is its essential assumption and confirmation. As Bakunin wrote:

> I mean . . . the liberty which knows no other restrictions but those set us by the laws of our own nature. Consequently there are, properly speaking, no restrictions, since these laws are not imposed on us by any legislator from outside, alongside, or above ourselves us. These laws are subjective, inherent in ourselves; they constituting the very basis of our being. Instead of seeking

---

17 Emerson, *Essential Writings*, 22.

> to curtail them, we should see in them the real
> condition and the effective cause of our liber-
> ty—that liberty of each man which does not find
> another man's freedom a boundary but a con-
> firmation and vast extension of his own; liberty
> through solidarity, in equality.[18]

In "Man, Society and Freedom," Bakunin states that we are
"truly free only when all human beings, men and women, are
equally free. The freedom of other men, far from negating or
limiting my freedom, is, on the contrary, its necessary prem-
ise and confirmation. . . . My personal freedom, confirmed by
the liberty of all, extends to infinity."[19]

Emma Goldman warned about the danger of "rugged individualism," as it was thought to be

> only a masked attempt to repress and defeat
> the individual and his individuality. So-called
> Individualism is the social and economic *laissez-
> faire*: the exploitation of the masses by the [rul-
> ing] classes by means of legal trickery, spiritual
> debasement and systematic indoctrination of the
> servile spirit. . . . That corrupt and perverse "indi-
> vidualism" . . . has inevitably resulted in the great-
> est modern slavery, the crassest class distinctions
> driving millions to the breadline.[20]

According to Malatesta, the freedom the anarchists want
for themselves and for others "is not an absolute metaphysical, abstract freedom which in practice is inevitably translated into the oppression of the weak; but it is real freedom,

---

18   Dolgoff, *Bakunin on Anarchy*, 261–62.
19   Ibid., 237–38.
20   Emma Goldman, *Red Emma Speaks: An Emma Goldman Reader*
(Amherst, NY: Humanity Books, 1996), 112.

possible freedom, which is the conscious community of interests, voluntary solidarity."[21]

Using the terminology of game theory, one can say that freedom (in contrast to property, for example) is not a zero-sum game because more freedom for others does not mean less freedom for us. This is a positive-sum game where at least the following holds true: more freedom for others means more freedom for us. As Proudhon remarked, "The liberty and security of the rich do not suffer from the liberty and security of the poor; far from that, they mutually strengthen and sustain each other!"[22]

The (neo)liberal emphasis on negative freedom raises the obvious dilemma of how to actually achieve an open society with closed (egoist) individuals? It seems that the anarchists' statement that negative freedom is not enough because positive freedom is the essence of all, is right to the point. People are not only the most individual but also the most social creatures in this world. Society is a prerequisite for our existence since, outside society, a person cannot be free and cannot exist as a human being capable of talking, thinking, and creating. According to Max Stirner and his egoist criticism of negative freedom:

> Of what use is a freedom to you, indeed, if it brings in nothing? And, if you became free from everything, you would no longer have anything; for freedom is empty of substance. . . . I have no objection to freedom, but I wish more than freedom for you: you should not merely be rid of what you do not want; you should not only be a "freeman," you should be an "owner" [*Eigner*] too.[23]

---

21   Malatesta, *Anarchy*, 43.
22   Proudhon, "What Is Property?" 93.
23   Stirner, *The Ego and Its Own*, 142.

Transcendentalism as Cultural Anarchism

One of the main characteristics of anarchism is its opposition to and negation of traditionalisms. Transcendentalism waged war against traditional patterns of behavior, expression, and action at multiple levels—in literature by struggling against traditional forms of cultural expression and in everyday life through the dissidence of their participants. In their works, Emerson and Thoreau drew attention to the tepidness reigning over American literature that had turned many American literates into mere imitators of the British "fathers." In this regard, it is worth mentioning Emerson's instruction in his poem "Merlin" (1847) that the poet's goal must not be the literary form but only the substance, where a lack of rhythm, freedom of verse, and innovation are also permitted:

> Great is the art,
> Great be the manners of the bard.
> He shall not encumber,
> With the coil rhythm and number.[24]

This tepidness certainly ended with Walt Whitman who, writing in free verse, dispelled the last doubts about the existence of a genuine American literature. His free verse has probably been the greatest American contribution to poetry and at the same time the greatest monument to American literary independence. Without any formal education, Whitman overrode the classical tradition of verse form and as a basic poetic unit used a sentence, a thought.

---

24 Ralph W. Emerson, *Essays and Poems* (New York: Barnes & Noble, 2004), 452. Emerson stresses that genuine poetry is not written for publication, because engaged poetry lacks the finality that ordinary literature requests from its authors. Genuine poetry is a work in progress. See also Joel Myerson, ed., *Transcendentalism* (New York: Oxford University Press, 2000), 491.

His prose is rhythmic, mainly without rhyme and without meter.[25]

Whitman's omission of the traditional metric scheme and introduction of free verse today classify him as the pioneer of modern American poetry.[26] The verse unit is not a traditional metrical foot but a message that is most often an independent clause.

Of course, Transcendentalism has many other literary merits. For the first time in the history of American literature, the Transcendentalist articulation of the self resulted in American society being described as a unity-in-difference. In the works of the Transcendentalists, we find the first signs of stream of consciousness, a modern technique that came into full swing a few decades later. For Uroš Mozetič, the foundation of the stream of consciousness is a "Transcendentalist idea about man's current perception of the universe, about the Over-Soul as opposed to the chaotic world."[27]

In this sense, one could speak about Transcendentalism as cultural anarchism seeking to abolish the tendency of traditional cultural forms of expression to establish and strengthen authoritarian values and views, and to demolish cultural forms of expression as such. By undermining literary form

---

25 In professional circles there is often a dilemma as to whether Whitman's expression (mingling traditions) is prose or poetry. This dilemma is substantiated the most by his "O Captain! My Captain!"

26 Though puritanical society was ready to condone Whitman's unconventional poetic form, it was unwilling to do so with the substance of his poems. The themes and narration of the undestined reformer of the American cultural and artistic mentality strongly overstepped all limits of the generally accepted probity and education. A paradoxical situation thus occurred: America first rejected Whitman, even though his entire opus can be understood as a hymn to the country and its people. Thus, Whitman was able to receive the well-deserved accolades in today's anthologies of American literature largely due to his optimism, persistence, and the help of his literary friends.

27 Uroš Mozetič, "Walt Whitman—bard za vse čase" in *Travne bilke*, Walt Whitman (Mladinska knjiga: Ljubljana, 1999), 152.

and substance, Transcendentalism tried to develop symbolic forms that would reveal different aspects of the domination system, along with placing these aspects as the opposite of the value systems based on freedom and equality.

As John Clark points out in *The Anarchist Moment*, cultural struggle can be reasonably considered an essential element of a broader struggle against the material and ideological levers of the ruling classes' power. Transcendentalism drove this cultural struggle to the extreme as well. The importance of a cultural struggle is even greater considering that the authoritarian values of the existing dominant system cannot be eliminated by an economic or political struggle, unless this struggle is accompanied by a crucial cognitive transformation.

7
TRANSCENDENTALISM AND THE AMERICAN ANARCHIST TRADITION

The Beginnings of American Tradition of Protest

IN HIS REMARKABLE, OFTEN OVERLOOKED STUDY, *THE AMERICAN as Anarchist*, David DeLeon identifies three factors that have contributed to the creation of an original type of anarchism in the United States: Protestantism, capitalism, and an environment of great physical space.[1] All three factors have underpinned the search for completely new political structures and practices as an answer to new steps toward the accumulation of power and privileges. They have facilitated the creation of self-sufficient communities and, through the continental westward movement, a withdrawal from the parochial centers of power on the East Coast. The openness of the political map enabled an exodus time and again, making it more difficult to establish highly centralized and hierarchical structures and resulted in a strong individualism, or a kind of "political Protestantism."[2]

---

1 David DeLeon, *The American as Anarchist: Reflections on Indigenous Radicalism* (Baltimore, MD: John Hopkins University Press, 1978), 5.
2 According to F.O. Matthiessen, the word *individualism* appeared for the first time in the English translation of a famous work by Alexis

In this environment, people did not seek help or protection from the state, but instead created ad hoc structures, reaffirming Kropotkin's theory of mutual aid. Norman Ware thus speaks about anarchism as the "only bona fide American radical tradition"; for Lillian Symes and Travers Clement, anarchism is "undoubtedly a philosophy which is closest to the American temperament"; and Staughton Lynd concludes that "American revolutionaries sought a society in which the state would wither away."[3] The absence of a political or any other tradition in the United States has thus been a driving force toward fluidity, improvisation, experiments, skepticism—all of which inevitably lead to anarchist sensibility.

In 1636, Roger Williams warned that forced belief is "soul-rape," because each person must have the right to "try all things."[4] In that period, Anne Hutchinson initiated a protoanarchist movement who fought against the unjust fetters of (man-made) laws. They followed the idea that religious people are not bound by laws if they cleanse themselves with a divine oath, with "the Holy Spirit in us." She organized meetings at her home where all those who were delayed or absent from the recent masses could catch up, based on summaries of the sermons she had heard on Sunday and Thursday of the preceding week. Her decision to give the assembled only a summary of sermons soon turned into commenting on and scrupulously analyzing the things said,which was, of course, a serious offense for both religious and secular authorities.

After Henry Vane was elected governor of Massachusetts and Henry Wheelwright, who supported the antinomians,

---

de Tocqueville, *Democracy in America*, where this neologism was formulated to describe a completely new state of relationships and affairs. See Marcus Cunliffe, *The Literature of the United States* (Baltimore: Penguin Books, 1959), 16.

3   DeLeon, *American as Anarchist*, 41; Lynd, *Intellectual Origins of American Radicalism*, 162.

4   Ibid., 16.

started preaching about rebellion against authority and about establishing a free society, the authorities were compelled to react. Vane was defeated in the next elections, and the antinomianists were found guilty of inciting public revolt. In 1638, Hutchinson was forced to leave the Massachusetts Bay Colony, and thirty-five families followed her to Rhode Island.

Following the English Revolution, a mass immigration of Quakers, only strengthened the general hatred and mistrust of (secular) laws in the country, along with disdain for political oaths, taxes, compulsory military service, and war. In the eighteenth century, the new waves of immigrants brought with them ideas of Enlightenment, thereby further strengthening the faith in human good and the possibility of limitless social progress. With the colonial expansion to the West, away from the Old World, the immigrants' distrust of any authority was only reinforced, along with their reluctance to pay compulsory taxes. This feeling of independence and individualism, which had developed among self-enthusiastic pioneers and immigrants in the seventeenth and eighteenth centuries, is the main reason that anarchism in the United States developed unique, distinctive characteristics justifying the currently used term "American anarchism."

After the War of Independence, the Founding Fathers acknowledged the need for a minimum government. Upon the adoption of the Articles of Confederation and Perpetual Union in 1777—these entered into force in 1781 after they had been ratified by all states—a minimum, liberal and decentralized government was established. Without having read Thomas Paine, the immigrants came to recognize that "Society in every state is a blessing, but Government, even in its best state, is but a necessary evil; in its worst state an intolerable one."[5] Moreover, they were so successful at organizing

---

5   Thomas Paine, *Collected Writings* (New York: Library of America, 1995), 6.

their everyday lives, that Benjamin Franklin had to alert the delegates of the (federal) Constitutional Convention in Pennsylvania to speed up the establishment of the new government: "Gentlemen, you see that in the anarchy in which we live society manages much as before. Take care, if our disputes last too long, that the people do not come to think that they can very easily do without us."[6]

Even though Franklin's ideal was a society of free and enlightened people helping each other and exchanging goods, he still remained at the level of *laissez-faire* liberalism and minarchism. It is not surprising that the growing influence (of a conservative reading) of the English and French Enlightenment political literature, particularly John Locke's *Second Treatise of Government*, resulted in a small but vital discontinuity between the radical ideas of the Declaration of Independence, the moderate propositions of the new federal Constitution (1787), and the Bill of Rights (1791). Under the Declaration, government was understood only as an artificial formation necessary to protect a person's right to life, liberty, and the pursuit of happiness. The constitutional wording, however, perceives government in a completely different way: as an instrument for maintaining and reproducing social differences through the protection of a person's right to life, liberty, and private property.

According to Richard Hofstadter, it should be obvious that all the Founding Fathers despised democracy.[7] Madison defined the main task of the government as "protection of the rich minority from the majority that would want to equally divide property or some other similarly perverted goal." John Jay requested that the "people who own the country should also govern it." Just more proof of the anarchist

---

6   Franklin quoted in Leonard Krimerman and Lewis Perry, eds., *Pattern of Anarchy: A Collection of Writings on the Anarchist Tradition* (Garden City, NY: Anchor Books, 1966), xv.

7   Richard Hofstadter, *The American Political Tradition and the Men Who Made It* (New York: Vintage Books, 1989), 6–7.

claim that authority and the state are not based on a social agreement but on a social conflict.

The only possible exception is Thomas Jefferson, who warned about the "violent" and "greedy" nature of the state and as an ideal ("the happiest") social system proposed a governmentless society ("the same as our American Indians have"). Jefferson came closest to anarchism in his famous maxim that "the best government is that which governs least."[8] In the Declaration of Independence, he wrote, using the style of the most radical thinkers:

> We hold these truths to be self-evident, that all men are created equal, that they are endowed by their Creator with certain unalienable Rights, that among these are Life, Liberty and the pursuit of Happiness. That to secure these rights, Governments are instituted among Men, deriving their just powers from the consent of the governed. That whenever any Form of Government becomes destructive of these ends, it is the Right of the People to alter or to abolish it, and to institute new Government, laying its foundation on such principles and organizing its powers in such form, as to them shall seem most likely to effect their Safety and Happiness.[9]

Under the Declaration of Independence, the people have not only the right but the duty to abolish the government when it becomes despotic. According to Jefferson, a little rebellion now and then is a medicine necessary for the sound health of government: "The tree of liberty must be

8   Although Jefferson is attributed authorship of the maxim "that government is best which governs least," it has in fact never been identified in his works. Nonetheless, this maxim is still considered his most remarkable idea, the topicality of which only increases with the years.
9   Jefferson quoted in Zinn, *A People's History of the United States*, 71.

refreshed from time to time with the blood of patriots and tyrants."[10]

Moreover, Jefferson warned about the growing concentration of power and wealth in certain banking institutions and industrial corporations and pinpointed a phenomenon of a new class of precapitalists—the "aristocrats." As suggested by Chomsky, "The aristocrats of his day were the advocates of the rising capitalist state, which Jefferson regarded with much disdain, clearly recognizing the quite obvious contradictions between democracy and capitalism."[11] Nevertheless, Jefferson was also unable to make this step toward the complete abolition of political power. He dedicated himself to broadening the public's participation in government. As a member of the slave-holding plantation nobility, he was unable to take a step beyond private property or toward its abolition.

Thomas Paine was even closer to the anarchist position. At the beginning of the American War of Independence, he made a groundbreaking analysis of the differences between society and government in his famous pamphlet *Common Sense* that—by explicitly distrusting the functioning of the government—heavily influenced the subsequent analyses of the "classics of anarchism":

> Some writers have so confounded society with government, as to leave little or no distinction

---

10   Ibid., 95. Although every revolt against authority should not be understood as anarchist, before 1760 the "New World" witnessed eighteen revolts whose aim was to destroy the colonial authorities, six revolts of slaves and over forty unrests due to unbearable and unjust social conditions. Revolution indeed meant victory over England, yet it failed to solve the internal class conflicts as the United States was for many years shaken by rebellions claiming a more just social, economic, and political system.

11   Noam Chomsky, *Powers and Prospects: Reflections on Human Nature and the Social Order* (Cambridge, MA: South End Press, 1996), 88.

between them. They are not only different, but have different origins. Society is produced by our wants, and government by our wickedness; the former promotes our Positively by uniting our affections, the latter Negatively by restraining our vices. The one encourages intercourse, the other creates distinctions. The first a patron, the last a punisher. Society in every state is a blessing, but government even in its best state is but a necessary evil; in its worst state an intolerable one . . . Government, like dress, is the badge of lost innocence.[12]

Paine's opposition to the government was only reinforced over time. Perhaps the reason for this growing wrath lies in the problems he had with the so-called revolutionary governments for his frankness and veracity. In his work *Rights of Man* sixteen years later, he put elaborated on the positive effects of natural (social) instincts, already discussed in Peter Kropotkin's famous work *Mutual Aid:*

Great part of that order which reigns among mankind is not the effect of government. It has its origin in the principles of society and the natural constitution of man. It existed prior to government, and would exist if the formality of government was abolished. The mutual dependence and reciprocal interest which man has upon man, and all the parts of civilized community upon each other, create that great chain of connection which holds it together. The landholder, the farmer, the manufacturer, the merchant, the tradesman, and every occupation, prospers by the aid which each receives from the other,

12   Paine, *Collected Writings*, 6.

and from the whole. Common interest regulates
their concerns, and forms their law; and the laws
which common usage ordains, have a greater influence than the laws of government.[13]

In the same work, Paine emphasizes that the more a civilization is perfect, the less there is room for government because
society handles its affairs autonomously and is governed by
itself. In his views and demands, Paine almost approached
the anarchist pantheon from which, according to Woodcock,
he differed only by lacking optimism about achieving a better society in the future.[14]

American anarchism is thought to boast a double tradition—the autochthonous and the immigrant. The beginning of the autochthonous tradition dates back to the
nineteenth century when individualist anarchism developed
under the influence of the liberal ideas of Jefferson, Paine,
and Protestantism. The reason that anarchism had not manifested itself earlier and was not practiced was probably that
the collective desire for liberation from foreign supremacy
blurred the internal social differences which only became apparent in the nineteenth century.

The first self-proclaimed anarchist in the United States
was the musician and inventor Josiah Warren, who founded
the pioneering American anarchist newspaper *The Peaceful
Revolutionist* in 1833. Warren, also known as the "American
Proudhon," was first a member of the New Harmony, a utopian experiment by Robert Owen, but he left the community
in 1827 due to the provisions prohibiting private property
and establishing a system of collective authority. To his mind,
these provisions were unacceptable as they prevented independence, creativity, and responsibility as well as curtailed
man's individuality. In his analysis of the causes of the failed

13   Ibid., 551.
14   Woodcock, *Anarchism*, 46.

experiment, he wrote: "It seemed that the difference of opinion, tastes and purposes increased just in proportion to the demand for conformity. . . . It appeared that it was nature's own inherent law of diversity that had conquered us."[15]

This experience did not ward him off from further communal experiments, but only strengthened his belief that a community should adjust to the needs of an individual person and not vice versa. Even though he formulated his ideas based on his own research work, both practical and theoretical, he arrived at almost identical conclusions to those of Proudhon. Warren defines private property as the foundation of personal freedom. Every person is entitled to the results of their work, yet they cannot achieve absolute self-sufficiency. Due to the division of labor as required by the modern production method, Warren also proposed a redistribution (Proudhon suggested an "exchange bank") which should be founded on the mutual trust of all those participating in the production process who are prepared to exchange their products at their actual cost of production and the amount of labor time. Like Proudhon, Warren suggested that checks should serve as nominal funds. Their value would be defined by the number of working hours (labor for labor) required to produce each individual good, but the difficulty and intensity of the work would also be considered.

Immediately after abandoning New Harmony, Warren founded the Time Store in Cincinnati, where the buyer was expected to pay proportionately for the purchased goods with their "time" or working checks, obliging them to put their activity at the disposal of the merchant for the number of working hours equivalent to the price of the goods. In this way, he tried to make his customers enthusiastic about the ideas of mutualism and to recruit members for his communal life experiment already in the pipeline. Consequently, he established the utopian community Village of Equity in

15   Ibid., 391.

Ohio with a group of supporters and disciples in 1834. In contrast to the Owenist and Fourierist communities (organized around the ideas of Robert Owen and Charles Fourier) the Village of Equity replaced a strict hierarchy with a system of free mutual agreements. The community, similarly to most utopian experiments throughout the rich history of utopianism in the United States, fell through due to a series of epidemics rather than internal disagreements or a collapse of the distribution system.

Persuaded by the practicability of his theories, Warren established a community in Ohio in 1846 with the meaningful name Utopia, composed mainly of former members of the failed Fourierist communities. The community was so successful in its activities that it achieved self-sufficiency and for several years lived completely independently from the external society. Counting more than a hundred members at its peak, Utopia thrived on the mutualist principles for over twenty years (until the 1860s), even after Warren left the community in 1850. In the same year, Warren established a new community in Long Island, named the City of Modern Times, which like Utopia thrived on mutualist principles for several years until it gradually transformed into a more or less ordinary village, adhering more explicitly to the principles of mutual cooperation. Warren's ideas contributed to the emergence of a new generation of individualist and social anarchists (Spooner, Andrews, and Greene), while also enriching the liberal discourse with the concept of "sovereignty of the individual" in the United States. In their efforts to abolish the state and establish an association of voluntary unions, these radical individualists emphasized the sovereignty of the individual on one hand and the positive meaning of private property and free market on the other—like Proudhon, they considered private property a guarantee of personal freedom. Hence, the American radical individualists can also be labeled "left-wing libertarians" who still see in capitalism a catalyst of anarchy and in work a means and point of emancipation.

The Advent of Transcendentalism

Genuine anarchist ideas only started to be generated in the United States in the mid-nineteenth century with the advent of Transcendentalism. If protoanarchist ideas and demands for the liberation of society and the individual can be traced back before the emergence of Transcendentalism, then Transcendentalism is remarkable for identifying the basic types of hierarchy and exploitation—that is, the modern state and capitalism—and marks the beginning of a genuine anarchist sensibility in the New World. Emerson considered the nation-state and its laws as enemies of freedom and virtue because the very existence of political institutions encroaches on human dignity: "Every actual State is corrupt. Good men must not obey the laws too well. . . . Wild liberty develops iron conscience. Want of liberty, by strengthening law and decorum, stupefies conscience."[16]

The economic depression of 1837 further confirmed his beliefs that the capitalist economy is "a system of selfishness . . . of distrust, of concealment, of superior keenness, not of giving but of taking advantage."[17] His anticapitalist stance resulted in a political appeal that "there is nothing more important in the culture of man than to resist the dangers of commerce," since the "invasion of Nature by Trade with its Money, its Steam, its Railroad, threatens to upset the balance of man and establish a new Universal Monarchy more tyrannical than Babylon or Rome."[18] We can only imagine what Emerson would say about the current state of affairs if we recall his statement that "trade is the lord of the world nowadays and government only a parachute to this balloon."

Emerson built up his libertarian vision—and thus his opposition to the state and capitalism—on a belief in the

---

16 Emerson, *Essential Writings*, 382.
17 West, *American Evasion of Philosophy*, 27.
18 Ibid.

"potential perfection of the reason" of each individual as well as the finding that "man has everything necessary for them to govern." Conscience leads us to the moral truth and therefore every individual must be a state in themselves; as a rational and moral creature they must develop their character and discard the violent and superfluous institutions of the state. In his essay "Politics," Emerson offered a criticism of statism that was later eternized and radicalized by Thoreau:

> Hence the less government we have the better— the fewer laws, and the less confided power. The antidote to this abuse of formal government is the influence of private character, the growth of the Individual. To educate the wise man the State exists, and with the appearance of the wise man the State expires. The appearance of character makes the State unnecessary. The wise man is the State.[19]

In accordance with the basic postulate of Transcendentalism— the omnipresence of the divine in the world in which every thing and creature is a "microcosm" of the entire reality—Emerson argues that "the world globes itself in a drop of dew."[20] As the world is ruled by a Higher Law, we do not need human laws and the state. Instead of the state, Emerson suggests public assemblies that would serve as decision-making forums. When the U.S. Congress adopted the infamous Fugitive Slave Bill of 1850, under which the fugitive slaves who had been captured in the North of the United States were returned to their owners in the South, he commented on this sordid act by saying: "I will not obey it, by God!"[21] In

---

19   Thoreau, *Walden and Other Writings*, 386.
20   Ibid., 158.
21   The adoption of the law was part of the broader Compromise of 1850, which tried to reconcile both sides arguing about the issue of slavery. After this agreement, California joined the Union as a free

the same period he wrote some cynical lines about the spirit of the time, which were later frequently quoted by Benjamin Tucker and thus entered the American anarchist tradition:

> When the Church is social worth,
> When the state-house is the hearth,
> Then the perfect State is come,
> The republican at home.[22]

Thoreau offered an even more radical criticism of the state and its institutions. In his *Walden; or, Life in the Woods* (1854) Thoreau described in detail his transcendentalist experiment—to live in a simple way, in nature and with it, in a material shortage but in a spiritual abundance—which lasted exactly two years, two months, and two days at Walden Pond. Thoreau was driven in this experiment by a desire to simplify society and free people from their artificial wants, requirements, and the complexity of modern life. Thoreau explains his wishes and demands by his belief in the natural that differs substantially from human laws, which is why everyone who is faithful to their libertarian views should assign more importance to spontaneous impulses than to mechanical abidance to the rules.

---

state; whereas to satisfy the other side a federal act was adopted requiring authorities to fully cooperate in the return of fugitive slaves. Reluctance to participate in the "democratic" procedure of returning "property" was punished by a penalty of $1,000. To at least give an appearance of democracy, the final decision about the fate of the fugitive slaves was adopted by special government agents. They received prize money for performing their work: if they decided in favor of the slaveholder they were paid $10, and if the decision favored the fugitive slave they were paid $5. In ten years (1850–60) government agents returned 332 people to slavery and freed only eleven. For more about Emerson's struggle against slavery, see Gary Collison, "Emerson and Antislavery" in *A Historical Guide to Ralph W. Emerson*, ed. Joel Myerson, (New York: Oxford University Press, 2000).

22   Emerson, *Essential Writings*, 378.

Although Thoreau attempted to consciously move away from society and its distresses, he could not escape from its tentacles. In 1845, after refusing to pay taxes in his symbolic protest against the war with Mexico and slavery, he was arrested overnight. The upshot of this experience was his essay "On the Duty of Civil Disobedience" (1849), considered to be Thoreau's greatest contribution to anarchist thought. Even today, Thoreau's essay is one of the greatest justifications of the right to rebellion and the practice of civil disobedience.[23] On one hand, the essay exposes Thoreau's faith in the reason of each individual and, on the other, his lack of confidence in and disdain for any authority:

> I heartily accept the motto—"That government is best which governs least"—and I should like to see it acted up to more rapidly and systematically. Carried out, it finally amounts to this, which I also believe—"That government is best which governs not at all"—and when men are prepared for it, that will be the kind of government which they will have. Government is at best an expedient; but most governments are usually, and all governments are sometimes, inexpedient. . . . But, to speak practically and as a citizen, unlike those who call themselves no-government men, I ask for, not at once no government, but *at once* a better government.[24]

Thoreau did not limit freedom to the sphere of politics but instead broadened it to the economic, social, and moral spheres.

---

23   For more about the influence of Thoreau's essay on subsequent protest movements, see Lawrence A. Rosenwald, "The Theory, Practice, and Influence of Thoreau's Civil Disobedience" in *A Historical Guide to Henry David Thoreau*, ed. William E. Cain (New York: Oxford University Press, 2000).

24   Thoreau, *Walden and Other Writings*, 667.

He legitimately pointed out that the War of Independence did in fact liberate people in political terms, but that most of these people were still economically and morally enslaved. Thoreau thus approached completely the anarchist interpretation of exploitation and domination, since he looked for exploitation and disciplining not only within class antagonism and the state but mainly within ourselves. Similarly to Stirner, he warned about the internalization of repressive mechanisms as a result of which (self)repression was implemented chiefly by the individual, not by the state: "Do we call this the land of the free? What is it to be free from King George and continue the slaves of King Prejudice? What is to be born free and not to live free? What is the value of any political freedom, but as a means to moral freedom?"[25]

As a consistent anarchist, he offered a lucid critique of man-made laws since "law never made men a whit more just; and, by means of their respect for it, even the well-disposed are daily made the agents of injustice." A common result of undue respect for law or civil obedience is "a file of soldiers, colonel, captain, corporal, privates, powder-monkeys, and all, marching in admirable order over hill and dale to the wars, against their wills, ay, against their common sense and consciences, which makes it very steep marching indeed, and produces a palpitation of the heart."[26]

He defines voting as a game with a slight moral aftertaste, a play with justice and injustice, with moral issues; accompanied, of course, by a bet. By rebuffing "majoritarian democracy," Thoreau evokes the anarchist vision of participatory democracy that instead of supporting people's sovereignty supports the sovereignty of the individual. According to Thoreau, representative democracy is an oxymoron, a highly discordant and simultaneously homogenizing institute leading to unstable and one-dimensional societies:

25 Ibid., 765.
26 Ibid., 673.

I cast my vote, perchance, as I think right; but I am not vitally concerned that the right should prevail. I am willing to leave it to the majority. Even voting *for the right* is *doing* nothing for it. It is only expressing to men feebly your desire that it should prevail. A wise man will not leave the right to the mercy of chance, nor wish it to prevail through the power of the majority. There is but a little virtue in the action of masses of men. When the majority shall at length vote for the abolition of slavery, it will be because they are indifferent to slavery or because there is but a little slavery left to be abolished by their vote. They will then be the only slaves.[27]

If Stirner, with his apothegm that a master is a thing established by their servant, emphasized the state's dependence on our willingness to be dominated and disciplined, then Thoreau also sought a solution for our liberation from the tyranny of the majority of one and civil disobedience. Accordingly, all individuals act according to their own conscience and not dictated national laws:

Cast your whole vote, not a strip of paper merely. A minority is powerless while it conforms to the majority; it is even a minority then; but it is irresistible when it clogs by its whole weight. If the alternative is to keep all just men in prison, or give up war and slavery, the State will not hesitate which to choose. If a thousand men were not to pay their tax-bills this year that would not be a violent and bloody measure, as it would be to pay them, and enable the state to commit violence and shed innocent blood. This is, in fact,

27 Ibid., 368.

the definition of a peaceable revolution, if any
such is possible. . . . Under a government which
imprisons unjustly, the true place for a just man
is also a prison. . . . I was not born to be forced. I
will breathe after my own fashion![28]

Thoreau is important for American progressive thought not
simply for his ideas about the revolt and civil disobedience,
but for his precursory gestures toward green anarchism.
In his works, he describes the consequences of industrialization, modern life, scrambling for profit and power that
inevitably lead to alienation from nature, work, society
and, finally, from oneself. Thoreau justifiably warns that to
preserve wild nature is to preserve humanity. Based on the
finding that capitalism is not only the main reason for preserving slavery in the South but that, by creating fictitious
needs and illusory conceptions about people, it inevitably
results in the "self-enslavement" of otherwise free people,
Thoreau found his exodus in nature: "I went to the woods
because I wished to live deliberately, to front only the essential facts of life, and see if I could not learn what it had
to teach, and not, when I came to die, discover that I had
not lived."[29]

For Thoreau, the forest is more magnificent and important than any cathedral; for Emerson, nature is also a place
showing us that life beyond states is not only possible but
also necessary if we want the human and social habitat to
become freer and to provide people with a greater degree of
good and freedom:

At the gates of the forest, the surprised man of
the world is forced to leave his city estimates of
great and small, wise and foolish. The knapsack

---

28 Ibid., 679–80.
29 Ibid., 86.

> of custom falls off his back with the first step
> he makes into these precincts. Here is sanctity
> which shames our religions, and reality which
> discredits our heroes. . . . Here no history, or
> church, or state, is interpolated on the divine sky
> and the immortal year.[30]

Though Thoreau strived to remain faithful to his individualism and belief in the rejection of political life or any organized political movement, he still became part of the abolitionist movement. Transcendentalism was inseparably linked with the abolitionist movement through the famous Underground Railroad that helped fugitive slaves gain freedom in the North as well as the radical movement called Come-outers (due to their leaving of the church) or Cape-Codders (they were particularly common on Cape Cod) that escalated from the opposition to slavery in the South to an absolute and uncompromising resistance to the church, government, and all types of social constraints. In their aspiration for a "harmonious self-government" many renounced money and private property.

While Walt Whitman was never a member of the Transcendental Club, many researchers of American history and literature justifiably pigeonhole him in the Transcendentalist milieu. In contrast to other Transcendentalists, Whitman finished his formal schooling at the age of eleven and took up many side jobs until he settled in printing and journalism. He was first an editor of the democratic newspaper *Eagle* from where he was dismissed for supporting abolitionism. Further on, he established his own newspaper *Freemen* that ran aground in its first year of publication.

Although Emerson welcomed Whitman's *Leaves of Grass* with the words "I greet you at the beginning of a great career,

---

30   Emerson, *Essential Writings*, 364–65.

which yet must have had a long foreground somewhere, for such a start. I rubbed my eyes a little, to see if this sunbeam were no illusion; but the solid sense of the book is a sober certainty," the reality proved otherwise. Despite Whitman's intent to cultivate and radicalize "small" people when he was writing his prosaic poetry, his collection received no particular attention—the working class had never bothered much about the transcendental quest for the cosmic truth. His work was appreciated and understood by literary connoisseurs, who were not his target audience. Whitman's poetry—besides the poetic form—is first and foremost defined by a strong egalitarian impulse. In the poem "By the Roadside," he wrote:

> Of Equality—as if it harm'd me, giving others
>   the same chances and rights as myself—as if
>   it were not indispensable to my own rights
>   that others possess the same.[31]

Like other Transcendentalists, Whitman emphasized both individualism—his most famous poem bears the title "Song of Myself"—and solidarity. His poems were an attempt to sow the ideas and values of communal individualism, "not only because that is a great lesson in nature, amid all her generalizing laws, but as a counterpoise to the leveling tendencies of Democracy."[32]

Whitman's deep-seated hatred for the state and politics not only stemmed from ontological radicalism, but was due to all the injustices he had witnessed during his life. He was a voluntary nurse in the Washington Hospital during the Civil War and poured his sympathy for the victims and his hatred of war into the soul-stirring poem "Drum-Taps." Whitman had a reasonable cause to cynically name the politicians of

---

31 Whitman, *Poetry and Prose*, 414.
32 Ibid., 667.

the world "scum floating atop of the waters," while calling upon working women and men in his poem, "To the States":

> To the States or any one of them, or any city of
> the States, *Resist much, obey little,*
> Once unquestioning obedience, once fully
> enslaved,
> Once fully enslaved, no nation, state, city of the
> earth, ever afterward resumes its liberty.[33]

Identity Building

At the end of the nineteenth century, Benjamin R. Tucker thrust anarchism in the United States again in the individualist direction. Many consider Tucker the most visible and most important American anarchist author. In his works, he intertwined the ideas of Warren and Proudhon which, thanks to his contribution, had become more acceptable to capitalist America.

He referred to anarchists as unterrified Jeffersonian Democrats, and defined anarchism as a method of organizing social and political life that leads to complete *laissez-faire.* He claimed that to achieve a better society all monopolies had to be abolished, including states that are nothing more than monopolies of political power in a given territory. Tucker reached beyond the minarchist position by emphasizing that the protection of personal freedom and property is possible through voluntary associations and cooperatives. In an ideal social system where the law of equal liberty—"the largest amount of liberty compatible with equality and mutuality of respect, on the part of individuals living in society, for their respective spheres of action"—has been achieved, there would be no moral law or the law would say "mind your own business" and the only crime would be interfering

---

33 Ibid., 172.

in other people's affairs.[34] Educational institutions, cooperatives, banks, syndicates, and other alternative institutions, are crucial to achieving such changes, as the collapse of the state would result of mass civil disobedience and general strikes. With the reinforcement of American anarchocommunism and anarcho-syndicalism, Tucker's individualist starting position became increasingly vague and inconsistent over time.

Tucker is also notable as a publicist. In 1878, he established the *Radical Review*, and edited and published the anarchist newspaper *Liberty* from 1881 to 1907. For several years, *Liberty* provided the main forum of American radicalism through which authors such as Henry Louis Mencken, George Bernard Shaw, and Walt Whitman spread their subversive ideas. Even if Tucker's vision of a free society was essentially different from the anarcho-communist conception of Peter Kropotkin, the latter still supported and welcomed Tucker's work, admitting that his "criticism of the state was very insightful and his defense of the individual very strong."[35]

In the United States, social anarchism, primarily anarchocommunism, was initially widely spread among Christian radicals who understood submission to divine authority as an inevitable rejection of all secular authorities. In the 1830s, Adin Ballou, who later importantly influenced Tolstoy's ideas, attempted to reach freedom in and with the community. He believed that the only guiding principle of humankind should be absolute divine authority. As secular authority has no intrinsic authority or moral power, it has no right to demand the submission and subordination of the individual. If divine authority is founded on belief and love, secular authority is founded on coercion and physical power that

---

34   Corrine Jacker, *The Black Flag of Anarchy: Antistatism in the United States* (New York: Charles Scribner's Sons, 1968), 123.

35   DeLeon, *The American as Anarchist*, 68.

manifest themselves in prisons and wars and people must withdraw their support for secular authority by boycotting elections, the legislative procedure, and warfare. Instead of secular authority, Ballou proposed that a society be based on communes and voluntary associations where public opinion would already be enough to prevent anomalies. He attempted to implement his ideas in the Hopedale Community in Massachusetts. In the following decade, the Christian radical John Humphrey Noyes in New York State established what was believed to be the most controversial utopian experiment, the Oneida Community, which announced the beginning of the end of American utopianism.[36]

The individualist Lysander Spooner applied John Locke's arguments to the anarchist conclusions. In *Natural Law; or, The Science of Justice* (1882), he wrote that justice could only be achieved through absolute respect for the freedom and property of every individual. When people ignore justice, the state of nature results in a war of all people against all people; therefore, a free society must facilitate a free and voluntary association of people and the related right as well as joint protection against (external and internal) transgressors. Spooner's most important contribution is probably his theoretically justified rejection of the social contract theory of the state and the U.S. Constitution. According to Spooner, it is impossible to say that every person has concluded a contract with the government. People may conclude contracts for themselves alone, and forming binding political contracts for future generations is absurd. Accordingly, any government that builds its authority on an invalid social contract is illegitimate. The individual has the right to oppose such a government: "And if he makes war upon it, he does it so as an open enemy, and not as a traitor."

---

36 The community was based on the principle that people as God's children cannot sin. The community practiced an extreme version of communism where not only property but also love was in "joint ownership."

Spooner does not see the main reason for maintaining this unnatural state only in the monopoly of coercion available to the rulers, but more in the institute of elections that give people the illusion they are free and have an influence. If elections were able to change anything, the rulers would have long ago deprived people of this right. Today, his ideas are mainly quoted by contemporary minarchists and anarcho-capitalists such as Murray Rothbard and Robert Nozick, but with his demands for freedom and equality, Spooner is rightly classified among the left-wing individualist anarchists.

Likewise, the lawyer and linguist Stephen Pearl Andrews took individualism to the boundaries of anarchism. In line with his conviction that Warren's principle of the sovereignty of the individual refers to each and every individual, Andrews organized a fundraising campaign for the redemption of all slaves in the federal state of Texas and also called for the sovereignty and self-proprietorship of both genders. He believed that sexual and family life should not be controlled by the state and religion as they are matters for the sovereign individual.

Immigrant Tradition

As already noted we can identify two closely linked but separate anarchist traditions in the United States: the American and the European. If at the beginning there were many attempts to make strong links between the two—one example was the so-called "Forty-Eighters," a loose group of Proudhonian anarchists that included the natives as well as the immigrants, prominent within European anarchist movement—the differences between both camps became more prominent and eventually resulted in open conflict. In the section that follows, I will focus on the "foreign" tradition that was becoming more and more threatening to the basic features of American individualist anarchism, while contributing to its rationale and sentiment.

Though the United States was participating in the international workers' movement through the membership of Lysander Spooner and William B. Greene in the First International, the development of a true American workers' movement occurred at end of the nineteenth century. With the new influx of immigrants from Europe, the United States witnessed a rift between statists (Marxists) and anarchists. After the end of the International Social Revolutionary Congress in 1881, two labor federations were organized in the United States. In 1883, groups of immigrants, mostly from Germany and the Austro-Hungarian monarchy, gathered in Pittsburgh to establish the revolutionary International Working People's Association, also called the Black International. One year earlier, groups of American socialists established the International Workingmen's Association or the Red International that was associated with the International in London.

At the beginning of the twentieth century, trade unions started consolidating and gathering strength. In 1905, the radical syndicalist organization Industrial Workers of the World (IWW) was founded and was dominated by libertarian socialists. In contrast to other trade union organizations, the IWW (also known as Wobblies) also offered membership to immigrants, Native Americans, women, African Americans, and unskilled workers. In line with their anarcho-syndicalist position, they rejected the tendencies of other workers' organizations that only advocated better working conditions or higher wages. Namely, they were convinced that capitalism could not be modified or made more humane, but only destroyed and replaced by a socialist system.

The year 1907, with a fire in Tucker's office and the abolition of *Liberty*, marked the end of the predominant individualist direction within American anarchism. In the second half of the nineteenth century, new European immigrants in the United States fueled the development of social anarchism and the period of an immigrant tradition started. Unlike

American anarchists who objected to the state for curtailing personal freedom and property, the European immigrants objected to the state because they saw in it the main pillar of private property and privileges. In contrast to the American individualists who emphasized the freedom of the individual, the discourse of the immigrant social anarchists highlighted the benefits of solidarity and community.

Another impetus to social anarchism was provided by the immigration of the former German member of parliament, Johann Most. Soon after his arrival in the United States in 1882, he settled down in New York and established the anarchist newspaper *Die Freiheit*, attracting a circle of militant immigrant workers who shared only one goal: the destruction of the state and capitalism. With his activism, publishing, and mainly enthusiastic support for the revolutionary violence, Most influenced and forecast the subsequent development of anarchism in the United States.

The general American public first became acquainted with anarchism because of an incident at Haymarket Square in Chicago on May 4, 1886. The so-called Haymarket Tragedy took place during a rally in support of an eight-hour workday and commemoration of the victims of police violence in the McCormic Harvester Works factory, when a fight broke out between policemen and protesters. After an unknown person threw a dynamite bomb, the blast and ensuing gunfire resulted in the deaths and injuries of both police and civilians. After the incident, eight anarchists were arrested, including Albert Parsons, the editor of the anarchist newspaper *Alarm*, and August Spies, one of the editors of the daily newspaper *Chicagoer Arbeiter-Zeitung*, its Sunday issue *Fackel*, and the weekly issue *Vorbote*. Of the eight anarchists who were tried, seven were given the death penalty. This is not surprising considering that State's Attorney Grinnell addressed the jury—composed of entrepreneurs and a relative of one of the policemen who had died—with the following words: "Law is on trial. Anarchy is on trial. These men have been selected, picked out by the grand jury and indicted because they are leaders. They are no more guilty than the thousands who follow them. Gentlemen of the jury: convict these men, make examples of them, hang them and you save our institutions, our society."[37]

This clear political motive of the trial is also confirmed by the explanation provided to the "Chicago eight" by the chief judge Joseph E. Garry: "Not because you caused the Haymarket bomb, but because you are Anarchists, you are on trial."[38] These events in Chicago are also important from a broader perspective as the incident provided fertile grounds for the prejudices of the general American public to any type of anarchism. Even though anarchists in the United States did not resort to violence in the following years, two incidents had received so much attention that they further cemented the public's prejudices and hatred toward anarchism.

In 1892, the Russian immigrant Alexander Berkman carried out an attempt on the life of the financial magnate Henry Clay Frick, as revenge for the massacre of workers during the Homestead strike, and the American public's perception of anarchism as a terrorist movement was only reconfirmed. In 1901, a young Polish immigrant Leon Czolgosz almost struck a fatal blow to anarchism in the United States, when he assassinated President McKinley. In December of the same year the new, President Theodore Roosevelt, in his address to Congress, labeled anarchism "a crime against the whole human race" and called on humankind to "band together against the anarchist." All these incidents helped bring to an end the period where the anarchist movement in the United States had enough potential to mobilize the broad public and ensure the necessary support and legitimacy for its activities.

---

37   Jacker, *Black Flag of Anarchy*, 113.
38   Goldman, *Anarchism and Other Essays*, 87.

Anarchism and the Short Twentieth Century

Although anarchism in the United States had reached its nadir after World War I, its ideas kept spreading, mainly owing to a number of isolated but active Jewish, Italian, Spanish, and Russian immigrants and their newspapers. Worth mentioning here are *Fraye Arbeter Stimme* (Yiddish), *Cultura Proletaria* (Spanish), *Dielo Truda* (Russian), and *Il Martello* and *L'Adunata dei Refrattari* (Italian). In the Russian immigrant community Alexander Berkman and Emma Goldman came to the forefront of American anarchism not only in their tireless propagation of anarchist ideas across the entire U.S. territory but also in the publication of the well-known newspapers *Mother Earth* (1906–1917) and *The Blast!* (1915–1917). Berkman and Goldman were also active in the organization and propagation of progressive schools (Free Ferrer Schools) established in the federal states of New York (Manhattan) and New Jersey (Stelton) based on the pedagogical ideas of the Spanish anarchist Francisco Ferrer.[39] These initial attempts encouraged the development of the Modern School Movement, influencing larger movements for progressive and alternative teaching in the United States.

George Woodcock once remarked that Goldman—in her struggle for the freedom of speech, advocating of women's right to abortion, practicing free love, and acquainting the American public with the works of Thoreau, Emerson, Whitman, Shaw, Strindberg, Ibsen, and others—overstepped

---

39 According to these ideas, it is possible to achieve the primary objective of education—the development of critical and independent individuals—only based on free and non-authoritarian teaching. Children should be enabled to explore those things that interest them the most, in their own way and in their own time framework. For more, see Paul Avrich, *Anarchist Voices: An Oral History of Anarchism in America* (Princeton, NJ: Princeton University Press, 1995); Paul Avrich, *The Modern School Movement: Anarchism and Education in the United States* (Oakland: AK Press, 2005).

the framework of even such a broad and variegated intellectual current as anarchism. Whether all of these activities can be understood as anarchism in the genuine, full meaning of the word is thus a matter of personal judgment. Undoubtedly, the value of Woodcock's assessment lies in the fact that it reveals the complex and multifaceted nature of the anarchist rebellion.

American anarchism again caught the world public's attention with the Sacco and Vanzetti case. In 1921, the Bostonian anarchists Nicola Sacco and Bartolomeo Vanzetti were sentenced to death for alleged double murder during an armed robbery. This politically motivated trial had become a *cause célèbre* that not only united socialist ranks in the United States but allied the new generation of anarchists all over the world. It received wide public attention not just because of the unfair and partial trial, but because of the idealism to which the convicted clung until their execution. This can be discerned from Vanzetti's statement when the death penalty was pronounced:

> If it had not been for this, I might have lived out
> my life talking at street corners to scorning men.
> I might have died, unmarked, unknown, a failure.
> Now we are not a failure. This is our career and
> our triumph. Never in our full life can we do such
> work for tolerance, for justice, for man's under-
> standing of man, as we now do by an accident.
> Our words, our lives, our pains—nothing! The
> taking of our lives—lives of a good shoemaker
> and a poor fish-peddler—all! That last moment
> belong to us—that agony is our triumph![40]

Over the years, the last letter Sacco sent his son before he was executed has become an inspiring call to millions to finally take the path to creating a better world:

---

40 Woodcock, *Anarchism*, 400.

So, Son, instead of crying, be strong, so as to be
able to comfort your mother. . . . Take her for
a long walk in the quiet country, gathering wild
flowers here and there. . . . But remember always,
Dante, in the play of happiness, don't you use all
for yourself only. . . . Help the persecuted and the
victim because they are your better friends. . . .
In this struggle of life you will find more and love
and you will be loved.[41]

Persecution by the authorities, disapprobation and fears in
the public, the surge of communism as a logical result of the
Russian Revolution, were followed by the relative economic
progress which further undermined the American anarchist
movement after the Great Depression. Before World War II,
Emma Goldman returned to the United States on the wish
of her Spanish friends, yet her agitation to assist the Spanish
anarchists received only modest attention as she—at one
time "the most dangerous woman in the world"—was now
perceived as a remnant of the past.

During World War II, anarchist ideas were resuscitated,
primarily thanks to new generations of radicalized young intellectuals influenced by the madness and slaughter of the
war. On the East Coast, a heterogeneous group united around
the progressive magazine *Why?*, later renamed *Resistance* and
New York–based magazine *Retort* succeeded in amalgamat-
ing anarchist theory with literary creation. In 1944, Dwight
McDonald, the former editor of the journal *Partisan Review*,
established an important anarcho-pacifist journal *Politics* that
also published contributions from authors such as George
Orwell, Ignazio Silone, and Simone Weil. On the West
Coast, there were two main centers of anarchist activities:
San Francisco and the small village of Waldport in Oregon
with a center (prison) for military dissidents. Here, young

---

41 Zinn, *A People's History of the United States*, 376.

intellectuals and literates (including William Everson) published various publications with strong libertarian tendencies. San Francisco, with its long and rich tradition of labor radicalism, also offered the social pedigree needed for the new heyday of anarchism. In the early 1940s saw the birth of the San Francisco Anarchist Circle, where old Italian and Jewish anarchists joined forces with young intellectuals and artists such as Kenneth Rexroth. The Circle, with its gazette *The Ark*, can undoubtedly be considered as a main seedbed for the emergence of the subsequent Beat Generation and counterculture in general.

At the end of the 1950s, the New Left rapidly developed in the United States, rediscovering and upgrading the ideas of libertarian socialism. The New Left was often unaware of its anarchist aspirations. Since it lacked explicit historical inclinations, it drew anarchist conclusions after analyzing the current state of affairs and pragmatically accepting the practical ideas; of all ideas available at the time, the anarchist ones were the most applicable. The "new" anarchism, with its pragmatic activism and rejection of dogmatic purism, was not different merely in terms of substance but also in terms of character and form. This was confirmed by an interesting survey conducted in the 1960s among readers of the British anarchist newspaper *Freedom*.[42] Of 457 readers who agreed to take part in the survey, 40 were from industrial activities, of whom 6 were managers; 23 were from agriculture, including 8 independent farmers and a farm manager; 19 came from transport and communications. Managers excluded, the readership of the magazine consisted of only 15 percent of the traditional anarchist "ranks," that is, workers and farmers. On the other hand, the readers included 52 teachers, 30 students, 20 architects, 16 journalists and writers, 23 independent artists, 12 bookshop owners, 25 scientists, 25 health and social care workers and, last but not least,

---

42 For more about the survey, see Woodcock, *Anarchism*, 403.

40 administrative and managerial workers from all walks of life. The predominance of nonmanual or white-collar workers was evident, as was the predominance of young people. While in the 1940s, the anarchist movement had been populated by elder, nostalgic veterans, the *Freedom* survey showed that two decades later, as much as 65 percent of the readers were under forty years old. Changes also occurred in class affiliation. If the readers above sixty years of age included 45 percent of those with a worker background, those in their thirties only accounted for 23 percent; readers aged twenty to thirty years represented just 10 percent. Of course, it should be mentioned that the survey only had a limited scope as it was conducted on a (relatively small) sample and only in the UK; however, it indicates or extrapolates a trend that only strengthened over the years.

The civil rights movement, the peace movement, and the New Left also manifested through the activities of the Student Nonviolent Coordinating Committee (SNCC), Students for Democratic Society (SDS), Youth International Party (commonly known as Yippies) who helped raise awareness among the public at large about the coercive and violent fetters of the state, militarism, capitalism, and materialism. To achieve their primary demands for freedom, peace, and consistent adherence to the democratic principle "one man, one vote," the protesters were very inventive in their manifestations of civil disobedience. The authority answered the protesters' demands with brutal force, which for many young people was a traumatically formative experience. As Carl Oglesby, one of the visible members of the SDS, wrote: "The policeman's riot club functions like a magic wand, under whose hard caress the banal soul grows vivid and the nameless recover their authenticity—a bestower, this wand, of the lost charisma of the modern self: 'I bleed, therefore I am!'"[43]

---

43   Marshall, *Demanding the Impossible*, 540.

The ideas of the Situationist International mushroomed not only across Europe but soon reached North America, especially New York and San Francisco. The Situationists' theoretical assumption that, in the future, rebellion would adopt new forms of political struggle was confirmed in the United States by the "long hot summer" of 1965 when riots erupted in Watts, a Los Angeles ghetto. It was only with the intervention of the army, backed by tanks, that "order" was reestablished. The Situationist International defined the Watts riots as "a rebellion against the commodity, against the world of the commodity in which worker-consumers are *hierarchically* subordinated to commodity standards. . . . Through theft and gift they rediscover a use that immediately refutes the oppressive rationality of the commodity, revealing its relations and even its production to be arbitrary and unnecessary."[44]

In New York, the Black Mask group which later transformed into the Up Against the Wall Motherfuckers or simply the Motherfuckers, linked the Watts riots with their own struggle against the American establishment: "A new spirit is rising. Like the streets of Watts we burn with revolution. We assault your Gods. . . . We sing of your death. DESTROY THE MUSEUMS!"[45] In the meantime, a new generation of poets and writers emerged in the United States, demanding that the world diverts from its current path that is fatal for humanity. They rejected conformism and uniformism that had survived American society in the 1950s. They emphasized spontaneity, creativity, and spirituality and gave intuition precedence over reason, eastern mysticism over Western institutionalized religion.

Although the philosophical background of the beatniks defies definition, it can be said that their political philosophy

44 Dark Star Collective, eds., *Beneath the Paving Stones: Situationists and the Beach, May 1968* (Oakland: AK Press, 2001), 99.

45 Josh MacPhee and Erik Reuland, eds., *Realizing the Impossible: Art Against Authority* (Oakland: AK Press, 2007), 153.

was precisely anarchism as can be discerned in the poetry of
Allen Ginsberg, Kenneth Rexroth, Diane di Prima, and Tuli
Kupferberg. In his poem "Greenwich Village of My Dreams,"
Kupferberg also included sailors (anarchists) from Kronstadt
in a dream image of the New York quarter:

> The Charleston on Charles St
>   featuring my Sister Eileen
>   & the Kronstadt sailors . . .
> Civilians telling cops to move on . . .
> The world an art
> Life a joy
> The village comes to life again . . . [46]

In his elegy on the Hungarian revolt "Noretorp-Noretsyh"
(or correctly: Hysteron-Proteron) in 1956, Kenneth Rexroth
offers a true epitome of revolutionary (anarchist) history:

> In clotting nights in smoking dark,
> The Kronstadt sailors are marching
> Through the streets of Budapest. The stones
> Of the barricades rise up and shiver
> Into form. They take the shapes
> Of the peasant armies of Makhno.
> The streets are lit with torches.
> The gasoline drenched bodies
> Of the Solovetsky anarchists
> Burn at every street corner.
> Kropotkin's starved corpse is borne
> In state past the offices
> Of the cowering bureaucrats.
> In all the Politisolators
> Of Siberia the partisan dead are enlisting.
> Berneri, Andreas Nin,

---

46   Kupferberg quoted in Harper, *Anarchy*, 160.

Are coming from Spain with a legion.
Carlos Tresca is crossing
The Atlantic with the Berkman Brigade.
Bukharin has joined the Emergency
Economic Council. Twenty million
Dead Ukrainian peasants are sending wheat.
Julia Poyntz is organizing American nurses.[47]

The members of the Beat Generation manifested their desire for absolute freedom in both the form and substance of their literary works. Jack Kerouac typed his novel *On the Road* on a 120-foot roll of teletype paper. This "book," which lacked punctuation and was not divided in paragraphs, is considered one of the greatest monuments to free life or a tribute to free life. With his poem "Howl," Allen Ginsberg offered a lucid criticism of the modern civilization. Thus, 520 copies of his work were confiscated and the author was charged with "obscenity and indecency." Following a successful defense in the court, Ginsberg received wide approval that prompted other artists—regardless of the form or means of expression used in their (artistic) works—to revolt. Through their works, all of these artists and authors announced and encouraged the subsequent social revolution in the 1960s.

After the protests at UC Berkeley in 1964 and 1965, the radical ideas on the West Coast of the United States started gaining ground once again. In San Francisco, the Diggers, assuming the name from the protoanarchist movement in England in the seventeenth century, tried to establish infrastructure for thousands of young people who had left home, school, and work. First, they organized a free clinic to help curb the growth of venereal diseases and offer addicts necessary help and counseling. They also established a store where donated goods could be "purchased" for free, followed by communes offering free housing to artists, turncoats, etc.

---

47 Rexroth quoted in ibid., 161–62.

They transformed the entire Haight-Ashbury district of the city into a commune and declared it a Free City.[48]

The federal authorities reacted to the New Left's growing power by establishing COINTELPRO (Counter Intelligence Program) whose primary objective was to systematically "expose, disrupt, misdirect, discredit and otherwise neutralize" the leftist activists and political organizations. The words of the document with which the program was enforced are merely a euphemism for the many assassinations of visible members of the movements.[49] The repression gained momentum after the increasingly stronger responses to the calls by Fred Hampton, one of the most prominent members of the Black Panther Party, that a revolutionary Rainbow Coalition—not to be mistaken by the organization bearing the same name founded in the 1970s by Jesse Jackson—should be established so as to include and integrate all previously separated struggles and movements. The government's activities resulted in smashing this initiative and, consequently, most movements redefined their radicalism into individual campaigns or single-issue themes.

From the New Left to New Anarchism

In Europe, the peak of the revolutionary tumult was marked by the general strike of French workers in 1968; in the United States, the peak was marked by protests and unrests which followed the Chicago convention of the Democratic Party in the same year. As a result of the despair that the anarchist movement and its ideas were on the wane, military groups started forming on both sides of the Atlantic—for example Weathermen,

---

48 For an excellent history of the Diggers movement, see Emmett Grogan, *Ringolevio: A Life Played for Keeps* (New York: New York Review Books, 2009).

49 For more about the COINTELPRO program, see Alexander Bloom and Wini Breines, eds., *"Takin' It to the Streets": A Sixties Reader* (New York: Oxford University Press), 317–24.

Direct Action, and Black Liberation Army in the United States, Baader-Meinhof and Rote Armee Fraktion (RAF) in Germany, Brigate Rosse in Italy, Action Directe in France, and the Angry Brigade in Great Britain—which, based on their methods and goals of political struggle, cannot be classified in the libertarian tradition as understood by the present work.

Even though the New Left was building its theoretical analysis and political practice on anarchist heritage, an absolute rift with old orthodoxy and dogmatism came in the 1970s with the second wave of feminism. The latter was a direct response to the undemocratic inclinations of many collectives and movements whose militant nationalism often resulted in an uncritical and nonreflected reproduction of gender roles or direct chauvinism and rejection of decentralized organizational structures and consensus decision-making.

The new anarchist movement in the United States cannot be regarded as an extension of the New Left, even though it largely builds on the feminist, environmental, and antinuclear movement in which the complex methods of consensus decision-making, adopted from the Quaker decision-making model, were implemented in full for the first time.[50] American progressive movements are unsurprisingly associated with Quaker traditions since the peace network A Quaker Action Group (AQAG) was one of the main initiators of the Movement for a New Society, which represented new convergence point for progressive social movements after the bifurcation period at the beginning of the 1970s. According to Andrew Cornell, the Quaker model of the Movement for a New Society that favors consensus decision-making over majority vote is the closest match to the internal organizational and decision-making structure of contemporary anarchist collectives in the United States.[51] Even more, Quakerism influenced the most

50   Francesca Polletta, *Freedom Is an Endless Meeting: Democracy in American Social Movements* (Chicago: University of Chicago Press, 2002), 120–75.
51   Andrew Cornell, *Oppose and Propose: Lessons from Movement for a New Society* (Oakland: AK Press, 2011) 155–86.

basic tools and solutions for optimizing consensual practices within anarchist collectives, such as the role of the facilitator and different types of vetoes and methods of exercising them. The anarchist idea of the affinity group as the basic organizational unit was resuscitated in the antinuclear movement. This movement lent itself to additional development and experimenting with the spokescouncil method, which is one of the hallmarks of global altermondialism today.[52]

In the 1970s and 1980s, individualist anarchism was reborn in the United States, drawing from the ideas of Spooner and Tucker. The Libertarian Party, which incorporated a series of ideational starting points and goals of anarcho-capitalism (e.g., abolition of the federal government, taxes, social care, and privatization of health care, schools, and parks) in its program, became the third largest political party. Due to its extremely conservative and egoist position, their libertarian credentials should be taken *cum grano salis*.

In this period, anarchist collectives acted in solidarity with anti-imperialist and indigenous struggles in Latin America, the struggles of lesbian and gay groups, people suffering from AIDS (the AIDS Coalition to Unleash Power— ACT UP), and with local indigenous movements. To some extent, anarchism can take the credit for the (relative) success of other (single-issue) social struggles, though they developed a (synergic) relationship of mutual cooperation. The emergence of many anarchist affinity groups as well as radical book, magazine, and newspaper publishers paved the way for a new generation of anarchists. All these events and projects contributed to a new global movement against capitalism which was unleashed in the broad public during a meeting of the World Trade Organization in Seattle, in November of 1999, and which derived the bulk of its creative energy particularly from anarchism.

---

52 See Epstein, *Political Protest & Cultural Revolution*, and Polletta, *Freedom Is an Endless Meeting*.

Over the past few years, the occurrence of a global movement against neoliberalism and capitalism—a broad coalition of collectives that are intrinsically complex, nonhierarchical, vague, and, at least in the United States, draw most of their energy from anarchism—has enriched the theory and practice of radicalism with the development of (internal) decision-making processes in groups or communities. This facilitates further development and empirical analysis of the functioning and applicability of various forms of direct democracy. The result of the experiment is a series of organizational instruments—which have already been tested in practice—aimed at creating and promoting democratic processes. On one hand, these processes enable the registering (transfer) of all initiatives (from the bottom up) and ensure the broadest support while, on the other, they render impossible the ignoring and suppression of dissenting voices, forming of leading positions and avant-gardes as well the forcing of individuals to agree with decisions they disapprove of.

The basic idea of consensus process is to avoid voting and to arrive at a proposal that is acceptable (or at least not unacceptable) to all. The process of this usually follows the same format: first, a proposal is made, then reservations are expressed and clarified. The basic proposal is supplemented or amended accordingly, considering all comments. Before consensus, everybody has a chance to reject the proposal (this veto can serve the individual to block decision-making and the adoption of a specific decision which would heavily infringe on that person's reasons and purpose of participating in the group) or to abstain from participating (the individual does not prevent or hinder the adoption of a certain decision but distances themselves from the decision, its consequences, and the ensuing obligations).

The aim of the spokescouncils is to coordinate different small affinity groups (before, during, and after important events and decisions). Each affinity group chooses a representative who is authorized to speak on behalf of the group.

Only these representatives can participate in the process of achieving a consensus at the council level. Before important decisions are accepted, these representatives who participate in the process of reaching consensus at the council level return to their groups, which then adopt a (consensus-based) position to be defended by their representative. Within the movement of movements, different tools were developed to facilitate and accelerate the decision-making process. Brainstorming is a common method for encouraging individuals to generate ideas and proposals (without assessing any of the proposals), whereas the fishbowl procedure in which two representatives (usually a man and a woman) are chosen from disagreeing sides to attempt to reach a consensus or generate a proposal that is acceptable to the entire group.[53]

When assessing the (un)successfulness and (un)reasonableness of developing these sensitive processes, we must obviously bear in mind their experimental nature. In fact, the creation and development of a democratic culture in an environment of persistent indoctrination to the opposite (which is why people have little experience with democracy and lack knowledge about it) is a demanding and unrewarding task, loaded with obstacles and missed attempts. Consensus-based decision-making is thus not only important in terms of improving the (quality of) adopted decisions and overall support, but also as a means of practicing participatory democracy and strengthening mutual ties and trust within a community.

Darij Zadnikar suggests that contemporary anarchism draws strength from precisely that which challenged it in the industrial era: in the postmodern period, the rejection of a solid and uniform organization enables plural organizational forms of rebellion; the rejection of authoritative levers enables prefigurative parallel living and community spaces; the

---

53   For more about decision-making practices within the modern anarchist movement, see Graeber, *Direct Action*.

failure to focus on strategic goals enables diffuse counterpowers; and, finally, theoretical inconsistencies enable heterogeneous experiences of direct action.[54] This was confirmed in a study by the U.S. military think tank RAND Corporation, which in its report on anarchist elements within the anticapitalist movement assessed:

> Anarchists, using extremely good modern communications, including live internet feeds, were able to execute simultaneous actions by means of pulsing and swarming tactics coordinated by networked and leaderless "affinity groups." It became an example of the challenges that hierarchical organizations face when confronting networked adversaries with faster reaction cycles. This loosely organized coalition, embracing network organization, and tactics, frustrated police efforts to gain the situational awareness needed to combat the seemingly chaotic . . . disturbances.[55]

---

54 Zadnikar, "Le vkup, le vkup, uboga gmajna!" 5.
55 Quoted in CrimethInc., *Anarchy in the Age of Dinosaurs* (Olympia, WA: CrimethInc. Ex-Workers' Collective, 2003), 128.

8
TRANSCENDENTALISM AS AN INSPIRATION AND ASPIRATION

Transcendentalism as Anarchy of Daily Life

More important than the Transcendentalists' struggle in literature is their general social and political struggle fought in everyday lives against European-influenced conservative forces and the local repressive "puritan Leviathan." A condensed version of a Transcendentalist antimanifesto of sorts, revealing their radical and holistic outlook, can be found in Walt Whitman's preface to the first edition of *Leaves of Grass* (1855), where he addressed all poets (i.e., rebels) with the following words:

> This is what you shall do: Love the earth and sun and the animals, despise riches, give alms to every one that asks, stand up for the stupid and crazy, devote your income and labor to others, hate tyrants, argue not concerning God, have patience and indulgence toward the people, take off your hat to nothing known or unknown or to any man or number of men, go freely with powerful uneducated persons and with the young and with

the mothers of families, read these leaves in the open air every season of every year of your life, re-examine all you have been told at school or church or in any book, dismiss whatever insults your own soul; and your very flesh shall be a great poem and have the richest fluency not only in its words but in the silent lines of its lips and face and between the lashes of your eyes and in every motion and joint of your body.[1]

The multiple dimensionality of the Transcendentalists' revolutionary struggle can also be understood as the first manifestation of the anarchy of everyday life that rejects the primariness of political struggle against the forces shaping the world. Viewing economic reductionism as a futile fight against Hydra, the many-headed monster, with capitalism as only one of the anomalies that must be eliminated, Transcendentalists highlighted the necessity for a sociocultural transformation that must necessarily start in private life, through a conscious personal transformation and a prefiguration of democratic society that transcends the boundaries of the existing political, economic, and social system. Transcendentalist utopian communities, for example, persistently rejected goods such as cotton and sugar that underpinned the economy of the slaveholding South and built alternative political structures and practices even though their result was only Thoreau's democratic and moral majority of one.

In his quest for genealogical links between the "old" and the "new" anarchism in the United States, Gerald Runkle found that the new generations of American anarchists—from Boston to Berkeley—did not arrive at the above findings and views by delving into Godwin, Bakunin, or Tucker but by reading the works of Thoreau, Emerson, and

---

1   Whitman, *Poetry and Prose*, 11.

Whitman.[2] It is thus understandable that the new anarchism, at least in the United States, was in many respects identical to Transcendentalism. A recapitulation of all characteristics of the new American anarchism shows they perfectly match the characteristics of the Transcendentalists' revolt against the conservative conventionalities of the Puritan culture and society. As has already been mentioned, the Transcendentalists first developed individualism to the extreme and on its basis redefined the individual's relation in society and his attitude toward it. They contended that the individual should break away from all fetters of traditionalism that unjustly determine his life, and thus live his own life and his own history. In the introduction to his essay "Nature" (1849), Emerson wrote:

> Our age is retrospective. It builds the sepulchres of the fathers. It writes biographies, histories, and criticism. The foregoing generations beheld God and nature face to face; we, through their eyes. Why should not we also enjoy an original relation to the universe? Why should not we have a poetry and philosophy of insight and not of tradition, and a religion by revelation to us, and not the history of theirs? . . . The sun shines to-day also. There is more wool and flax in the fields. There are new lands, new men, new thoughts. Let us demand our own works and laws and worship.[3]

Secondly, the nonconformism manifest in Transcendentalists' literary works and everyday lives focused on civil disobedience and de-statism. Needless to say that most Transcendentalists also declined all institutional forms of

---

2   Runkle, *Anarchism*, 199.

3   Emerson, *Essential Writings*, 3.

life and activity, usurping the individual's independence and autonomy.[4] The results of this overall state of mind and life-style included other (anarchist) attributes such as respect for mutual differences, feminism, environmental awareness, a commitment to the independence of the individual and the group, an emphasis on "do-it-yourself" principles, pacifism, an ethical commitment to justice and solidarity, an objection to materialism and, last but not least, an emphasis on moving from theory to practice.

The last characteristic, tendency for actionization of theory, probably equips Transcendentalism with the necessary emancipatory potential and, most importantly, the topicality that makes their ideas appealing even today. Even today the new anarchists tread on the path to achieving a better world with a "revolution of everyday life" (Vanegeim), by turning into vegans or freegans, boycotting the goods of multinational corporations, returning to horticulture and through various attempts to establish collectives and communities in revolt. This revolution is not limited to political change, but also incorporates cultural change and, above all, the personal change that Emerson describes in his essay "Self-Reliance": "Whoso would be a man must be a nonconformist. He who would gather immortal palms must not be hindered by the name of goodness, but must explore if it be goodness. Nothing is at last sacred but the integrity of your own mind."[5]

This understanding of anarchism is apparent in the works of the collective CrimethInc. that evokes, through its conceptualization of "folk anarchy," Stephen Pearl Andrews and his perception of a dinner with friends—where all structures of authority are substituted by harmony, fluidity, and

---

4   For instance, Thoreau established in *Walden; or, Life in the Woods*: "But wherever a man goes, men will pursue and paw him with their dirty institutions, and, if they can, constrain him to belong to their desperate odd-fellow society." Thoreau, *Walden and Other Writings*, 162.

5   Emerson, *Essential Writings*, 134–35.

spontaneity—as the best example and proof of the functioning of anarchist society: "Freedom only exists in the moment of revolution. And those moments are not as rare as you think. Change, revolutionary change, is going on constantly and everywhere—and everyone plays a part in it, consciously or not."[6]

The Heritage of Disobedience

The key message of Thoreau's essay "Civil Disobedience" also appears in the Declaration of Independence: governments are artificial creations established solely for one purpose—to serve the people. In his essay, Thoreau proffered a (universal) conception of human rights and duties, for decades now providing an important inspiration to activists, dissidents—all people:

> Must the citizen ever for a moment, or in the last degree, resign his conscience to the legislator? Why has every man a conscience, then? I think we should be men first, and subjects afterward. It is not desirable to cultivate a respect for the law, so much as for the right? The only obligation which I have the right to assume is to do at any time what I think right.[7]

In this spirit, the progressive social movements in the United States remained faithful to Thoreau's idea that the basic moral principles should first be adhered to and considered, and only then arbitrary laws. By disrespecting local regulations, for example, the Wobblies found their right and freedom only in prisons, and the points of contestation

---

6   CrimethInc., "Indulge . . . & Undermine," http://www.crimethinc.com/texts/atoz/indulge.php.

7   Thoreau, *Walden and Other Writings*, 668–69.

at places where they were least expected.[8] Similarly, in Washington before the onset of World War I, the suffragettes protested—even though it was prohibited—against the madness of war on the one hand and for the right to vote on the other. In the 1930s, during the global economic crisis workers employed in the automotive and rubber industry, gained their right to organize a trade union only by calling a strike. In the 1960s, African Americans in the South only secured their equality by disrespecting racist laws that required them to "tolerate" racial segregation. They took seriously Thoreau's words, "I quietly declare war with the State, after my fashion!"

They came to realize that the government does not protect their constitutional rights and that the only solution to this problem, which concerns them as citizens and even more as people, was struggle. The idea and practice of civil disobedience evolved with time from a movement for civil rights to an antiwar movement. The individuals who were the first to resist the draft—and sanctioned for this with long prison sentences—included young African Americans from the South.[9] The spirit of rebelliousness soon overwhelmed priests and nuns who broke into draft offices during the Indochina war. By destroying the files on conscription they saved many young lives from the terror of war and, conversely, by burning and destroying, further dramatized their protest against the war. Disobedience also proliferated within military ranks. In the last years of the war the number of pilots who rejected the pointless bombing of Vietnamese villages and towns was growing, and ever more soldiers refused to

---

8   The Wobblies continue to follow this tradition even today, as one of their main campaigns is the unionizing of Starbucks coffeehouses.

9   One of the most dramatic and symbolic acts of civil disobedience against the war in Vietnam was undoubtedly young boxing star Muhammad Ali's refusal to take part in the "white man's war," as he named it. The authorities punished him by stripping him of his heavyweight champion title.

take part in the ordered expeditions or military actions. Of course, the war in Indochina did not end because politicians had realized the immorality of the war. It ended because of the disobedience of "small" people whom the rulers could no longer ignore. As Thoreau wrote:

> A man has not everything to do, but something. . . . If any think that their influence would be lost there, and their voices no longer afflict the ear of the State, that they would not be as an enemy within its walls, they do not know by how much truth is stronger than error, nor how much more eloquently and effectively he can combat injustice who has experienced a little in his own person. Cast your whole vote, not a strip of paper merely, but your whole influence . . . If the alternative is to keep all just men in prison, or give up war and slavery, the State will not hesitate which to choose. . . . When the subject has refused allegiance, and the officer has resigned his office, then the revolution is accomplished.[10]

With their struggle for a genuine democracy, people (again) witnessed an empirical confirmation of Thoreau's theoretical statement that elections and other "legal" remedies "take too much time, and a man's life will be gone." They once again proved Thoreau's idealist conviction that good always prevails over evil. Occasionally Thoreau is "interpreted as defending a simple escapism, sheer negative freedom. The move toward wildness is taken as a movement back to nature, a romance with primitivism."[11]

---

10 Thoreau, *Walden and Other Writings*, 679–80.
11 Douglas R. Anderson, "Awakening in the Everyday: Experiencing the Religious in the American Philosophical Tradition" in *Pragmatism and Religion*, ed. Stuart Rosenbaum (Chicago: University of Illinois Press, 2003), 147.

Although a number of studies labeled Thoreau as pessimist, fatalist, or escapist, the truth, of course, is different. Thoreau did not give up on good. Even more, Thoreau is one of the few whose acts and words can serve, even in such hostile times as today's, as a meaningful example that the fight for a better world is worthwhile, even with a seemingly small possibility of success. With Thoreau, optimism can be drawn from nature, which reminds us with the scent of a white water-lily that "the season we had waited for had arrived." Thoreau added that the scent also reminds us of "what kind of laws have prevailed longest and widest, and still prevail. . . . What confirmation of our hopes is in the fragrance of this flower! It suggests that the time may come when man's deeds will smell as sweet."[12]

"Do I Contradict Myself?"

The new anarchism also remains faithful to Transcendentalism by rejecting the creation of a consistent philosophical system. On one hand, this enables its universal flexibility; on the other, it can be an obstacle to its practical application. This is perhaps best justified by Ralph Waldo Emerson, who intentionally avoided the construction of a logical intellectual system as it contradicted romantic beliefs of intuition and flexibility. He wrote about contradiction in his illustrious essay "Self-Reliance":

> A foolish consistency is the hobgoblin of little minds, adored by little statesmen and philosophers and divines. . . . Speak what you think now in hard words and to-morrow speak what to-morrow thinks in hard words again, though it contradict every thing you said to-day—"Ah, so you shall be sure to be misunderstood."—Is it so bad then to be misunderstood? Pythagoras

---

12 Thoreau, *Walden and Other Writings*, 713.

was misunderstood, and Socrates, and Jesus, and Luther, and Copernicus, and Galileo, and Newton, and every pure and wise spirit that ever took flesh. To be great is to be misunderstood.[13]

The idea that to adopt rigid views and final conclusions means to reach a point where one actually stops thinking was poetically described in Whitman's "Song of Myself" with the following famous words that best summarize the (eclectic) spirit of the new anarchism:

Do I contradict myself?
Very well then I contradict myself,
(I am large, I contain multitudes.)[14]

Since new anarchism remains complex and internally highly diversified, it retains much needed historical flexibility. The new anarchists also adopted the Transcendentalists' concept of revolution, no longer perceived as a cataclysmic overnight event but more as a sociocultural evolution that will erode the fossil remnants of authority and compulsion. Victory, in this case, will not only be achieved with an external physical fight but also with a change within us even before the authoritarian institutions are radically transformed or eliminated:

I learned this, at least, by my experiment. That if one advances confidently in the direction of his dreams, and endeavors to live the life which he has imagined, he will meet with a success unexpected in common hours. He will put some things behind, will pass an invisible boundary; new, universal, and more liberal laws will begin to establish themselves around and within him; or

13   Emerson, *Essential Writings*, 138.
14   Whitman, *Poetry and Prose*, 87.

the old laws be expanded, and interpreted in his
favor in a more liberal sense, and he will live with
the license of a higher order of beings. . . . If you
have built castles in the air, your work need not
be lost; that is where they should be. Now put
the foundations under them.[15]

This is what Henry D. Thoreau thought at the end of his
Walden Pond experiment. A similar concept of revolution as
a complex process was also offered by Alexander Berkman. As
the creation of a new society can only start with a prior personal transformation, a revolution need not wait for the right
time or the final implementation of the (revolutionary) theory:

If your object is to secure liberty, you must learn
to do without authority and compulsion. If you
intend to live in peace and harmony with your
fellow-men, you and they should cultivate brotherhood and respect for each other. If you want to
work together with them for your mutual benefit,
you must practice cooperation. The social revolution means much more than the reorganization
of conditions only: it means the establishment
of new human values and social relationships, a
changed attitude of man to man, as of one free
and independent to his equal; it means a different spirit in individual and collective life, and
that spirit cannot be born overnight. It is a spirit
to be cultivated, to be nurtured and reared, as the
most delicate flower is, for indeed it is the flower
of a new and beautiful existence. . . . We must
learn to think differently before the revolution
can come. That alone can bring the revolution.[16]

---

15 Thoreau, *Walden and Other Writings*, 303.
16 Berkman, *What Is Anarchism?*, 185.

The new anarchism is ahistorical because it refuses to refer to any historical achievements of past struggles. It rejects the (exclusively) theoretical discussion of classical anarchist texts so as to divulge what the author "really" meant. The new anarchism rejects theoretical purity and unity because what matters is solidarity in practice. As noted above, Featherstone, Henwood, and Parenti warn that today's anti-historical and anti-ideological position within the anarchist movement has been carried to such an extreme that it is now possible to speak of a new (post)ideology of activistism or actionism.[17] This should obviously be understood not as a criticism of activism as such, but as a warning against problems in the future, when the anarchist movement requires transformation and, hence, a self-reflection.

The new anarchism recognizes differences and plurality, but emphasizes similarities and inclusivity. It is global, just as exploitation and poverty are global, and flexible just as capital and our jobs are flexible. As each struggle for a better world stems from specific (local) circumstances, it is understandable that the new anarchists have different visions of liberation, requiring different organization models and solutions. Accordingly, anarchism strives to achieve a world of many worlds whose point in common would only be that they enable people the greatest degree of self-realization and maximizing of their (internal) creative potential. It is impossible to take a walk through the woods in a predefined (ideational) direction since one has to take the obstacles into account and either go around them or remove them.

Today, many anarchist organizations, infoshops, squats, media centers, and publishing houses are thriving in the United States. The value of such collectives is not only in their basic activities (e.g., publishing), though these undoubtedly contribute

---

17 Featherstone, Henwood, and Parenti, "Activistism," 309–14. The contours of this danger can be discerned in activistism and actionism of the new ideologists of insurrectionism.

to a change in the world, but in their existence as liberated areas showing what anarchist society can be. Using the terminology of Hakim Bey, these organizations are important as "autonomous zones," helping to further spread the ideas of TAZ (theories and practices of temporary autonomous zones). They are the best means to overcome the artificial division between political and private with which individuals actualize the world outside the boundaries of commodification or spectacle. They are a political laboratory, a "place where the present transforms into the future," "the seeds of future society."

As today's anarchist struggle is total, anarchism is no longer only a political engagement but also incorporates all other resistances to nonpolitical forms of authoritarianism and hierarchical structures. In conclusion, we could define the new anarchism as a visual, tactical, and political tension: a tension between the (historical) way things are (*natura naturata*) and the (philosophical) way things could become (*natura naturans*); between what it is to be and to become; between Utopianism and historical realism; between the attractiveness of a one-off act and the inevitability of the complex process; between activistism and intellectualism; between (short-term) goals and (long-term) visions; between despair and joy; between solitude and solidarity; between individualism and communism; between theoretical purism and practical pragmatism; between equality and freedom; between ontological radicalness and the need to reach compromises; between the rejection of violence and the recognition of the limitations of pacifism.[18]

The new anarchism is also a hope, teaching us that a world of many worlds can only be achieved by a revolution in everyday life that depends on the ability of the anarchist movement to "think like no other social movement has ever thought," to act like no other rebellion has ever acted.[19]

18 Sheehan, *Anarchism*, 158.
19 Starhawk quoted in *We Are Everywhere: The Irresistible Rise of Global Anti-capitalism*, eds. Notes from Nowhere (London: Verso Books, 2003), 506.

9
THE ANATOMY OF REVOLT

THOMAS L. FRIEDMAN, A FAMOUS *NEW YORK TIMES* COLUMNIST, concluded his analysis of the effects of (economic) globalization with the daring statement that people should be grateful to be living in a world in which a historical question has been resolved, and the answer is free-market capitalism. In a world, in other words, in which the invisible hand of the market cannot function without a hidden fist, and McDonald's cannot flourish without McDonnell Douglas, the designer of fighter jets.[1]

The neoliberal conception of globalization, says Friedman, forces nation-states to finally put on the Golden Straitjacket of liberalization, privatization, and fiscal discipline that fosters economic growth, although on the political front the Golden Straitjacket narrows the political and economic policy choices to relatively narrow parameters. "Once your country puts it on, its political choices get reduced to Pepsi or Coke—to slight nuances of taste, slight nuances of policy, slight alterations in design to account for local traditions, some loosening here or there, but never any major deviation from the core golden rules."[2] Friedman admits that

---

1   Thomas Friedman, *The Lexus and the Olive Tree: Understanding Globalization* (New York: Anchor Books, 2000), 464.
2   Ibid., 106.

its "one-size-fits-all" ideology does not suit the specifics of various societies and therefore the only way to enlarge it is to wear it ever tighter:

> To fit into the Golden Straitjacket a country must either adopt, or be seen as moving toward, the following golden rules: making the private sector the primary engine of its economic growth, maintaining a low rate of inflation and price stability, shrinking the size of its state bureaucracy, maintaining as close to a balanced budget as possible, if not a surplus, eliminating and lowering tariffs on imported goods, removing restrictions on foreign investment, getting rid of quotas and domestic monopolies, increasing exports, privatizing state-owned industries and utilities, deregulating capital markets, making its currency convertible, opening its industries, stock and bond markets to direct foreign ownership and investment, deregulating its economy to promote as much domestic competition as possible, eliminating government corruption, subsidies and kickbacks as much as possible, opening its banking and telecommunications systems to private ownership and competition and allowing its citizens to choose from an array of competing pension options and foreign-run pension and mutual funds. When you stitch all of these pieces together you have the Golden Straitjacket.[3]

Although Friedman sums up his apotheosis of the Golden Straitjacket, *ergo* the neoliberal conception of globalization, with the conclusion that "the tighter you wear it, the more

---

3   Ibid., 105.

gold it produces and the more padding you can then put into it for your society," its stitches have finally broken.[4]

While the past few decades have been considered and depicted as decades of progress, the human toll in this "story of success" is often concealed. Namely, this success has been bolstered by the toil of girls who started working in factories at the age of twelve and died at twenty-five; the toil of immigrants who worked themselves to death in the heat of summer and cold of winter; the toil of the common people, or the *etceteras*, as Howard Zinn or Studs Terkel have named them, who have had to fight by themselves for their eight-hour workday and other rights, with their life at stake.

Politicians, managers, and scientists still measure progress with indicators of their own financial standing such as growth in the (value of) stocks, and joint production of goods and services which are available only to those who can pay. With some exceptions—the casual cyclic stagnations in some parts of the world (in Latin America) and the declining per capita revenue in the poorest countries of Africa—these indicators have been generally favorable, proving that the promises made by the elite of the richer world due to programs have been fulfilled. However, in one of his brighter moments, Robert Kennedy commented:

> Gross National Product counts air pollution and cigarette advertising, and ambulances to clear our highways of carnage. It counts special locks for our doors and the jails for the people who break them. It counts the destruction of the redwood and the loss of our natural wonder in chaotic sprawl. It counts napalm and counts nuclear warheads and armored cars for the police to fight the riots in our cities. . . . Yet the GNP

---

4 Ibid., 106.

does not allow for the health of our children, the quality of their education or the joy of their play. It does not include the beauty of our poetry or the strength of our marriages, the intelligence of our public debate or the integrity of our public officials. It measures neither our wit nor our courage, neither our wisdom nor our learning, neither our compassion nor our devotion to our country, it measures everything in short, except that which makes life worthwhile.[5]

"Ordinary" people measure progress using indicators of their own welfare. For quite some time, these popular indicators have shown that the situation is not that bright after all and that the world is becoming poorer. It has been clear for quite some time that the rising tide of economic globalization does not mean progress for all—this rising tide does not lift all boats, but only yachts. According to UNICEF, more people die of hunger all over the world every two years than the number of casualties of both world wars put together; every hour, one thousand children die of the consequences of easily curable diseases and, with a shortage of basic medicines and treatment during pregnancy, at least twice as many women die or suffer serious injuries. Data from the Food and Agriculture Organization (FAO) of the United Nations show that the number of chronically starving people is constantly on the rise. In our world, some people enjoy unimaginable wealth while two hundred million children who are under five are undernourished due to the shortage of food. Every year, about twenty million children die of famine and related diseases. One hundred million children are forced to live and work on the streets.

---

5   Robert F. Kennedy, "Remarks at the University of Kansas, March 18, 1968," http://www.jfklibrary.org/Research/Ready-Reference/RFK-Speeches/Remarks-of-Robert-F-Kennedy-at-the-University-of-Kansas-March-18-1968.aspx.

This tragedy is not just limited to poor countries. Even in a rich country such as the United States, 10 percent of the population (thirty-one million people), have insufficient funds to provide for their basic living needs. Thirty-one million Americans live in poverty and hunger, while the wealthiest 5 percent own 81.9 percent of all stocks and bonds and 57.4 percent of the entire (net) wealth of the United States. It is harrowing that in many districts of big U.S. cities, the life span and mortality of infants equal those of the poorest countries in the world. The maxim "the rich get richer and the poor get poorer" is not only a worn-out catchphrase or cliché but a sad fact, far from real democracy in which all individuals should have equal opportunities regarding their (political) participation.[6]

Another way to drive home the above observations is to add a frightening detail: in the time you need to read this page a hundred people will die of easily curable diseases and hunger. Half of them will be children younger than five. As Cindy Milstein has observed, we live in a period of hyperproduction while millions of people are being deprived of food; a period of the high-speed development of technology while most people work more; a period of unbelievable breakthroughs in medicine while unimaginable masses of people die of easily curable diseases.[7] A good question arises here of whether this situation could come any closer to "anarchy" in the pejorative, subverted meaning of the word?

Further, the current financial meltdown and economic crisis reveal a crisis of politics: a crisis pointing not at the incompetence of politics to mitigate the contradictions inherent to the current economic model, but at its incompetence to transcend the very same economic model. Nicos

---

6   For more, see for example John Cavanagh, ed., *Alternatives to Economic Globalization: A Better World Is Possible, A Report of the International Forum on Globalization* (San Francisco, CA: Berrett-Koehler Publishers Inc., 2002).

7   Milstein, *Anarchism and Its Aspirations*, 44.

Poulantzas has warned that with the overuse of the word *crisis*, the word loses its content and clarity. We should then be careful to theoretically elaborate the concept of crisis and our own understanding of it. Namely, in the past a crisis—economic and political—has been perceived merely as an anomaly or rupture within the harmonious working of a self-regulatory system, as a dysfunctional moment that will be overcome when the balance of the system is restored. This concept of crisis results in myopia that:

1. overlooks many crises that are present, but are not perceived as such, because of their positive role in consolidating and reproducing the status quo, despite their undemocratic and even antidemocratic inclinations; and

2. equates with a crisis various ruptures that are inherent to the hegemonic economic paradigm and do not represent a threat to its functioning since they are a permanent part of its consolidation and reproduction.[8]

The current crisis is therefore an economic and political crisis in the proper meaning of the word, a "crisis of crisis," since we face such a concentration of contradictions inherent to the system that they now represent a threat to its stability and very survival. Hence, the proper question we should ask is not how to redesign the basic contours of the Golden Straitjacket but how to get rid of it.

Not everything is as bad as it seems, of course. It is worth remembering, for example, a (true) story about a penguin in the Lacandon rainforest, recorded by Subcomandante Marcos in one of his communiqués. The story describes how the inhabitants of a Zapatista village, before a planned

8   Nicos Poulantzas, "The Political Crisis and the Crisis of the State" in *The Poulantzas Reader: Marxism, Law and the State*, ed. James Martin, (New York: Verso, 2008).

retreat to a safe area, were faced with the dilemma of whether they should cook and eat their chickens or leave them in the village to be eaten by members of paramilitary groups and the Mexican army. After a thoughtful consideration, the chickens ended up in the pot one by one, thus adding some variety to the monotonous food of the *indigenas*.

When the day came to leave the village and only one chicken was left, the villagers noticed, to their great surprise, in the yard instead of a chicken, an indefinable creature trying to walk upright and infiltrate the groups leaving the base. The Zapatistas soon understood the chicken's trick and its unnatural and clumsy walk resembling—due to its anatomical makeup—a penguin rather than an EZLN soldier. Though the chicken's plot was exposed, it still achieved the goal—it won the sympathies of the Zapatistas and, more importantly, saved its own life. Marcos concludes:

> It occurs to me now that we are like Penguin, trying very hard to be erect and to make ourselves a place in Mexico, in Latin America, in the World. Just as the trip we are about to take is not in our anatomy, we shall certainly go about swaying, unsteady and stupidly, provoking laughter and jokes. Although perhaps, also like Penguin, we might provoke some sympathy, and someone might, generously, protect us and help us, walking with us, to do what every man, woman or penguin should do, that is, to always try to be better in the only way possible, by struggling.[9]

Since the contemporary world has removed the feasibility of revolutions in the old sense, and rendered customary methods of political action obsolete, Howard Zinn has

---

9   Subcomandante Marcos, "A Penguin in the Selva Lacandona," http://www.zmag.org/znet/viewArticle/5745.

predicted that revolutionary change will be "a process, with periods of tumult and of quiet, in which we will, here and there, by ones and twos and tens, create pockets of concern inside old institutions, transforming them from within."[10] We should not perceive revolutionary change as something that concerns an alternation in hegemonic economic and political arrangements only but we should rather understand it as something immediate: "We must begin *now* to liberate those patches of ground on which we stand—to 'vote' for a new world (as Thoreau suggested) with our whole selves all the time, rather than in moments carefully selected by others."[11] Consequently, we need "tactics short of violent revolution, but far more militant than normal parliamentary procedure, it seems to me. It will take systematic, persistent organizing and education, in the ghettos, in the universities, plus coordinated actions of various kinds designed to shock society out of its lethargy."[12]

Through his activist work, Zinn learned that working through electoral politics will corrupt one's ideals. The solution, therefore, is prefigurative politics as an attempt to create the future in the present through political and economic organizing alone, or at least to foresee social changes for which we aspire. Since in the struggle for social change, "there is no act too small, no act too bold," Zinn does not deny the importance of what we shall call revolutionary reformism. His experience with the GI Bill, that enabled him to enroll in New York University and later to continue with graduate studies at Columbia, resulted in the provocative idea that in every system of domination and control it is still reasonable to achieve its change already within the limits it allows; when the system itself becomes an impassable obstacle to progress the solution is, of course, a conflict, a fight,

---

10   Zinn, *Politics of History*, 14.
11   Ibid.
12   Zinn, *Zinn Reader*, 684.

and revolutionary changes.[13] He saw the possibility of and need for government intervention to solve the precarious situation of the ordinary people and to rebuild the levees to defend them from the deadly flood of the so-called financial Hurricane Katrina. In this way, we can defend pockets of resistance, even empower them, so that we can overcome this anachronistic institution we know as the nation-state in the long run. Even the present social/economic/political framework could be reinterpreted in a fashion that is "moving away from the deification of precedent":

> Why should not the equal protection clause of the Fourteenth Amendment be applied to economics, as well as race, to require the state to give equal economic rights to its citizens: food, shelter, education, medical care. . . . Why should not the "cruel and unusual punishment clause" of the Eighteenth Amendment be applied in such a way as to bar all imprisonment except in the most stringent of cases, where confinement is necessary to prevent a clear and immediate danger to others? Why should not the Ninth Amendment, which says citizens have unnamed rights beyond those enumerated in the Constitution be applied to host of areas: rights to carry on whatever family arrangements (marriage, divorce, etc.) are desired, whatever sexual private activities one wants to carry on, so long as others are not harmed (even if they are irritated).[14]

---

13   The opposition between the so-called "reformists" and "revolutionaries" is thus unreasonable. Only the most extreme revolutionaries completely reject the reasonableness of partial changes, and only the most conservative reformists completely reject the possibility of revolutionary changes.

14   Howard Zinn, *Disobedience and Democracy: Nine Fallacies on Law and Order* (Cambridge, MA: South End Press (2002 [1968]), 116.

If such a stance is denounced as social democratic reform-ism, then it is revolutionary reformism that transcends the binary position of revolution vs. reform. It clearly builds on the pragmatism and realism much needed in contemporary anarchism. That is also why Zinn believed that the difficult task of defying authority within as well as without, of consis-tently refreshing our radical politics from the spring of anger and love, still lies ahead of us.[15]

In this way, our vision will not be blurred by some grand utopia squelching our immediate goals. In, this way, we can also see the subversiveness of Zinn's infrapolitics of the seem-ingly nonpolitical: "Let's not speak anymore about capital-ism, socialism. Let's just speak of using the incredible wealth of the earth for human beings. Give people what they need: food, medicine, clean air, pure water, trees and grass, pleasant homes to live in, some hours of work, more hours of leisure. Don't ask who deserves it. Every human being deserves it."[16]

My outline of the forgotten currents of anarchist thought and practice may only be a negligible contribution to the process of changing the existing social relations, but I hope it offers chance to critically reconsider them. Like Noam Chomsky, I observe that over the years, anarchism seems to have bred highly authoritarian personality types "who legis-late what the Doctrine *is*, and with various degrees of fury (of-ten great) denounce those who depart from what they have declared to be the True Principles. Odd form of anarchism."[17] Like Chomsky, I think—and hope that this work has dem-onstrated—that anarchism cannot be understood as a naïve, utopian fantasy but as a criticism of the existing social, eco-nomic, and political system as well as a strategy for achiev-ing a different world—a world of many worlds. As such, anarchism remains one of the most important and topical

---

15   Zinn, *SNCC*, 275.

16   Howard Zinn, *Marx in Soho* (Cambridge, MA: South End Press, 1999), 47.

17   Neal, "Anarchism: Ideology or Methodology?"

intellectual currents of the modern world which for quite some time, given current developments, has not been a mere ideal but a practical possibility or even necessity. Compared to other "isms," anarchism, according to Woodcock, remains an untarnished and pristine image of an idea which, in practical terms, has had nothing but a future because it has not come to power and has never been discredited in power.[18]

It has shouldered the demanding task of a prefigurative adventure in new political structures and practices through which it should be guided by an instruction by the Martinican philosopher Frantz Fanon, who warned that in our search for the new we do not pay tribute to the decadent past by establishing new states, institutions, and societies copied from it: "Humanity expects other things from us than this grotesque and generally obscene emulation. . . . If we want humanity to take one step forward, if we want to take it to another level . . . then we must innovate, we must be pioneers."[19] Let us innovate and be pioneers, then!

18   Woodcock, *Anarchism*, 415.
19   Frantz Fanon, *The Wretched of the Earth* (New York: Grove Press, 2004), 239.

REFERENCES

ACME Collective, "N30 Black Bloc Communiqué," http://theanarchistlibrary.org/HTML/ACME_Collective__N30_Black_Bloc_Communique.html.

Albert, Michael. *Parecon: Life after Capitalism*. New York: Verso, 2003.

Amster, Randall, ed. *Contemporary Anarchist Studies: An Introductory Anthology of Anarchy in the Academy*. London: Routledge, 2009.

Anderson, Benedict. *Under Three Flags: Anarchism and the Anticolonial Imagination*. New York: Verso, 2007.

Anderson, Douglas R. "Awakening in the Everyday: Experiencing the Religious in the American Philosophical Tradition." In *Pragmatism and Religion*, edited by Stuart Rosenbaum. Chicago: University of Illinois Press, 2003.

Antliff, Allan, ed. *Only a Beginning: An Anarchist Anthology*. Vancouver: Arsenal Pulp Press, 2004.

Appadurai, Arjun. "Grassroots Globalization and the Research Imagination." In *The Anthropology of Politics: A Reader in Ethnography, Theory, and a Critique*, edited by Joan Vincent. Malden, MA: Blackwell Publishers, 2004.

Apter, David E., and James Joll, eds. *Anarchism Today*. New York: Anchor Books, 1972.

Archer, Julian P.W. *The First International in France, 1864–1872*. Lanham, MD: University Press of America/Rowman & Littlefield, 1997.

Avrich, Paul. *Anarchist Voices: An Oral History of Anarchism in America*. Princeton, NJ: Princeton University Press, 1995.

———. *The Modern School Movement: Anarchism and Education in the United States*. Oakland: AK Press, 2005.

Bakunin, Mikhail. *God and the State*. Mineola, NY: Dover Publications, 1970.

Barclay, Harold. *People Without Government: An Anthropology of Anarchy*. London: Kahn & Averill, 1996.

Berkman, Alexander. *What Is Anarchism?* Oakland: AK Press, 2003.

Bernstein, Barton J., ed. *Towards a New Past: Dissenting Essays in American History*. New York: Pantheon Books, 1968.

Bey, Hakim. *T.A.Z.: The Temporary Autonomous Zone, Ontological Anarchy, Poetic Terrorism*. Brooklyn: Autonomedia, 2003.

Blair, Walter, Theodore Hornberger, and Randall Stewart. *The Literature of the United States, An Anthology and a History, Vol I: From the Colonial Period through the American Renaissance*. New York: Scott, Foresman and Company, 1946.

Bloom, Alexander, and Wini Breines, eds. *"Takin' It to the Streets": A Sixties Reader*. New York: Oxford University Press, 2003.

Bookchin, Murray. *Anarchism, Marxism, and the Future of the Left: Interviews and Essays, 1993–1998*. San Francisco: AK Press, 1999.

———. *Post-Scarcity Anarchism*. Oakland: AK Press, 2004.

———. *Social Anarchism or Lifestyle Anarchism: An Unbridgeable Chasm*. San Francisco: AK Press, 1995.

———. *Social Ecology and Communalism*. Oakland: AK Press, 2007.

Bradley, Edward S. *The American Tradition in Literature*. New York: Norton & Company, 1961.

Breines, Wini. *Community and Organization in the New Left, 1962–1968: The Great Refusal*. New Brunswick, NJ: Rutgers University Press, 1982.

Brown, Susan. *The Politics of Individualism: Liberalism, Liberal Feminism, and Anarchism*. Toronto: Black Rose Books, 2003.

Buell, Lawrence. *Emerson*. Cambridge, MA: Belknap Press, 2003.

———. "Henry Thoreau Enters the American Canon." In *New Essays on Walden*, edited by Robert F. Sayre. Cambridge: Cambridge University Press, 1992.

————, ed. *Ralph Waldo Emerson: A Collection of Critical Essays*. Upper Saddle River, NJ: Prentice-Hall Inc., 1993.

Buhle, Mary Jo, Paul Buhle, and Harvey J. Kaye, eds. *The American Radical*. New York, NY: Routledge, 1994.

Cain, William E., ed. *A Historical Guide to Henry David Thoreau*. New York: Oxford University Press, 2000.

Capper, Charles, and Conrad Edick Wright. *Transient and Permanent: The Transcendentalist Movement and Its Contexts*. Boston: Massachusetts Historical Society, 1999.

Carter, April. *The Political Theory of Anarchism*. New York: Harper Torchbooks, 1971.

————. *The Political Theory of Global Citizenship*. London: Routledge, 2001.

Cavanagh, John, ed. *Alternatives to Economic Globalization: A Better World Is Possible (A Report of the International Forum on Globalization)*. San Francisco, CA: Berrett-Koehler Publishers Inc., 2002.

Cavell, Stanley, and David Hodge. *Emerson's Transcendental Etudes*. Palo Alto, CA: Stanford University Press, 2003.

Chernus, Ira. *American Nonviolence: The History of an Idea*. Maryknoll, NY: Orbis Books, 2004.

Chomsky, Noam. *American Power and the New Mandarins*. New York: The New Press, 2002.

————. *Chomsky on Anarchism*, edited by Barry Pateman. Oakland: AK Press, 2005.

————. *The Chomsky Reader*. New York: Pantheon Books, 1987.

————. *Language and Politics*, edited by Carlos-Peregrín Otero. Oakland: AK Press, 2004.

————. *Language and Problems of Knowledge*. Cambridge, MA: The MIT Press, 1988.

————. *New Horizons in the Study of Language and Mind*. New York: Cambridge University Press, 2004.

————. *Powers and Prospects: Reflections on Human Nature and the Social Order*. Cambridge, MA: South End Press, 1996.

————. *Radical Priorities*. edited by Carlos-Peregrín Otero. Oakland: AK Press, 2003.

————. *Somrak demokracije*. Ljubljana: Studia humanitatis, 1997.

Christie, Stuart, and Albert Meltzer. *The Floodgates of Anarchy*. Oakland: PM Press, 2010.

Cohn-Bendit, Daniel, and Gabriel Cohn-Bendit. *Obsolete Communism: The Left-Wing Alternative*. San Francisco: AK Press, 2000.

Collison, Gary. "Emerson and Antislavery." In *A Historical Guide to Ralph W. Emerson*, edited by Joel Myerson. New York: Oxford University Press, 2000.

Cornell, Andrew. *Oppose and Propose: Lessons from Movement for a New Society*. Oakland: AK Press, 2011.

CrimethInc. *Anarchy in the Age of Dinosaurs*. Olympia, WA: CrimethInc. Ex-Workers' Collective, 2003.

————. *Days of War, Nights of Love: Crimethink for Beginners*. Olympia, WA: CrimethInc. Ex-Workers' Collective, 2003.

————. *Expect Resistance: A Crimethink Field Manual*. Salem, OR: CrimethInc. ExWorkers' Collective, 2008.

————. *Fighting for Our Lives*. Olympia, WA: CrimethInc. Ex-Workers' Collective, 2003.

————. *Recipes for Disaster: An Anarchist Cookbook*. Olympia, WA: CrimethInc. ExWorkers' Collective, 2004.

Cunliffe, Marcus. *The Literature of the United States*. Baltimore, MD: A Pelican Book, 1959.

Curran, Giorel. *21st Century Dissent: Anarchism, Anti-globalization and Environmentalism*. New York: Palgrave, 2006.

Dark Star Collective, eds. *Beneath the Paving Stones: Situationists and the Beach, May 1968*. Oakland: AK Press, 2001.

————. *Quiet Rumors: An Anarcha-Feminist Reader*. Oakland: AK Press, 2003.

Day, Richard J. F. *Gramsci Is Dead: Anarchist Currents in the Newest Social Movements*. London: Pluto Press, 2005.

Delano, Sterling F. *Brook Farm*. Cambridge, MA: Harvard University Press, 2004.

Delanty, Gerard. *Citizenship in a Global Age: Society, Culture, Politics*. New York: Open University Press, 2006.

DeLeon, David. *The American as Anarchist: Reflections on Indigenous Radicalism*. Baltimore, MD: The John Hopkins University Press, 1978.

Dupuis-Déri, Francis. "Qui a peur du peuple? Le débat entre l'agoraphobie politique et l'agoraphilie politique," *Variations: Revue internationale de théorie critique*, no. 15 (2011): 49–74.

Dolgoff, Sam, ed. *Bakunin on Anarchy*. New York: Alfred A. Knopf, 1972.

———. *The Relevance of Anarchism to Modern Society*. Chicago: Charles H. Kerr Publishing Company, 1989.

Ehrlich, Howard J., ed. *Reinventing Anarchy, Again*. San Francisco: AK Press, 1996.

Ellul, Jacques. *Anarchy and Christianity*. Grand Rapids, MI: Wm. B. Eerdmans Publishing Company, 1991.

Eltzbacher, Paul. *Anarchism*. London: A.C. Fifield, 1908.

Emerson, Edward Waldo. *Henry Thoreau as Remembered by a Young Friend*. Mineola, NY: Dover Publications, 1999.

Emerson, Ralph Waldo. *Essays and Poems*. New York: Barnes & Noble, 2004.

———. *The Essential Writings of Ralph Waldo Emerson*. New York: The Modern Library, 2000.

———. *Selected Writings of Ralph Waldo Emerson*. New York: Modern Library, 1992.

———. *Self-Reliance and Other Essays*. Mineola, NY: Dover Publications, 1993.

Engels, Friedrich. "Letter from Engels to Philipp Van Patten (1883)." http://www.marxists.org/archive/marx/works/1883/letters/83_04_18.htm.

———. "Letter from Engels to Theodore Cuno (1872)." http://www.marxists.org/archive/marx/works/1872/letters/72_01_24.htm.

Epstein, Barbara. "Anarchism and the Anti-globalization Movement." *Monthly Review* 53, no. 4 (2001): 1–14.

———. *Political Protest & Cultural Revolution: Nonviolent Direct Action in the 1970s and 1980s*. Berkeley: University of California Press, 1991.

Esteva, Gustavo. "The Other Campaign, APPO and the Left: Reclaiming an Alternative." In *Teaching Rebellion: Stories from the Grassroots Mobilization in Oaxaca*, edited by Diana Denham and C.A.S.A. Collective. Oakland: PM Press, 2008.

Fanon, Frantz. *The Wretched of the Earth*. New York: Grove Press, 2004.

Fischer, Jasna. "Johann Most in slovensko delavsko gibanje." In *Anarhizem in Komunizem Kapital in delo*, Johann Most. Ljubljana: Knjižnica revolucionarne teorije, 1986.

———. "Radikalizacija delavskega gibanja v Sloveniji v os-emdesetih letih 19. stoletja." *Časopis za kritiko znanosti, domišljijo in novo antropologijo* 7, no. 35–36 (1979): 7–21.

Foerster, Norman, ed. *American Poetry and Prose*. Cambridge, MA: The Riverside Press, 1957.

Fogarty, Robert S. *All Things New: American Communes and Utopian Movements, 1860–1914*. Lanham, MD: Rowman & Littlefield Publishers, 2003.

Francis, Richard. *Transcendental Utopias: Individual and Community at Brook Farm, Fruitlands, and Walden*. Ithaca, NY: Cornell University Press, 1997.

Fraser, Ronald, et al. *1968: A Student Generation in Revolt*. New York: Pantheon Books, 1988.

Freeman, Jo. "The Tyranny of Structurelessness." http://www.jofreeman.com/joreen/tyranny.htm.

Fremion, Yves. *Orgasms of History: 3000 Years of Spontaneous Insurrection*. Oakland, CA: AK Press, 2002.

Friedman, Thomas. *The Lexus and the Olive Tree: Understanding Globalization*. New York: Anchor Books, 2000.

Frost, Robert. *The Poetry of Robert Frost: The Collected Poems, Complete and Unabridged*. New York: Henry Holt and Company, 1969.

Furlong, Paul, and David Marsh. "A Skin not a Sweater: Ontology and Epistemology in Political Science." In *Theory and Methods in Political Science*, edited by David Marsh and Gerry Stoker. New York: Palgrave Macmillan, 2002.

Geldard, Richard G., ed. *The Essential Transcendentalists*. New York: Penguin, 2005.

Gibson, Nigel, and Andrew Rubin, ed. *Adorno: A Critical Reader*. Malden, MA: Blackwell Publishers, 2002.

Gilmore, Ruth Wilson. *Golden Gulag: Prisons, Surplus, Crisis, and Opposition in Globalizing California*. Berkeley: University of California Press, 2007.

Goldman, Emma. *Anarchism and Other Essays*. Mineola, NY: Dover Publication, 1969.

———. *Red Emma Speaks: An Emma Goldman Reader*. Amherst, NY: Humanity Books, 1996.

Goodman, Paul. *Drawing the Line Once Again: Paul Goodman's Anarchist Writings,* edited by Taylor Stoehr. Oakland: PM Press, 2010.

Goodway, David. *For Anarchism: History, Theory, and Practice*. London: Routledge, 1989.

———, ed. *For Workers' Power: The Selected Writings of Maurice Brinton*. Oakland, CA: AK Press, 2004.

Gordon, Uri. *Anarchy Alive! Anti-authoritarian Politics from Practice to Theory*. London: Pluto Press, 2008.

Graeber, David, and Andrej Grubačić. "Anarchism; or, the Revolutionary Movement of the Twenty-First Century." http://www.zcommunications.org/znet/viewArticle/9258.

Graeber, David. *Direct Action: An Ethnography*. Oakland: AK Press, 2009.

———. *Fragments of an Anarchist Anthropology*. Chicago: Prickly Paradigm Press, 2004.

———. *Possibilities: Essays on Hierarchy, Rebellion, and Desire*. Oakland: AK Press, 2007.

Grafton, John, ed. *The Declaration of Independence and Other Great Documents of American History, 1775–1865*. Mineola, NY: Dover Publications, 2002.

Graham, Robert, ed. *From Anarchy to Anarchism, 300 CE to 1939*. Vol. 1 of *Anarchism: A Documentary History of Libertarian Ideas*. Montreal: Black Rose Books, 2004.

———. *The Emergence of the New Anarchism, 1939–1977*. Vol. 2 of *Anarchism: A Documentary History of Libertarian Ideas*. Montreal: Black Rose Books. 2009.

Gray, Christopher. *Leaving the 20th Century: The Incomplete Work of the Situationist International.* London: Rebel Press, 1998.

Grodzins, Dean. *American Heritage: Theodore Parker and Transcendentalism.* Chapel Hill, NC: University of North Carolina Press, 2002.

Grogan, Emmett. *Ringolevio: A Life Played for Keeps.* New York: New York Review Books, 2009.

Grubačić, Andrej. "Towards Another Anarchism." In *World Social Forum: Challenging Empires*, edited by Jai Sen and Peter Waterman. New Delhi: The Viveka Foundation, 2004.

Grossman, Richard, ed. *A Year with Emerson.* Boston: David R. Godine Publisher, 2003.

Guérin, Daniel. *Anarchism: From Theory to Practice.* New York: Monthly Review Press, 1970.

———. *No Gods, No Masters: An Anthology of Anarchism.* Oakland: AK Press, 2005.

Gura, Philip F. *American Transcendentalism: A History.* New York: Hill and Wang, 2006.

Gutek, Gerald, and Patricia Gutek. *Visiting Utopian Communities: A Guide to Shakers, Moravians, and Others.* Columbia, SC: University of South Carolina Press, 1998.

Harding, Walter. *The Days of Henry Thoreau: A Biography.* Mineola, NY: Dover Publications, 1982.

Hardt, Michael, and Antonio Negri. *Empire.* Cambridge, MA: Harvard University Press, 2001.

Harper, Clifford. *Anarchy: A Graphic Guide.* London: Camden Press, 1987.

Hayden, Tom. *The Port Huron Statement: The Visionary Call of the 1960s Revolution.* New York: Thunder's Mouth Press, 2005.

Heckscher, Zahara. "Long before Seattle: Historical Resistance to Economic Globalization." In *Global Backlash: Citizen Initiatives for a Just World Economy*, edited by Robin Broad. Manham, MA: Rowman & Littlefield Publishers, 2002.

Herman, Edward S., and Noam Chomsky. *Manufacturing Consent: The Political Economy of the Mass Media.* New York: Pantheon, 2002.

Hinds, William Alfred. *American Communities and Cooperative Colonies*. Honolulu, HI: University Press of the Pacific, 2004.

Hofstadter, Richard, *The American Political Tradition And the Men Who Made It*. New York, NY: Vintage Books, 1989.

Holloway, John. *Change the World Without Taking Power: The Meaning of Revolution Today*. London: Pluto Press, 2002.

Holloway, Mark. *Utopian Communities in America, 1680–1880*. Mineola, NY: Dover Publications, 1966.

Horowitz, Irving L., ed. *The Anarchists*. New Brunswick, NJ: Aldine Transaction Publishers, 2005.

Indjić, Trivo. *Razvoj anarhističkih ideja na tlu jugoslovenskih zemalja*, unpublished manuscript.

Jacker, Corrine. *The Black Flag of Anarchy: Antistatism in the United States*. New York, NY: Scribner, 1968.

Jeffs, Nikolai. "All You Need Is Love (nasilje, emancipacija, pa tudi nekaj uvodnih besed . . .)." *Časopis za kritiko znanosti, domišljijo in novo antropologijo* 26, no. 188 (1998): 9–42.

———."Intelektualci, novi razredi, anarhizmi." In *Somrak demokracije*, Noam Chomsky. Ljubljana: Studia humanitatis, 1997.

Joll, James. *The Anarchists*. London: Routledge, 1979.

Jordan, Tim. *Activism! Direct Action, Hacktivism and the Future of Society*. London: Reaktion Books, 2002.

Kempton, Richard. *Provo: Amsterdam's Anarchist Revolt*. Brooklyn: Autonomedia, 2007.

Kennedy, Robert F. "Remarks at the University of Kansas, March 18, 1968." http://www.jfklibrary.org/Research/Ready-Reference/RFK-Speeches/Remarks-of-Robert-F-Kennedy-at-the-University-of-Kansas-March-18-1968.aspx.

Kesić, Stojan. *Odnosi između radničkih pokreta u jugoslovenskim zemljama do 1914.godine*. Belgrade: Narodna knjiga, Institut za savremenu istoriju, 1976.

Kesten, Seymour R. *Utopian Episodes: Daily Life in Experimental Colonies Dedicated to Changing the World*. Syracuse, NY: Syracuse University Press, 1996.

Kingsnorth, Paul. *One No, Many Yeses*. London: Free Press, 2004.

Klein, Naomi. *Fences and Windows*. London: Flamingo, 2002.

Knabb, Ken, ed. *Situationist International Anthology.* Berkeley,
    CA: Bureau of Public Secrets, 2006.

Krimerman, Leonard, and Lewis Perry, eds. *Pattern of Anarchy:
    A Collection of Writings on the Anarchist Tradition.* Garden
    City, NY: Anchor Books, 1966.

Kristan, Anton. *O delavskem in socialističnem gibanju na
    Slovenskem do ustanovitve jugoslovanske socijalno-demokratične
    stranke (1848–1896).* Ljubljana: Zadružna založba, 1927.

Kropotkin, Peter. *Anarchism: A Collection of Revolutionary
    Writings.* Mineola, NY: Dover Publications, 2002.

———. *Mutual Aid: A Factor in Evolution.* London: Freedom
    Press, 1998.

———. *Revolutionary Pamphlets.* Cambridge, MA: The MIT
    Press, 1970.

Landauer, Carl. *European Socialism: A History of Ideas and
    Movements.* Los Angeles: University of California Press, 1959.

Landauer, Gustav. *Revolution and Other Writings: A Political
    Reader.* Oakland: PM Press, 2010.

de León, Juana Ponce, ed. *Our Word Is Our Weapon: Selected
    Writings of Subcomandante Marcos.* New York: Seven Stories
    Press, 2001.

de Ligt, Bart. *The Conquest of Violence.* London: Pluto Press, 1989.

Lister, Ruth. "Citizenship and Difference: Towards a
    Differentiated Universalism. *European Journal of Social
    Theory* 1, no. 1 (1998): 71–90.

———. *Citizenship: Feminist Perspectives.* New York: New York
    University Press, 1998.

Lynd, Staughton. *From Here to There: The Staughton Lynd Reader.*
    Edited by Andrej Grubačić. Oakland: PM Press, 2010.

———. *Intellectual Origins of American Radicalism.* New York:
    Cambridge University Press, 2009.

MacPhee, Josh, and Erik Reuland, ed. *Realizing the Impossible:
    Art Against Authority.* Oakland: AK Press, 2007.

Madden, Edward H. *Civil Disobedience and Moral Law in
    Nineteenth-Century American Philosophy.* Seattle, WA:
    University of Washington Press, 1970.

Malatesta, Errico. *Anarchy*. London: Freedom Press, 2001.

———. "Sedem ločenih kosov globalne sestavljanke—Neoliberalizem kot sestavljanka: brezplodna globalna enotnost, ki razdvaja in pogublja narode." *Časopis za kritiko znanosti, domišljijo in novo antropologijo* 30, no. 209–210 (2002): 37–57.

Marshall, Peter. *Demanding the Impossible: A History of Anarchism*. Oakland: PM Press, 2010.

Maserati, Ennio. "Attività anarchica in Dalmazia nel primo Novecento." *Clio:Rivista Trimestrale di Studi Storici* 18, no. 1 (1982).

Matthiessen, Francis O. *American Renaissance: Art and Expression in the Age of Emerson and Whitman*. Oxford: Oxford University Press, 1968.

May, Todd. "Jacques Rancière and the Ethics of Equality." *SubStance* 36, no. 2 (2007): 20–36.

———. *The Political Philosophy of Poststructuralist Anarchism*. University Park, PA: Pennsylvania State University Press, 1994.

McCarthy, Timothy P., and John McMillian. *The Radical Reader: A Documentary History of the American Radical Tradition*. New York: The New Press, 2003.

McDonough, Tom, ed. *Guy Debord and the Situationist International: Texts and Documents*. Cambridge, MA: The MIT Press, 2002.

McGilvray, James, ed. *The Cambridge Companion to Chomsky*. Cambridge: Cambridge University Press, 2005.

McLean, George N. *The Rise and Fall of Anarchy in America*. New York: Haskell House, 1972.

Meltzer, Albert. *Anarchism: Arguments For and Against*. San Francisco: AK Press, 1996.

Meltzer, Milton, and Walter Harding. *A Thoreau Profile*. Lincoln, MA: The Thoreau Society, 1998.

Mertes, Tom, ed. "Grass-roots Globalism." *New Left Review* 17 (September–October 2002): 101–10.

———. *A Movement of Movements: Is Another World Really Possible?* New York: Verso, 2004.

Milgram, Stanley. "Behavioral Study of Obedience." *Journal of Abnormal & Social Psychology* 67, no. 4 (1963): 371–78.

Miller, David. *Anarchism*. London: J.M. Dent & Sons Ltd., 1984.

Miller, Perry, ed. *The American Transcendentalists: Their Prose and Poetry*. Garden City, NY: Doubleday Anchor Books, 1957.

———, ed. *The Transcendentalists*. Cambridge, MA: Harvard University Press, 2001.

Milstein, Cindy. *Anarchism and Its Aspirations*. Oakland: AK Press, 2010.

Mott, Wesley T., ed. *Encyclopedia of Transcendentalism*. Westport, CT: Greenwood Press, 1996.

Myerson, Joel, ed. *The Cambridge Companion to Henry David Thoreau*. Cambridge: Cambridge University Press, 1995.

———, ed. *Transcendentalism*. New York: Oxford University Press, 2000.

Neal, Dave. "Anarchism: Ideology or Methodology?" http://www.connexions.org/CxLibrary/Docs/CX6984-MethodologyAnarchism.htm.

———, ed. *The Selected Letters of Ralph Waldo Emerson*. New York: Columbia University Press, 1997.

Nettlau, Max. *A Short History of Anarchism*. London: Freedom Press, 1996.

Nordhoff, Charles. *American Utopias*. Stockbridge, MA: Berkshire House Publishers, 1993.

Notes from Nowhere, eds. *We Are Everywhere: The Irresistible Rise of Global Anti-capitalism*. London: Verso Books, 2003.

Nozick, Robert. *Anarchy, State, and Utopia*. New York: Basic Books, 1977.

O'Byrne, Darren J. *The Dimensions of Global Citizenship: Political Identity Beyond the Nation-State*. London: Taylor & Francis, 2003.

Paine, Thomas. *Collected Writings*. New York: Library of America, 1995.

Panikkar, Raimon *The Intrareligious Dialogue*. Mahwah, NJ: Paulist Press, 1999.

Pennock, Roland J., and John W. Chapman, eds. *Anarchism: Nomos xix*. New York: New York University Press, 1978.

People's Global Action (PGA), http://www.nadir.org/nadir/initiativ/agp/en/.

Perlin, Terry M., ed. *Contemporary Anarchism*. New Brunswick, NJ: Transaction Books, 1979.

Perry, Bliss, ed. *The Heart of Emerson's Journals*. Mineola, NY: Dover Publications, 1995.

Perry, Lewis. *Radical Abolitionism: Anarchy and the Government of God in the Antislavery Thought*. Knoxville, University of Tennessee Press, 1995.

Petrović, Gajo. *Čemu Praxis*. Zagreb: Praxis, 1972.

——. *Mišljenje revolucije: Od ontologije do "filozofije politike."* Zagreb: Naprijed, 1978.

——. *Praksa/istina*. Zagreb: Kulturno-prosvjetni sabor Hrvatske, 1986.

Pitzer, Donald E., ed. *America's Communal Utopias*. Chapel Hill: University of North Carolina Press, 1997.

Polletta, Francesca. *Freedom is an Endless Meeting: Democracy in American Social Movements*. Chicago: University of Chicago Press, 2002.

Pope, Daniel, ed. *American Radicalism*. Malden, MA: Blackwell Publishers, 2001.

Porte, Joel, ed. *Emerson in His Journals*. Cambridge, MA: The Belknap Press, 1982.

Porte, Joel, and Saundra Morris. *The Cambridge Companion to Ralph Waldo Emerson*. Cambridge: Cambridge University Press, 1999.

Poulantzas, Nicos. *The Poulantzas Reader: Marxism, Law, and the State*, edited by James Martin. New York: Verso, 2008.

Purkis, Jonathan, and James Bowen, eds. *Changing Anarchism: Anarchist Theory and Practice in a Global Age*. Manchaster: Manchaster University Press, 2004.

Rediker, Marcus. *Villains of All Nations: Atlantic Pirates in the Golden Age*. London: Verso, 2004.

Restrepo, Eduardo, and Arturo Escobar. "Other Anthropologies and Anthropology Otherwise: Steps to a World Anthropologies Framework." *Critique of Anthropology* 25, no. 2 (2005): 99–129.

Reynolds, David S. *Beneath the American Renaissance: The Subversive Imagination in the Age of Emerson and Melville.* Cambridge, MA: Harvard University Press, 1989.

Richardson, Robert Jr. *Emerson: The Mind on Fire.* Berkeley: University of California Press, 1995.

———. *Henry Thoreau: A Life of the Mind.* Berkeley: University of California Press, 1986.

Ritter, Alan. *Anarchism: A Theoretical Analysis.* Cambridge: Cambridge University Press, 1980.

Rizman, Rudi, ed. *Antologija anarhizma.* Ljubljana: Knjižnica revolucionarne teorije, 1986.

———. *Globalizacija in avtonomija: Prispevki za sociologijo globalizacije.* Ljubljana: Znanstvena založba Filozofske fakultete, 2008.

———. "Semantika nasilja—družbena misel Noama Chomskega." In *Somrak demokracije*, Noam Chomsky. Ljubljana: Studia humanitatis, 1997.

Rocker, Rudolf. *Anarcho-Syndicalism: Theory and Practice.* Oakland: AK Press, 2004.

Roddick, Anita, ed. *Take It Personally: How to Make Conscious Choices to Change the World.* Berkeley, CA: Conari Press, 2001.

Rozman, Franc. *Socialistično delavsko gibanje na slovenskem Štajerskem.* Ljubljana: Založba Borec, 1979.

Runkle, Gerald. *Anarchism: Old and New.* New York: Delacorte Press, 1972.

Salkie, Raphael. *The Chomsky Update: Linguistics and Politics.* London: Unwin Hyman, 1990.

Santos, Boaventura de Sousa, ed. *Another Knowledge Is Possible: Beyond Northern Epistemologies.* New York: Verso, 2008.

———. *Cognitive Justice in a Global World: Prudent Knowledges for a Decent Life.* Lanham, MD: Lexington Books, 2007.

———, ed. *The Rise of the Global Left: The World Social Forum and Beyond.* London: Zed Books, 2006.

———. "The World Social Forum: Toward a Counter-Hegemonic Globalisation (Part I)." In *World Social Forum: Challenging Empires*, edited by Jai Sen and Peter Waterman. New Delhi: The Viveka Foundation, 2004.

Sayre, Robert F., ed. *New Essays on Walden*. Cambridge: Cambridge University Press, 1992.

Scott, James C. *The Art of Not Being Governed: An Anarchist History of Upland Southeast Asia*. New Haven, CT: Yale University Press, 2010.

———. *Domination and the Arts of Resistance: Hidden Transcript*. New Haven, CT: Yale University Press, 1990.

———. *Seeing Like a State: How Certain Schemes to Improve the Human Condition Have Failed*. New Haven, CT: Yale University Press, 1999.

———. *Weapons of the Weak: Everyday Forms of Peasant Resistance*. New Haven, CT: Yale University Press, 1985.

Sheehan, Sean M. *Anarchism*. London: Reaktion Books, 2003.

Shepard, Odell, ed. *The Heart of Thoreau's Journals*. Mineola, NY: Dover Publications, 1962.

Sher, Gerson S. *Praxis: Marxist Criticism and Dissent in Socialist Yugoslavia*. Bloomington: Indiana University Press, 1977.

Shukaitis, Stevphen, David Graeber and Erika Biddle, eds. *Constituent Imagination: Militant Investigations—Collective Theoretization*. Oakland: AK Press, 2007.

Skirda, Alexandre. *Facing the Enemy: A History of Anarchist Organization from Proudhon to May 1968*. San Francisco: AK Press, 1996.

Smith, Adam. *An Inquiry into the Nature and Causes of the Wealth of Nations*. University Park, PA: Penn State University Press, 2005.

Smith, Guy E. *American Literature: A Complete Survey*. Totowa, NJ: Littlefield, Adams & Co., 1970.

Smith, Neil. *Chomsky: Ideas and Ideals*. Cambridge: Cambridge University Press, 2004.

Sonn, Richard D. *Anarchism*. New York: Twayne Publishers 1992.

Starhawk. *Truth or Dare: Encounters with Power, Authority, and Mystery*. New York: HarperCollins Publishers, 1987.

Starr, Amory. *Global Revolt: A Guide to the Movements Against Globalization*. London: Zed Books, 2005.

Stirner, Max. *The Ego and Its Own*. Cambridge: Cambridge University Press, 1995.

Streissguth, Thomas. *Utopian Visionaries*. Minneapolis: Oliver Press, 1998.

Subcomandante Marcos. "A Penguin in the Selva Lacandona." http://www.zmag.org/znet/viewArticle/5745.

Suissa, Judith. *Anarchism and Education: A Philosophical Perspective*. Oakland: PM Press, 2010.

Taylor, Michael. *Community, Anarchy and Liberty*. Cambridge: Cambridge University Press, 1982.

Thoreau, Henry David. *Civil Disobedience and Other Essays*. Mineola, NY: Dover Publications, 1993.

———. *The Journal of Henry D. Thoreau* (volumes i–xiv). New York: Dover Publications, 1962.

———. *Walden and Other Writings*. New York: Modern Library, 2000.

Turner, Bryan. "Outline of a theory of citizenship." In *Citizenship: Critical Concepts*, edited by Bryan Turner and Peter Hamilton. London: Routledge, 2002.

Vaneigem, Raoul. *Revolution of Everyday Life*. London: Rebel Press, 1983.

Vodovnik, Žiga, ed. *Ya Basta! Ten Years of the Zapatista Uprising: Writings of Subcomandante Insurgente Marcos*. Oakland: AK Press, 2004.

Walter, Nicolas. *About Anarchism*. London: Freedom Press, 2002.

Walzer, Michael. "Citizenship." In *Political Innovation and Conceptual Change*, edited by Terence Ball, James Farr, and Russell L. Hanson. New York: Cambridge University Press, 1995.

Ward, Colin. *Anarchism: A Very Short Introduction*. Oxford: Oxford University Press, 2004.

———. *Anarchy in Action*. London: Freedom Press, 1982.

———. *Autonomy, Solidarity, Possibility: The Colin Ward Reader*. Oakland: AK Press, 2011.

West, Cornel. *The American Evasion of Philosophy: A Genealogy of Pragmatism*. Madison, WI: The University of Wisconsin Press, 1989.

———. *Democracy Matters*. New York: Penguin Books, 2005.

Whicher, Stephen E., ed. *Selections from Ralph Waldo Emerson*. Boston: Houghton Mifflin Company, 1960.

Whitman, Walt. *Poetry and Prose*. New York: Library of America, 1982.

———. *Travne bilke*. Ljubljana: Mladinska knjiga, 1999.

Woodcock, George. *Anarchism: A History of Libertarian Ideas and Movements*. Peterborough: Broadview Press, 2003.

Yuen, Eddie, Daniel Burton-Rose, and George Katsiaficas, ed. *Confronting Capitalism: Dispatches from a Global Movement*. New York: Soft Skull Press, 2004.

Zadnikar, Darij. "Kronika radostnega uporništva." In John Holloway, *Spreminjamo svet brez boja za oblast: pomen revolucije danes*. Ljubljana: Študentska založba, 2004.

———. "Le vkup, le vkup, uboga gmajna!" *Časopis za kritiko znanosti, domišljijo in novo antropologijo* 26, no. 188 (1998): 5–6.

———. "Que se vayan todos!" *Časopis za kritiko znanosti, domišljijo in novo antropologijo* 31, no. 212 (2003): 5–8.

Zinn, Howard. *Disobedience and Democracy: Nine Fallacies on Law and Order*. Cambridge, MA: South End Press, 2002 (1968).

———. *Justice in Everyday Life: The Way It Really Works*. Cambridge, MA: South End Press, 2002 (1974).

———. *Marx in Soho*. Cambridge, MA: South End Press, 1999.

———. *SNCC: The New Abolitionists*. Cambridge, MA: South End Press, 2002 (1964).

———. *Passionate Declarations: Essays on War and Justice*. New York: Harper-Perennial, 2003 (1990).

———. *A People's History of the United States: 1492–Present*. New York: Harper-Perennial, 2005 (1980).

———. *The Politics of History*. Chicago: University of Illinois Press, 1990 (1970).

———. *You Can't Be Neutral on a Moving Train: A Personal History of Our Times*. Boston: Beacon Press, 2002 (1994).

———. *The Zinn Reader: Writings on Disobedience and Democracy*. New York: Seven Stories Press, 2009 (1997).

INDEX

"Passim" (literally "scattered") indicates intermittent discussion of a topic over a cluster of pages.

About PM Press

politics • culture • art • fiction • music • film

PM Press was founded at the end of 2007 by a small collection of folks with decades of publishing, media, and organizing experience. PM Press co-conspirators have published and distributed hundreds of books, pamphlets, CDs, and DVDs. Members of PM have founded enduring book fairs, spearheaded victorious tenant organizing campaigns, and worked closely with bookstores, academic conferences, and even rock bands to deliver political and challenging ideas to all walks of life. We're old enough to know what we're doing and young enough to know what's at stake.

We seek to create radical and stimulating fiction and nonfiction books, pamphlets, T-shirts, visual and audio materials to entertain, educate, and inspire you. We aim to distribute these through every available channel with every available technology, whether that means you are seeing anarchist classics at our bookfair stalls; reading our latest vegan cookbook at the café; downloading geeky fiction e-books; or digging new music and timely videos from our website.

Contact us for direct ordering and questions about all PM Press releases, as well as manuscript submissions, review copy requests, foreign rights sales, author interviews, to book an author for an event, and to have PM Press attend your bookfair:

PM Press • PO Box 23912 • Oakland, CA 94623
510-658-3906 • info@pmpress.org

Buy books and stay on top of what we are doing at:

www.pmpress.org

MONTHLY SUBSCRIPTION PROGRAM

These are indisputably momentous times—the financial system is melting down globally and the Empire is stumbling. Now more than ever there is a vital need for radical ideas.

In the six years since its founding—and on a mere shoestring—PM Press has risen to the formidable challenge of publishing and distributing knowledge and entertainment for the struggles ahead. With over 250 releases to date, we have published an impressive and stimulating array of literature, art, music, politics, and culture. Using every available medium, we've succeeded in connecting those hungry for ideas and information to those putting them into practice.

Friends of PM allows you to directly help impact, amplify, and revitalize the discourse and actions of radical writers, filmmakers, and artists. It provides us with a stable foundation from which we can build upon our early successes and provides a much-needed subsidy for the materials that can't necessarily pay their own way. You can help make that happen—and receive every new title automatically delivered to your door once a month—by joining as a Friend of PM Press. And, we'll throw in a free T-shirt when you sign up.

Here are your options:

- $30 a month: Get all books and pamphlets plus 50% discount on all webstore purchases
- $40 a month: Get all PM Press releases (including CDs and DVDs) plus 50% discount on all webstore purchases
- $100 a month: Superstar—Everything plus PM merchandise, free downloads, and 50% discount on all webstore purchases

For those who can't afford $30 or more a month, we're introducing *Sustainer Rates* at $15, $10 and $5. Sustainers get a free PM Press T-shirt and a 50% discount on all purchases from our website.

Your Visa or Mastercard will be billed once a month, until you tell us to stop. Or until our efforts succeed in bringing the revolution around. Or the financial meltdown of Capital makes plastic redundant. Whichever comes first.